New Vision, New Reality

A Guide to Unleashing Energy, Joy, and Creativity in Your Life

DONALD C. KLEIN, PH.D.
WITH KATHLEEN MORROW

HAZELDEN®
INFORMATION & EDUCATIONAL SERVICES

Hazelden
Center City, Minnesota 55012-0176

1-800-328-0094
1-651-213-4590 (Fax)
www.hazelden.org

Library of Congress Cataloging-in-Publication Data

Klein, Donald C.
    New vision, new reality : a guide to unleashing energy, joy, and
creativity in your life / Donald C. Klein ; with Kathleen Morrow.
        p. cm.
    Includes bibliographical references and index.
    ISBN 1-56838-576-5
    1. Quality of life.   I. Morrow, Kathleen.   II. Title.
    BF637.C5 K57 2001
    158—dc21

                                                            2001016562

05 04 03 02 01   6 5 4 3 2 1

Cover design by Lightbourne
Interior design by Elizabeth Cleveland
Typesetting by Stanton Publication Services, Inc.

New Vision, New Reality

Lola Perl Klein, my precious love,
dearest friend, and cherished companion of fifty-three years.
She embraced the world, one person at a time.

There are two ways to live life.
One is as though nothing is a miracle.
The second is as though everything is a miracle.

—Albert Einstein

Contents

Exercises

Preface: Embracing the Psychology of Appreciation

□ □ □

THE POWER OF APPRECIATION. Those four words represent the essential, life-transforming teaching of this book. I ask you to keep those words in your mind—and in your heart—as you make your way through the following pages.

My hope is that (with the help of my colleague Kathleen Morrow) I succeed in stirring you to the depths of your being, enabling you to walk through a thin veil of obscuring consciousness to rediscover and put to use your inborn capacity for discerning wonderment. If I can do that, I will have succeeded in realizing one of my dreams, to make a significant difference in the lives of as many people as possible. That desire is what motivated me to begin writing this book ten years ago and, beyond teaching the power of Appreciation in many workshops and seminars, to persist in my determination to explain in book form the importance of reclaiming our capacity for Appreciative knowing.

The trip I invite you to make will feature a few side trips along less-traveled roads and many stops at spots we all consider—at first glance—to be more than familiar. At each stop and each side venture we will deal with aspects of human consciousness—what it is; how it organizes our lives; under what circumstances it dooms us to live in a world of personal and shared prescriptions for what life is and ought to be; how even the smallest dysfunctions can add up over time to produce enormous personal and societal misery; and what we can do to move beyond those prescriptions to tap into our capacity to live Appreciatively, in touch with the clarity, energy, creativity, and zest that is the human birthright.

We'll begin by exploring—playfully, I hope—how ordinary consciousness works, how we use it to organize cosmic life energy into a kind of mental scenery that includes all our important images and ideas about ourselves, others, and the world at large, and how we use those images as guides to our behavior. We'll shine a liberating spotlight on the mechanisms of humiliation and learn how humiliation—both deliberate and random—can hurt and enrage us, sometimes leading us to squander time, money, and energy on fruitless efforts to soothe our wounded pride. We'll examine the creativity we bring—as individuals and as members of society—to unconscious efforts to create the conditions that ensure that we continue to be confronted by the very conditions we wish to avoid. These initial chapters share a common theme and purpose—to help us understand why we have difficulties experiencing Appreciative consciousness.

Later chapters describe more fully the state of Appreciative knowing and the widely differing circumstances under which different people allow themselves to gain temporary access to that realm of human consciousness. These chapters emphasize the fact that—contrary to many religious and philosophic myths—the realm of Appreciative human consciousness is a perfectly "normal" state of mind, not at all esoteric and not at all dependent on special rituals and experiences.

The book does not propose to offer you a new road map to consciousness or to tell you how to use that map to enter the Appreciative realm. You need no special skill or technique to reap the benefits of Appreciation. You need only make the decision to refuse to mistake your personally filtered reality for the whole of life.

This book's contribution to your life, if you choose to embrace it, is to encourage you to set aside mental preconceptions (that is, lose your mind, if only temporarily) and allow yourself to take a leap of faith into the realm of Appreciative knowing. You will know when that leap is complete because your life will be remodeled. You will see things more clearly, no longer blurred by your egoistic mental scenery; you will be better able to discern the many promising possibilities in whatever situation confronts you; you will have renewed energy to cope with experiences and dilemmas that might once have exhausted you; and you will find yourself draped in a joyful mantle, emotionally "dressed up" for whatever life brings your way.

The surest way to escape being changed by a new idea or experience is to compare it to some concept or theory with which you are already familiar. By doing so, you simply add this new piece of information to the storage bin in which you've already collected one or more similar ideas. You thus avoid the possibility of allowing the new idea to enter into your consciousness, of giving yourself permission to fully experience it, and of determining from that complete experience whether you will make the new idea yours for the rest of your life.

A secondary method for ensuring that you will not absorb the teaching and make it yours is to turn your active, critical mind loose. Let it find and raise as many critical objections to the new idea as it can, the more the better. Let it also search for evidence that this new idea makes sense, feels right, and has definite merit. In this way you'll simply—again—be relegating the teaching to the mental storehouse of ideas and opinions you already have, the storehouse that informs the life you currently lead and helps you to maintain your present way of looking at the world. But no matter. What can you really lose by reinforcing and solidifying your commitment to the level of consciousness that has already created the many-faceted, delightful human being that you no doubt are?

The moral is simple. If you are truly interested in allowing the teaching to materialize in your life, do your best to keep your mind at rest. Note the comparisons it presents to what you already know; note the arguments it suggests that minimize and very likely negate the possibility that you will allow yourself to enter the Appreciative way, engage in Appreciative knowing, and discover from your own experience the profound power of Appreciation to transform your life in thousands of unexpected ways.

Acknowledgments

This book began to take shape in my mind almost twenty years ago after visiting with Sidney Banks, a sage who has been blessed with spontaneous spiritual enlightenment. My wife and I realized that we were in the presence of someone who had attained a kind of profound wisdom and knowing that we could not fully discern. We were, nonetheless, touched by Sidney's words and his presence. We also talked with and observed the home lives of several couples, old friends of Sidney's, who described truly wonderful changes in their lives that had taken place because of listening to him speak about his experience of reality. From two meetings with Sidney Banks and from visits with his family and friends, I took away a glimmer of understanding that over the years changed my way of being in the world and ultimately led to the insights that form the substance of this publication. Roger Mills, a colleague in the field of mental health, introduced me to Sidney's work and is currently engaged with others in making Sidney's work known to psychotherapists and others in the helping professions. I can make neither Sidney nor Roger responsible for the ideas in this book, however, and I suspect that they would question the wisdom of devoting chapters to "negative" material that dwells on the ways in which we human beings clutter our minds with ideas, beliefs, and images that interfere with the direct knowing that I call Appreciation.

The ideas came together in a book during the time I was on sabbatical leave from The Union Institute and in residence for an entire summer at Ashridge Management College in England. There on that beautiful campus, in an office high in what resembled an ancient medieval tower, I found the friendship, collegiality, and support needed to draft an initial manuscript. I am especially grateful to Margaret Doydge, my secretary at the college, who inspired me to push ahead with the work when she told me that reading the earliest version had made a significant difference in her life. I am also deeply grateful to then-President Michael Osbaldeston, Dean Peter Beddowes, Martin Bennett, Judith Coker, Bill Critchley, Brian Davies, Brian Ellison, Shirley Forder, Jack Hardie, Philip Hodgson, Tony Hulshof, Alex Knight, Keith Milmer, Carole Osterweil, Saroj Patel, Karen Sadler, Edgar Wille, and Stefan Wills for their hospitality to a sojourner in their midst as well as for their unflagging interest, encouragement, questions, and criticisms. I owe special thanks to Martin Bennett who went out of his way to arrange a special seminar for those in residence at the college that enabled me to sort out and present my ideas to a group of friendly critics.

In the years that followed I found further encouragement from many friends and colleagues at NTL Institute for Applied Behavioral Science. There are too many to mention everyone by name. But I do want to acknowledge Charles and Edith Seashore, John and Joyce Weir, and Rolf Lynton for their consistent friendship and support, and to single out Kenneth Benne, one of the three co-founders of NTL (initially known as National Training Laboratories), who is one of the few people I know who lived a life informed by the Appreciative knowing that is at the heart of this book. Because Ken was especially excited about the observations I was developing on the Humiliation Dynamic, he convened two gatherings of NTL colleagues in Safety Harbor, Florida, and in Bethel, Maine, to explore the personal and social ramifications of humiliation.

I've found important opportunities to present, discuss, and refine my observations with fellow faculty members and doctoral candidates at The Union Institute. This work could not have been done without the wholehearted support of those responsible for allocating funds and investing in the work of people like myself. The late President Robert Conley, Acting President Mervyn Cadwallader, and Vice President Mark Rosenmann were consistently supportive over many years, as were Deans Fontaine Belford, Dick Genardi, Al Hall, and John Tallmadge. Faculty colleagues who provided insights, encouragement, and help at critical junctures included John Adams, Rita Arditti, Marjorie Bell Chambers, Ellen Colburn, Bruce Douglass, Rose Duhon-Sells, Colin Greer, Jean Griffin, Bethe Hagens, Leland K. Hall Sr., Barry Heermann, Penny MacElveen-Hoehn, Robert McAndrews, William McKelvie, Elizabeth Minnich, Clark Moustakas, Michael Patton, Lawrence Ryan, Holloway Sells, Mary Sheerin, and Ross Speck.

I've also benefited from the interest and encouragement of colleagues within the Society for Community Research and Action (a division of the American Psychological Association), most notably David Chavis, James Kelly, J. Robert Newbrough, and Tom Wolff, as well as Leonard Duhl, an early companion in the mental health field, and Thomas Gullotta, former editor of *The Journal of Primary Prevention*.

Possibly the earliest inspiration for this volume was drawn from Dr. Erich Lindemann, whose pioneering work on grief inspired much of what has become accepted practice among those involved in the field of preventive psychiatry. My mentor and esteemed colleague in the 1950s, Erich was the first person in my experience to demonstrate the creative power of Appreciation in his way of working with colleagues and students.

Of the many other friends and colleagues who have supported this work directly or indirectly, I wish to mention a few and hope the others will pardon their omission: A. David Feinstein's searching comments on the first manuscript of this work inspired many important changes that ultimately led to the present version. Michael Broom, a treasured friend and colleague and co-author with me of a previous book, *Power: The Infinite Game*, has been a companion over many years in the explorations of levels of consciousness that are an important part of this book. Our ideas have been so intertwined that by now there is no way for me to say which of the ideas in this book about Self creation and ego-hooking are his and which are mine. Richard Yensen is a pioneer explorer of altered states of consciousness. His work as a researcher into the use of LSD for therapeutic purposes at the Maryland Psychiatric Research Center introduced me to the experience of direct awareness stripped of preconceptions about myself and the world. Judith Vogel and David Glaser have listened with encouragement to my ideas as they have emerged over the past decade, asking clarifying questions, sharing their own experiences, and in a variety of ways keeping me grounded to the realities of everyday life in organizations. Louise Diamond, a graduate of The Union Institute Ph.D. program, exemplifies the power of Appreciation in her worldwide work with intercommunal conflicts. Jack Pransky, another graduate of The Union Institute, has been deeply influenced by the teachings of Sidney Banks. In our discussions of the importance of Appreciation as a way of transforming one's understanding of oneself and the world, he has been consistently affirming and has helped to shape my understanding of related work going on under the aegis of Health Realization. Finally, James Rouse, developer of the planned new town of Columbia, Maryland, and an ardent advocate of healthy communities, modeled for me the zest for life and optimistic, forward-looking creativity that is the hallmark of someone who is in touch with his capacity for Appreciative knowing.

I am deeply grateful to my sons Stefan, Jonathan, Alan, and Jeremy, daughters-in-law Sally, Laura, and Tammie, and grandchildren Becca, Josh, and Kelly. Each of them has offered consistent love, interest in my ideas, and ego-boosting admiration, fortunately tempered from time to time with critical feedback designed to keep me grounded in humility.

In the final stages of its development, this work was enlivened and transformed by the dedicated efforts of writer/editor Kathleen Morrow. Her understanding of what I was trying to convey has been matched only by her ability to breathe life into the manuscript, to provide additional illuminating perspectives from her own experience, to ground the work in marvelously illustrative examples, and to weave connections between sections to show how they flow together to make a coherent whole.

Finally, I will always remember the excitement with which Stephen Lehman, Hazelden's acquisitions editor, greeted the book. From his first enthusiastic phone call after reading the manuscript to his most recent thoroughgoing editorial comments and suggestions, Stephen has been a consistently supportive and enormously helpful ally.

ONE

Our Shared Realities

◨ ◨ ◨

In her account of growing up as the daughter of immigrant Chinese parents, Maxine Hong Kingston tells how her mother, Brave Orchid, a Chinese healer, explained the psychotic behavior of Maxine's auntie, who had come from Hong Kong to live with Maxine and her family:

> Brave Orchid saw that all variety had gone from her sister. She was indeed mad. "The difference between mad people and sane people," Brave Orchid explained to the children, "is that sane people have variety when they talk-story. Mad people have only one story that they talk over and over."[1]

The mother's explanation strikes at the heart of human psychology, normal or abnormal. A so-called normal person's reality typically is what Harry Stack Sullivan, an interpersonal psychiatrist, describes as "consensual."[2] For Sullivan, the difference between "normal" people and emotionally disturbed or mentally ill individuals is that "normals" make effective connections between their own stories (personal life narratives) and the stories of others. Their talk-stories are "realistic" enough to mesh with the talk-stories of those around them and, therefore, "make sense."

As Brave Orchid and Harry Sullivan point out from their very different cultural perspectives, our lives are shaped by individual and collective images that we project onto the individuals and groups with whom we deal. Although few people realize it, our relationships are mediated by talk-stories. Rich and poor, business executives and hired hands, professional experts and their clients, community leaders, politicians, heads of state, and everyday

1

citizens—most people function by projecting their stories onto others. Transpersonal psychologist Willis Harman puts it this way:

> Research on perceptual illusions and "virtual reality" has demonstrated that the world we ourselves experience is a projection based on clues from "out there." Representations of external events do actually form within the subject's mind, but the mind models the world by projecting its own experiences out to the judged location of the events they represent. With this "reflexive" model of perception, the phenomenal world is a representation in the mind which only seems to be "out there." . . . The phenomenal world, the experienced world, is just a representation; it cannot be the "thing itself."[3]

These projections include dramatic individual and collective images that are crucial to the Self definitions of the participants. When one person's "mind models" come into contact with those of another person (or group of people), especially in a context of fear and threat, the result is often a collision of "realities" that feels Self diminishing, humiliating, and even life threatening to everyone concerned. The idea of projection is associated in most people's minds with psychopathology, more specifically the fear and suspicion associated with paranoia. The projection to which I refer, however, is a common, everyday, garden variety. It is the way ordinary, normal individuals pass judgment on one another, satisfy themselves that they understand one another's behavior, and convince themselves that they are justified in their reactions to one another. Projection is involved when a husband accuses his wife of being an unbearable nag. Projection is equally involved when the wife attacks the husband for being neglectful, unfeeling, and cold. Convinced that the images of one another that they carry in their minds are correct, neither one is prepared to take the steps needed to explore what's going wrong with their relationship or to make the changes needed to rediscover the love and mutual attraction that brought them together in the first place. Attack, counterattack, and mutual recriminations reinforce the projective images each has of the other until the relationship becomes unbearable, and another marriage fails. Projection is also involved in relationships that go wrong between colleagues, bosses, and subordinates in organizations, between teachers and students in schools, between opposing groups in communities, and, for that matter, between warring nations. At each of these levels, the parties involved are convinced that their antagonists are behaving in an altogether reprehensible manner toward them because they are incompetent, inconsiderate, indecent, or otherwise incapable of behaving acceptably toward them. The result of these mutual projections of characteristics is that differences become disagreements, which in turn escalate into mutually destructive conflicts. Each side is convinced of the rightness of its position. Each side blames the other for the situation in which it finds itself. And all too often, each side is prepared to sacrifice vast amounts of time, energy, money, property, and even lives in order to support the accuracy of its beliefs and its projections of inferiority, depravity, and malevolence onto its antagonists. Out of such everyday clashing projections come such conflagrations as divorce, fragmented communities, riots, industrial strife, business failure, international tension, murderous violence, and armed conflict.

Perhaps one of the most dangerous aspects of this tendency to live in a very personal "virtual reality," which we all share, is our even more pronounced tendency to assume that our personal projections represent the One True Reality. With few exceptions, Western psychologists treat the Psychology of Projection as the standard, the norm, busying themselves creating ingenious descriptions and theories about how perceptions, beliefs, attitudes, and ideas are created from data available through the senses. In this cultural context, reality testing has been not much more than a constant negotiation to achieve agreement about what is real and true.

By contrast, generations of Eastern students of psychology have been aware of the projective nature of what we Westerners call reality. Philosopher Jiddu Krishnamurti represents a long tradition in Hindu thought when he writes about the division between the observer and that which is observed, which he calls "the source of all human conflict":

> Thought brings about this division. You look at your neighbor, at your wife, at your husband or your boyfriend or girlfriend . . .

but can you look without the imagery of thought, without the previous memory? For when you look with an image there is no relationship; there is merely the indirect relationship between the two groups of images, of the woman or of the man, about each other; there is a conceptual relationship, not actual relationship.[4]

In the book *Changing Consciousness*, coauthor David Bohm, a remarkable combination of physicist and philosopher, enshrines thought as the single-most effective creator of the physical and social world in which we live, saying:

[A]lmost everything we see in the world around us was created from thought, including all the cities, all the buildings, all the science, all the technology, and almost everything that we call nature. Farmland was produced by thought, by people thinking what they're going to do with the land and then doing it. So without thought we wouldn't have farms; we wouldn't have factories; we wouldn't have ships; we wouldn't have airplanes; we wouldn't have governments. Supposing we have a company like General Motors. People have to think to know what they are supposed to be doing—if they all forgot this, the company would collapse and would cease to exist. So thought can take part in creativity. Thought has created a lot of good things. It is a very powerful instrument, but if we don't notice how it works, it can also cause great harm.[5]

To illustrate both the benefits and awful consequences of thought, Bohm points out that "every nation has come into existence through some thought that said, 'We exist; we declare that we exist; we have our independence,' or else it gradually came to that." On the flip side, "people are supposed to die for nations and give up all their possessions for them, and put their children into the army for them, and . . . sacrifice for them." In short, although nations are nothing more than cultural, political, and geographic entities created from thought, "they seem to be supremely precious realities . . . the world as a whole is ready to pay a thousand billion dollars a year to defend these nations."[6]

Unfortunately, as Bohm points out, thoughts and feelings have a way of becoming inseparable in our minds. Unsupported by thought, a momentary surge of joy or flash of anger may enliven the moment and convey our happiness or discomfort to those around us. "But then," as Bohm puts it, "if it doesn't work in that short burst, it's going to go wrong." Why is that? *Because to sustain an emotional reaction, such as anger, one has to think of a valid reason for that anger.* Once feeling and thought are combined, we feel justified in behaving in ways that hurt those who in our minds have become antagonists or even enemies. As Bohm says, "Anger can build up into terrible things if you sustain it. Going from that short outburst of anger to sustained anger is the crucial mistake. Therefore, thought, which is responsible for this, really has no place in anger."[7]

PSYCHOLOGY OF MIND
The creators of Psychology of Mind, a growing movement on the fringe of contemporary psychology and related fields, define Thought as one of three overriding principles of Mind, Thought, and Consciousness that explain how mental processes work. In this view, there is an "impersonal, universal intelligence of Mind."[8] By Mind they mean what spiritual teachers have variously referred to as the intelligence behind life, universal life force, or formless energy. Mind is the source of both individual Thought and Consciousness. Without the principle of Mind, neither Thought nor Consciousness would be possible. The principle of Thought refers to our remarkable ability to create what Brave Orchid's mother called talk-stories. In other words, through our perceptions, ideas, beliefs, and values we organize what we take in through our senses into patterns of thought. These thought patterns provide what we experience as coherence and meaning in our lives. The principle of Consciousness refers to the facility through which these thoughts and inner images become so real to us that we "become immersed in our reality to an extent that this self-limiting set of ideas is all we see and all we experience."[9]

Roger Mills, co-founder of Psychology of Mind, uses the metaphor of a movie projector to explain the way in which Mind, Thought, and Consciousness interact to create ordinary subjective reality. Mills likens Mind, the life force, to the power source that drives the projector. Consciousness is the apparatus of the projector itself, including the light that projects images onto the screen.

Thought is the film. The content on that film at any point in time is the story line that is projected onto one's mental screen.

In the book *Changing Consciousness*, philosopher physicist Bohm offers an analogy from physics that helps illuminate the importance of universal Mind as the context from which Thought emerges. In physics, he explains, sound is viewed "as a wave in a medium, such as air, which carries this wave."[10]

> Even in the absence of sound, the medium is always there and is present everywhere. However, the medium is in itself silent. So the fundamental being of sound is in something that could at least metaphorically be called a deeper ground that is not sound. Similarly, thoughts can be regarded as waves or ripples on a deeper ground that is not thought.[11]

Various observers of the human scene have called attention to the importance of liberating ourselves from the dictatorship of our thoughts and have suggested ways to do so. In *Changing Consciousness*, for example, Bohm suggests that, in order to access the "deeper ground" of knowing, silence of thought is essential. He says, "The silence is the deeper being, the true being, within which all the words, images, 'noise,' and so on can be held in wholeness. Only [in this way] can the subtle intelligence operate without impediment."[12]

WHAT IT'S ALL ABOUT

Beneath the thought-dominated individual and collective stories of all human beings all over the world lie the desires for happiness, love, and dignity, for opportunities to care for and be of service to others, and for lives free of humiliation and physical harm. These shared desires for connection and community are, indeed, the force that has often enabled warring parties to arrive at agreements in the face of apparently intransigent disputes. Efforts to arrive at such transformational agreements usually involve carefully designed opportunities for those involved to get beyond mutual blame and recriminations. Given the proper circumstances, people are often able to reach beyond their limiting projections and enter the realm of shared humanity. Together, they create a new, shared reality based on those basic human desires they hold in common—the dream of peace, happiness, love, and lives lived without fear of war and destruction.

Unfortunately, such transformations are usually limited to the carefully staged, peacemaking situation and tend to be short-lived, lasting only as long as the projections of all parties can remain reframed in ways that reduce threat and open up possibilities for rapprochement. In effect, when warring parties embrace one another within the framework of a shared new (but, too often, fragile and temporary) identity, they do so only within the framework of consensual reality. Their projective talk-stories have been modified or enlarged. They no longer clash, create sparks, and generate recriminations and violence because, for the (usually very transient) moment, they have agreed to inhabit a common reality. It often does not take much—a border incident, a slight or an insult from one party to the other—to bring forth all the old projective mental images and reduce the fragile consensual reality to shreds.

A WORLD WITHOUT PROJECTION?
Although good enough to allow the human species to squeak by for ten thousand years or so, our traditional projective orientation may have just about exhausted its value to civilization. With only occasional lapses into such elevated behaviors as love, compassion, and forgiveness, human beings throughout recorded history have inflicted all manner of humiliations on those they despised, tortured those with whom they disagreed, enslaved and killed those who couldn't prevail against their superior force, and wiped out entire civilizations. And they continue to do so.

Faced with the increasingly turbulent complexities of a rapidly changing, evermore high-tech environment, it would seem suicidal for us to continue to approach life and its problems in our customary projective fashion. I believe we stand challenged at this moment in history with nothing less than a major psychological transformation, a sea change in how we perceive, think about, and cope with one another and the world around us.

I am convinced that such a transformational change is within our grasp. The predisposition to live projectively is not all there is to the human condition. We also come predisposed to celebrate life, to be consumed with curiosity and awe, to bring fascination and wonder to our work and to our relationships. In short, we all come equipped with what it takes to celebrate the fullness of life and to live it appreciatively, complete with its challenges, frustrations, missed expectations, and mysteries. This point is eloquently made in the following quote from Gurudev Chitrabhanu, a Jain teacher:

> We come to this world so that we can find our ultimate center, which is happiness, joy. *But we keep hoping that joy will come to us from the outside, that someone or some circumstance will give us happiness.* [italics added] But really, friends, there is no need to wait. The happiness you wish for is already there, waiting for you, but you must open the door so it can come out.[13]

To open the door to a world free of projection, two basic steps are required.

The first step is for a majority of individuals to recognize clearly and unequivocally that it's unacceptably dangerous and dysfunctional to continue to confuse the images and ideas that populate our minds with reality. This step may be painful because in order to traverse it successfully, we must face up to the fact that by continuing to live as creatures of projection, we doom ourselves and future generations to an increasingly disordered—possibly extinct—world.

Just as cigarette smoking, once almost universally accepted, has become increasingly unacceptable in our society, so can we work on dethroning projection from its present position as a universally accepted given in social interaction. To do so the goal would be to make it unacceptable to project our own fears, impulses, and shortcomings onto others, or to act as if those projections of ourselves and others are real.

The second step is to tap into our inherent capacity for living within the guidance of a Psychology of Appreciation—a way of being in which we view life events through the lens of an intellectual/feeling state that frees us from preconceptions, pre-existing beliefs, concepts, analysis of relationships, and the like. It involves bringing the inner feeling that has been variously called fascination, delight, ecstasy, wonder, joy, and appreciation to bear on all situations, from the most mundane to the world-shaking. Appreciation is a way of seeing the world that is counter to the strategy of projection. It is a way of seeing the world around us through childlike eyes, not only under those special circumstances that evoke our capacity for wonderment, but also at all times and under all circumstances. As will be explained later, Appreciative knowing is our birthright. We were born with it and lose touch with it as we create defining ideas and images about ourselves and the world. In subsequent chapters of this book we will discuss how and why, despite negative consequences to ourselves and others, we do not activate our inherent ability to use Appreciation, even though it is a far more effective means of coping than the more commonly used and often destructive projective approach. I will also have much more to say about Appreciation itself and about the art of releasing our capacity for Appreciative knowing.

The recognition of the need for a psychological revolution is by no means original or new. It was expressed, for example, by Krishnamurti more than twenty years ago:

> Man is suffering, man is in travail, and our problem, *our question, is: whether the mind can transform itself completely, totally and thereby bring about a deep, psychological revolution* [italics added] –which is the only revolution. Such a revolution can bring about a different society, a different relationship, a different way of living.[14]

Looking back over the past century, we can see that it is long past time to take the transformational leap. We can no longer afford the luxury of maintaining this separation between our everyday lives of projection and our occasional exhilarating episodes of wonder. Each of us can reverse this state of affairs by taking seriously the fact that we're capable of illuminating everyday events and relationships with the transforming power of Appreciation. Let's reserve our projective abilities for short stories, novels, biographies, history, and other creative occasions.

Whether or not we transform our present psychology of individual and group behavior from Projection to Appreciation does not rest on abstract philosophical questions or moral issues. It involves the most practical and urgent question of all—namely, human survival.

The following material is organized to lead you gently through fascinating, but complex, information and ideas about how we humans create ourselves (usually as projective creatures) and about how we are free to re-create ourselves at any time.

You will also experience ample opportunity, through a series of guided exercises, to examine the choices you have made about who you are and how you want to function and to understand how you can remake those choices, thereby re-creating the person you have always known yourself to be.

TWO

How Free Are We, *Really?*

◘ ◘ ◘

The destiny of every human being is decided by what goes on inside his skull when he is confronted by what goes on outside his skull. Each person designs his own life.[1]
— Eric Berne, founder of transactional analysis

The thesis we explored in chapter 1—the idea that, in our current level of conscious development, we create much of our so-called reality by projecting images we form inside our brains onto the external world—lends support to Eric Berne's contention that "each person designs his own life."

On the surface, designing our own lives looks like an exceptionally good deal. If we take Berne's words at face value, we have almost infinite freedom to become whoever we want to become, to live however we want to live, to see the world around us in ways that nurture our deepest humanities. There's only one little problem—as many commentators, ranging from John Kennedy to Yogi Berra, have noticed: life's not fair. From the get-go, some people get a better deal than others.

Every evening, the broadcast news reports another series of bizarre human dramas, stories of individuals who would be easy to view as victims of their birth or circumstances: a selfless young woman accosted and killed by guerrillas while aiding citizens of a Latin American country; six thousand U.S. residents diagnosed with hepatitis C, a slowly lethal infection of the liver, in one year; huge numbers of African American young men imprisoned for drug use or trafficking during their potentially most productive years.

Anger, rage, malaise—they're everywhere. And is it really possible that every one of the angst-ridden denizens of our times is "making it all up," projecting their own internal anger and wrath on the world, thereby creating scenarios that fulfill their expectations? It's easy, in today's conflict-ridden, fault-finding, road-raging, terrorist-threatening world scene, to assume that Berne is exaggerating and oversimplifying in his zeal to make his point. It doesn't, after all, require an encyclopedic knowledge of how the world works to realize that different people are given very different materials with which to work in "designing" their lives. A Jewish child in Nazi Germany, for example, had to be a veritable artist at living to project a creative, joyful life onto the sordid stuff that comprised her external circumstances. Today's inner-city children—growing up in poverty-stricken, single-parent households in high-crime neighborhoods dominated by gangs and drug dealers—have a far different set of building blocks and design options than their contemporaries raised in affluent, stable, suburban settings.

As Paul Loeb, one recent skeptic of Berne's Self-design theory, puts it:

> It's easy for those of us blessed with comfortable circumstances to assume that everyone has options equal to our own. But, when we insist that we each have the power to shape the direction of our own lives, and that all problems are therefore individual problems, we ignore the social and economic context in which resources and opportunities are apportioned. Indeed, one reason for arguing that the poor choose poverty through their actions is that to think otherwise raises troubling questions about whether our own good fortune might in part be due to privilege or chance, and not merit.[2]

So, who's viewpoint is nearer the truth—Berne's or Loeb's? How free are we, really? Are we creatures of our own creation? Does what goes on inside our skulls really have the final power to impact and change what's going on "out there"? Or, do our psyches and lives depend (for better or worse) on the luck of the draw— the toss of the cosmic dice that dictates whether we're born rich or poor, black or white, to loving parents or to abusive parents, in a highly developed industrial nation or in some developmental backwater where the majority of citizens are unable to secure the food, shelter, education, and health care essential to even the most limited standard of living? In a world with such obvious inborn inequality, how is it possible for anyone to agree with New Age guru Deepak Chopra when he insists: "You are your own reality. You create it; you carry it around with you."?

My belief—and one of the primary tenets of this book—is that neither extreme position is correct. We're neither totally free nor completely at the mercy of external forces that act on us like so many pawns on a chessboard. Even the most starry-eyed adherent to any of the many (and multiplying daily) psycho-spiritual sects expounding personal transformation has to admit that half-starved refugees, exiled from their homes by famine, persecution, or war, have a vastly different set of life-transforming options from which to choose than do most middle-income Americans. The experiences that create the internal selves that perceive the external world are in no way equal for all people, or even for any two individuals growing up in the same family.

Nevertheless, there is one great equalizer in all the inequality we see around us. And that great equalizer is the inescapable fact that none of us can experience any external reality without screening it through an elaborate set of internal mental and emotional filters—the perceptions, ideas, and interpretations that we bring to an experience in order to shape and give meaning to it.

Despite the insistence of some in the new spirituality that we "choose" our parents before we are born, most of us are convinced that we had little control over the economic, social, and psychological resources that formed the environments into which we were born and lived the earliest, most formative, years of our lives.

What I believe we can control, to an extent most of us have only vaguely begun to realize, are the filters we bring to life's raw material, the perceptions we select to view the experiences that form the cores of our lives, the interpretations we give those experiences, and the discipline we exercise in selecting only those perceptions and interpretations that empower us in our never-ending efforts to define who we are, how we function, and why we deserve the respect and affection of other human beings.

All this is really nothing new. The finest minds of the human race have devoted entire lifetimes to the study of how "what goes on inside our skulls" interacts with and influences "what goes on outside our skulls." In the past, however, only the most privileged and committed—monks, saints, seers—have had the luxury of living their lives in such a way as to bring their internal worlds and their external circumstances into some semblance of congruence. One of the wonders of the current transmillennial age is that this luxury is now available to millions of us—in fact, to anyone willing and capable of devoting a minimal amount of time and energy to the exploration.

There is one discouraging note—many of us have tried to escape our inner prisons and been (or felt) defeated. In record numbers, Americans in the last half of the twentieth century read self-help literature, attended transformational workshops (and joined transformational religious groups), visited therapists, watched and taped Oprah Winfrey broadcasts, engaged in Himalayan retreats—on and on and on goes the exhausting menu of tried-and-not-quite-right consciousness-expanding options. And, on and on and on and *on* goes the list of failures and frustrations. The consciousness "dropout" rate increases as our ability to enjoy our lives decreases. The external pressures we face daily escalate, and our ability to cope with those pressures seems to contract.

I believe the reason for the sense of failure and futility that pervades the remnants of the once-glorious "peace-and-love" movements is very simple and exceedingly easy to correct. All we need to progress in our efforts to release the chains that bind us and move into a freer, more Appreciative approach to life are a few basic cognitive (intellectual) tools. We need to understand (1) the difference between the True (or Creative) Self and the False (or Created) Self; (2) the enormous pressures that are brought to bear on the Creative Self in the first years of life to engender a False Self with which to face the world; (3) the insidious process whereby that False Self—originally created to protect the tender, vulnerable (and joyous and free) True Self—becomes more and more rigid until it forms a tough crust over the entire personality, a Self-created prison that shields the True Self, not only from danger and attack, but also from joy, freedom, love, and creativity.

THE CREATIVE SELF

The "Creative Self" is the term I use to describe that part of every human being that, the minute he or she is born, begins to form, shape, and define the "Self" or "Me." The Creative Self never rests—it continually sifts experience, looking for those nuggets of information, those shards of incident, that reinforce the emerging sense of Self. It discards those experiences that refuse to fit coherently with the larger pattern, selects those that give the pattern coherence and form, and provides a standard by which the individual can define and evaluate his or her relationship to the larger world.[3]

Eric Berne (whom we met at the opening of this chapter) coined the phrase "Little Professor" to describe the innate, intuitive, and creative aspect of the human personality that emerges almost at birth to figure out what's going on in the external environment and to decide the best response to those external happenings.

> With no knowledge of psychology, a child intuits much of what is going on. Debby looks at her mother's face and figures out she'd better stop what she's doing. She catches her mother's nonverbal message sent through a disapproving look and responds to it. She then attempts to solve her problem with the use of her Little Professor, who "psyches out" the best move in a given situation.[4]

We never lose our Little Professors. According to Berne and his adherents, every grown-up carries within himself or herself a mature Little Professor who can unerringly spot and interpret the twinkle in a friend's eye or the tensing of a boss's jaw.

We unconsciously rely on our Little Professors in even the most mundane situations of daily life. Suppose you greet a friend, asking "How's it going?" The friend responds, "Fine." But your Little Professor notes her downturned mouth and slumping posture, two nonverbal clues that suggest she may not be as "fine" as she insists, that she may, in fact, be feeling sad or discouraged or downright desolate.

My years of practice have taught me that the most important single fact about your Self is that *you* (not your mother or your father or the church of your childhood) created it. You weren't born with that Self and nobody handed it to you. Yet, somehow, through all the complexity of experience, you managed to produce your Self, a splendidly complex character that is unlike any other that ever lived.

This magnificent creation, this Self that each of us so painstakingly develops (and fights to maintain), is far more complex, imaginative, and useful than any truly fictional character ever devised. You use this Self-created character to play the parts you have devised for your life—twenty-four hours a day, seven days a week, even while on vacation, throughout an entire lifetime. Not even Shakespeare or Dickens could do as well. The characters these authors worked so hard to create were designed for limited, predetermined plots, designated settings, and single story lines. The most ordinary human beings, on the contrary, are so flexible that they can step into any situation—no matter how unfamiliar or bizarre—and play their parts without missing much more than a beat or two. Even if awakened from a sound sleep at 3:00 A.M., you can count on your Self to speak lines that are appropriate to the person you know your Self to be—all this without benefit of script, prompter, or director.

Left to its own devices, the Creative Self gives enormous energy to its Self-defined job—the maintenance and protection of the ideas and beliefs that you have chosen to incorporate into your definition of "Me." The Creative Self will struggle to maintain your status quo even after you begin to feel dissatisfied, even when you consciously express the desire for change. It's as if the mechanism of Self remains faithful to the original instructions it was given unless and until the Creative Self realizes it can and must encourage the Self to operate differently, in a way that will produce a happier, more productive life.

THE ORIGINS OF STAGNATION

Early in the process of Self creation, within the first five years or so of life, something very important happens. We develop a kind of mental and emotional template, a mold or model which from that point on shapes (and often severely limits) how the Creative Self operates. From the moment this template emerges, the child (and the teenager and adult he or she will become) has fewer options from which to choose in going about the job of Self design. To understand how this template emerges and how powerful it is in determining the final product, visualize a sculptor busily imagining, designing, and finishing a statue. He finds a flawless piece of marble. He studies the stone carefully, until the color, shape, and patterns are engraved in his mind's eye. He strokes it with his fingers to detect tiny imperfections, places where its density may be greater or less than that of the whole. With a chisel, he removes tiny pieces of stone. Slowly, as he becomes more and more familiar with his material, he develops a compelling image of the sculpture he is creating. From the moment this image appears, the sculptor's work changes—he begins to work toward a goal, ignoring new options and opportunities in favor of those options he feels will most likely result in the creation in stone of the image he has in mind.

The mental image of the statue that has yet to be is analogous to the budding identity the Little Professor develops during the preschool years. This template (created before the person was even able to read) determines how the Creative Self will function, how it will fashion from the available social, economic, genetic, and interpersonal materials the adult who will emerge years later. Adherents of transactional analysis refer to this design template as a primitive "protocol," a basic premise about what life is and what it has in store for the individual. Gradually, the Creative Self expands this protocol, or life position, into what Berne calls a "life script":

> A script is an ongoing life plan formed in early childhood under parental pressure. It is the psychological force which propels the person toward his destiny, regardless of whether he fits it or says it is his own free will.[5]

So, for better *and* for worse, your Little Professor (long before it matured into your knowledgeable and experienced Creative Self) worked hard on your behalf, doing what it could to sort out and make sense of the millions of confusing signals to help you understand what you needed to do to maintain the love and attention of your parents, to avoid punishment, to reflect the basic attitudes and values of the people who were important to your safety, to learn how to survive—and, hopefully, thrive—in your strange new world. Most important, your Little Professor developed some basic convictions about your Self, the people around you, and the world into which you were born.

Unfortunately, as a life sculptor, the preschool-age Little Professor is more than slightly "challenged" in terms of brainpower and plain-old life experience. In view of the Little Professor's almost insurmountable limitations, then, it is not surprising that few of us survive to adulthood without picking up (or creating out of whole cloth) one or more dysfunctional personality quirks.

I'm reminded of the story of two Quaker sisters who had labored together their entire lives, performing many acts of Christian charity and supporting many good causes on behalf of those whom society rejected. One evening after an especially distressing day dealing with indifferent bureaucrats, discouraged victims, and reluctant philanthropists, one sister turned to the other and said, "Sister, there are times when I think the whole world is crazy, but for thee and me." The other sister sighed, nodded, and responded, "So true. So true. And, sometimes I misdoubt thee."

Eric Berne, too, misdoubts the competence of his Little Professor. On the one hand, he points out that even when we are very young, we are especially adept in figuring out both what is required of us and what we can get away with at any given moment. The Little Professor, he writes,

> becomes very adept at figuring out what people want or will tolerate, or at worst, what they will get the most excited or angry about, or perhaps feel the most guilt, helpless, scared, or hurt about.[6]

On the other hand, because of limitations of brainpower and experience, the child "has no way to tell the facts from the delusions, and the most everyday events are distorted."[7] Berne further writes:

> [T]he comedy or tragedy of each human life is that it is planned by an urchin of pre-school age, who has a very limited knowledge

of the world and its ways, and whose heart is filled mainly with stuff put there by his parents. Yet this wonder child is precisely who determines in the long run what will happen to kings and peasants and whores and queens.[8]

THE LITTLE PROFESSOR AT WORK

Years ago I witnessed a scene that has come to symbolize for me the process we all undergo to determine who we are and how we will relate to our world—the process, in other words, through which we literally sift and sort through all the possible options, choosing among millions of possibilities to *create* the people we believe ourselves to be as we interact with our personal universes.

I was attending a community conference in Virginia and had just completed three intense days. As I often do in such situations, I rose a little early to spend some time alone, wandering the lovely hill-strewn countryside and collecting my thoughts. I was returning to the conference center when I saw a young boy, not more than three years old, skipping merrily along ahead of his father, another early-rising conferee.

As I watched, hidden by the low-hanging branches of a dogwood tree, the child stumbled and fell. He grabbed his knee, examined it, and scrunched his face in pain. Then, he looked nervously around for his father, who was still lagging several hundred yards behind, outside the child's range of vision. At this point, the youngster did a remarkable thing: he simply picked himself up, brushed the dirt from his knee, and limped back along the path, his face relaxed and his pain miraculously eased. That miracle cure lasted until he saw his father rounding the bend in the path, at which time he grabbed his knee and emitted a terrible yelp of pain.

That child—looking around for an adult to validate his experience—is all of us. We all learn early to feel what we think significant adults want us to feel, to express what those giants appear ready to hear, to respond to the thousands of subtle (and not so subtle) cues they give about who we are and how we are to behave. Without his father's witness, the boy had difficulty knowing what he had experienced and how to react to that experience.

This may have a slightly sinister ring to it—as if we were all

Twilight Zone robots programmed at birth to accept whatever vision is reflected to us by the huge people around us. What saves our childhood scenarios from robotic inevitability is the active role we play, choosing our reactions to adult input, just as the little boy on that sunlit Virginia pathway decided to repress his discomfort until he found his father to serve as an audience.

Even with the most loving parents, frustration and shock are part and parcel of the everyday life of a young child. The life of an infant is a life lived at the behest of other people, people who appear as gods—large and knowing and all-powerful, people on whom the infant depends for the very basics of survival. Helpless, the infant wails for relief from hunger, discomfort, or boredom and waits for what must seem an eternity for relief to come. The infant knows periods of the most intense frustration— times when it is consumed by the most savage, unarticulated rage. It can feel overwhelming sorrow when cut off from those larger creatures, never knowing when such separation might occur. That same infant also knows moments of intense bliss— times when it is cuddled and held, when it experiences the sheer wonder of being alive, available to the full range of fascination and delight. These alternating moments of extreme emotion are built into the nature of infancy. Whatever our walk in life, our social status, our personality type, our political persuasions—none of us escaped these archetypal experiences. The memories of those inevitable traumas are buried deep within us, helping to form who we are and how we experience our existences.

RELIVING THE EMOTIONAL LIFE OF A CHILD
In the 1960s, before LSD was classified as a controlled substance, I participated in a study that I often use to remind myself of the life every human being lives before he or she learns to speak. The experiment, conducted by the Maryland Psychiatric Research Institute, was designed to evaluate LSD's potential to help people cope with physical illness, emotional problems, and impending death. I was invited, along with other mental health professionals, to participate in a comprehensive training and preparation program and to ingest LSD in a carefully controlled setting, allowing researchers to observe the drug's effects on our mental and emotional processes. We were asked to describe out loud

everything we experienced, and our comments were recorded for future study and analysis.

The session, as you might expect, was very intense, taking me into exciting, startling, sometimes primitive, often frightening realms of perception, feeling, and ideas. Many of these experiences started with an almost overwhelming feeling of anxiety, followed by a series of different primitive emotions. On one occasion I found myself begging forgiveness, knowing I would never be forgiven. At another time, I called desperately for help, realizing that no help would be forthcoming. Still later, I was engulfed by a savage, destructive rage—a rage so all-consuming that I felt capable of tearing the world apart with my teeth. The rage faded into a feeling of being totally alone and unlovable. The desolation, in turn, was followed by equally intense perceptions of myself wallowing in a combination of pleasurable sights, sounds, and other sensations that were almost sickening in their intensity.

These experiences—the sense of being, if only for brief moments, in the position of feeling deserted, deprived, helpless, unloved, and alone in a complex, often threatening world—are the nitty-gritty stuff that comprises the life of even the most cherished infant. It is, indeed, the shadowy memory of that helplessness, many theorists say, that often drives even the most emotionally healthy adult to behave in inexplicable ways.

OUR EARLIEST WORK—TO DEVELOP A
WORKING THEORY OF LIFE

Given our shared trauma—the trauma I was privileged to relive as an adult man cooperating with science—there is little wonder that we all begin, as soon as our developing intellectual powers let us, to attempt to create for ourselves a sense of safety. We form our own personal working "theories" about people and events and begin, very early, to develop ideas of the kind of person we need to be—a person who can negotiate with ease and success the maze of contradictory sensations that make up our slowly expanding worlds. In adulthood, most of us are content to limit our growth to the simple maintenance and updating of those early images, expectations, and interpretations of ourselves and the world around us. In essence, we spend our adulthoods piling up barriers against experience, learning new and more effective ways to buffer ourselves from whatever shocks the environment might hold—generating, in other words, more and more impenetrable barriers between our True (Creative) Selves and our False (Created) Selves. All the while, we insist on believing that we are free, growing adults—even when we are responding like robots to the demands of a terrified, tantrum-tossing child.

INTRODUCING SOME HELPFUL (BUT OPTIONAL) ACTIVITIES

Before we move on to examine the details of Self creation, I invite you to participate in the ongoing process of Self examination presented by the exercises that appear in almost every chapter of this book. The chart on page 23 serves as a basis for a series of short exercises, to be completed in three phases (in conjunction with other Self-analysis exercises) as we progress. This exercise—like all those that follow—is set off from the main body of text in *italics,* a typographic reminder of its optional nature. Some people enjoy completing formal exercises and acquiring the applied, personal insights they offer. Others find that stopping to complete an exercise distracts them from the flow of ideas. If you are among that second group of readers, feel free to skip over these *italicized* sections. You may return to them later or choose to eliminate them altogether from your experience of this book.

◨ **Exercise 1: Describing "Me"**

In the left-hand column of the chart on page 23, list up to ten words or phrases that you feel describe personal qualities or characteristics that you like about yourself. (Don't worry about the other two columns right now. We will return to them in chapter 8.)

Me | Not Me | Also Me

THREE

The Miracle of Self Creation

□ □ □

The Sense of Self is as much verb as noun.[1]
—John D. W. Andrews, psychologist and psychotherapist

Even those of us who recognize that we are almost completely creatures of our own creation tend to think of our "Selves" as highly individualized, personal, and private entities, separate and identifiable sets of qualities and attributes that exist in the same way a brick or a tree exists. Most experts, however, agree that what we call the Created Self exists only because it defines who we are *with respect to other people.* That thesis, in fact, is the basis on which all other theories of Self are built. So the first thing we need to remember in our examination of the Created Self, which was put together so diligently by that unheralded partnership between our Little Professors and our Creative Selves, is that the Created Self is a social Self.

THE CREATED SELF IS A SOCIAL SELF

As children, we learn to behave in ways that bring desired results from the adults on whom we depend for such basic human needs as food, clothing, and—most especially—love and affection. As adults, we continue our childhood tendency to use the reactions of other people as standards that dictate who we are and how we behave. This tendency is most evident in our predisposition to define ourselves in terms of the important interpersonal roles we play—mother, son, friend, or grandfather, for example. We also testify to the importance of others in determining our Self definitions when we refer to qualities (such as shyness, modesty, loyalty, or trustworthiness) that play major roles in our relationships, perhaps by making us more valuable or important to others.

◼ **Exercise 1-A**

Review the qualities you listed in the chart on page 23. Which of your Self descriptions, if any, defines who you are in respect to the other people in your life? Are words like "parent," "friend," or "spouse" important parts of your Self concept?

THE CREATED SELF IS A REFLECTED SELF

Early writers used the term "looking-glass self" to describe how young human beings develop and maintain their ideas of Self by incorporating into their psyches information from others about who they are and what their outstanding qualities might be.[2] Parents are the first such mirrors. Later, other mirrors—teachers and friends--provide children with additional input about their abilities and characteristics.

Like most powerful psychological tools, this "looking-glass" phenomenon is a double-edged sword, providing children with Self-fulfilling prophecies as they struggle to live up (or down) to the views and expectations of others. A daughter whose parents view her from the beginning as capable, loving, and intelligent usually will work to live up to those expectations, generating a set of circumstances that justify those parental attitudes. A child, on the other hand, whose parents choose (for whatever reason) to see her as less than capable, a problem child, is apt to honor those opinions by behaving in problematic ways, likewise generating situations that justify the initial parental judgment.

◼ **Exercise 1-B**

Look again at your ten Self descriptions. Do any reflect qualities your parents or other significant people admired? How much of your concept of Self consists of "mirrored" views that have influenced your thinking about your identity?

By now, you should sense how few of the qualities you've always claimed as "yours" were really your idea in the first place.

THE CREATED SELF SEEKS VALIDATION
  FROM OTHERS

To thrive, we need other people to support and affirm us in who
we have (half-consciously) chosen to be. To exist without such
validation is almost unthinkable. Gripping novels and plays have
been written about the pain of feeling invisible to others or of
being exiled from one's native community. In many primitive
communities, the most horrible punishment—worse, even, than
the punishment of death—is banishment. The banished person is
considered to have died to the good opinion and the validation of
the community. This is a living death, a death of the Self inside the
human body. Only the strongest human psyches can survive, un-
scathed, without the reflected glory of their colleagues' good
opinions.

◘ **Exercise 1-C**

How many of the Self-descriptive words in the chart on page 23 repre-
sent qualities that you feel make you more valuable to others? Words
such as "understanding," "loyal," and "leader" might fall into this
category.

THE CREATED SELF IS A REPORT-CARD SELF

More than most of us care to admit, our concepts about ourselves
overflow with positive and negative judgments. The Created Self
has something of the traditional schoolmarm in its makeup. That
is, it does more than describe and define—it also evaluates and
grades ourselves, our friends, everyone, in fact, with whom we
have the slightest personal or impersonal contact. We may value
objectivity in ourselves and others, but in defining who we are,
we rarely give ourselves the luxury and freedom of objectivity.
Except for those, however, who are clinically depressed or ha-
rassed by deep-seated doubts about their Self worth, we tend to
give ourselves passing grades or better when we evaluate our status as human beings. This bias is reflected in the very words we
choose to describe similar qualities in ourselves and in other
people. Consider for a moment how comfortable you and your
friends may be using negatively charged labels to describe

groups of people you have never met. Now (be honest) allow yourself to think about how often in the course of a routine day or week you succumb to the temptation to think you are a notch or so better than even a good friend in some talent, characteristic, or attitude.

I use the two word games described in the next pages to encourage my seminar and workshop participants to see how they bring the report-card aspect of their Created Selves to bear countless times each day, almost always to render positive judgment on themselves at the expense of others.

The I-You-They Game

The "I-You-They Game" illustrates how difficult it is for us to be objective in our constant evaluations of ourselves versus those we are close to versus those we have never met, especially those individuals who fit certain of our negative stereotypes—bureaucrats, politicians, "wild-eyed" liberals, artists, and so on. It's best to play this game when you and a good friend or colleague are feeling relaxed and playful.

The rules are simple: one of you selects a personal quality that neither of you finds admirable. Your friend, for example, might choose "stinginess," a quality that you agree is not one of your favorites. Now your job is to describe "stinginess" in a way that you would consider complimentary if it were applied to yourself. You might say, for example, "I am thrifty." Next think of a somewhat less positive, but still acceptable, word or phrase to describe your friend's stinginess. You could choose, perhaps, to say, "You are tight," leaving only those unknown others (individuals with no virtue-saving bond to either you or your friend) to live out the contempt you attach to being stingy. Your final judgment on the subject of stinginess is: "I am thrifty, you are tight, and *they* are stingy."

Examples abound:

- "I am organized, you are methodical, *they* are compulsive."
- "I am quick, you are impatient, *they* are impulsive."
- "I am calm, you are passive, *they* are lazy."
- "I am shrewd, you are crafty, *they* are sneaky."

The Disdain Game

At your next social gathering, watch how quickly (and sometimes subtly) people organize around the "Disdain Game." If the subject of politicians or the media or lawyers comes up, it's almost certain that someone will have some negative, possibly clever, comment.

Notice how much these negative comments resemble the "They" statements from the I-You-They game.

Now notice that all you have to do to short-circuit the game is introduce more positive ("I" or "You") terms to describe the group or behavior under attack. If someone says, "Lawyers are a sneaky bunch," for example, agree with the statement, but agree using an "I" term. You might say, "Yes, they are very shrewd, aren't they?"

My experience has been that it doesn't take more than a few "I" rounds to cause people to lose interest in playing the Disdain Game.

THE CREATED SELF IS A COLLECTIVE SELF

As we have just seen, the individual Created Self needs to feel a part of one or more groups, to develop what sociologists call "collective identities." We all identify with certain groups because we consider the individual members to be like us in some essential respect—nationality, gender, religion, race, social class, sexual orientation, occupation, age, political beliefs, level of education, or tribe. These groups play a major role in defining who we are, allowing us to feel known, recognized, and appreciated by people who share our basic values and beliefs.

An interesting human phenomenon is that we find it much easier to defend the Collective Self than the smaller, personal Self. To stick up for oneself alone can leave a person feeling vulnerable, selfish, and liable to criticism. To join with others in defending the rights of an entire group, however, is to leave all sense of isolation behind, to lose the smaller, personal Self in a common effort. There can be no indictment of selfishness when we choose to fight for the rights of something (the group) larger than we are as individuals. The sense of being puny or vulnerable, likewise, is lost as we combine our strength with that of other like-minded group members. We have no need to waste energy being defensive and uncertain; we can be proud and sure of our common cause.

Patriotism is the single-most powerful demonstration of the Collective Self at work. For those stirred by nationalistic fervor, love of country far transcends love of Self. People who in every-day life appear timid and cautious will risk death in defense of their nation; people who consider murder a sin on the individual level will in time of war kill their nation's enemies—and be proud of their contributions.

An often-overlooked corollary of the Collective Self, in which the individual Self identifies with one or more groups, is the Collective Non-Self, in which Collective Selves disdain certain other groups, considering their members to be lacking in some essential quality or qualities.[3] For every collective identity you incorporate into your Self, there are one or more groups with whom you definitely do not identify (indeed, *cannot,* at the risk of your loss of collective identity). This Collective Self/Non-Self dichotomy is so strong that we can almost think of them as matched sets—for every Collective Self identity, there has to be at least one Non-Self counterpart. If I am proud of my status as a property-owning citizen, I must look down on those who do not own property. If I believe my religious orientation is the only right and true route to spiritual happiness, I must hold some disparaging opinions about the members of other religious groups. If I hold strong convictions about the superiority of my gender or age group, I must hold similar convictions about the inferiority of the opposite gender or older or younger age groups. Collective identities are, in other words, more than a little judgmental, being based so rigidly on our beliefs about how members of other groups shape up in comparison with our own. One cannot have a collective identity without, at the same time, having a picture in one's mind of what that identity is not. Not only are members of other groups people with whom we don't identify—they are actually people with whom we *dis*-identify. That is, we view them as so unlike ourselves in certain important respects that we draw an important mental line between "us" and "them."

At best, our collective identities help us understand our places and roles in the larger social world. They help us determine those basic attributes that define who we are—nationality, gender, age, religion, race, sexual orientation, and social class. They give us a foundation for Self esteem, our sense of being valued and respectable, both in our own eyes and in the regard of others.

The lines we draw between our in-groups and out-groups can be comparatively unimportant in our lives. In my own mind, for example, I draw a line between "professional musicians" (who make a living with their talent) and "amateur musicians" like myself (who play, as a friend used to say, "for their own amazement"). The difference between "us" amateurs and "those" professionals has only minimal impact on my life. Other distinctions are important enough to become barriers between one group and another and make mutual understanding virtually impossible. The "us" in my mind who are philosophical liberals, for instance, feels inescapably at odds with the "them" (also in my mind) who are religious fundamentalists, whether Christian, Jew, or Muslim. A few of those lines qualify as earthshaking. They are the collective dis-identities that separate groups from one another by potentially explosive minefields of deadly suspicion, mistrust, and hatred. As a Jew who lived through the Nazi era, for example, I find that I almost automatically stereotype avowed anti-Semites as dangerous, despicable, and essentially subhuman "thems," individuals with whom I see no possibility for (or desirability in) achieving the shared reality discussed in chapter 1.

One's position in society almost always influences how one deals with one's own collective identities and those of others. Those at or near the top of society tend to view their collective identities in much more unreservedly positive terms than do members of marginal groups. Members of a dominant group—affluent, white, Anglo-Saxon, Protestant males, for example—take a certain amount of unabashed pride in those several collective identities, taken separately or together. But how do those same individuals feel about individuals who represent their collective dis-identities—people who are not affluent, white, Anglo-Saxon, Protestant, and male? The probability is that even the most "liberal" member of this dominant group will hold the members of at least one of those dis-identified groups in some minimal (or more) degree of disdain, associating them with nonproductivity, abnormality, immorality, intellectual and/or mental handicap, crime, political and social radicalism, and social marginality.

▣ Exercise 1-D

This exercise is designed to help your Collective Self explore the dis-identities that are so important to your Self definition.

Draw a line down the middle of a sheet of paper. Label the left-hand column "Us," the right-hand column "Them."

Again, review the list you composed for the chart on page 23, this time for words that reflect your collective affiliations—age, gender, national-ity, or religion, for example. Write those words in the left-hand column.

In the right-hand column, write words that reflect the Them groups that correspond to your Us groups. If you are a male, for example, and chose Man as one of your Us groups, it is likely that Woman or Boy might show up in your Them column.

Take a close look at your Them groups, considering why the distinction between your Us groups and Them groups is important to you.

What are your feelings about your Thems?

Do you consider Them to be in some way superior or inferior to your Us?

Does your Them represent any kind of threat to your Us?

Do you find it easy or difficult to communicate with Them? To under-stand Them? To agree with Them? To have one as a friend? To work with Them? To have one as a next-door neighbor? To welcome one into your home? To marry one?

COLLECTIVE IDENTITIES OF MARGINAL GROUPS

Not surprisingly, members of marginal and oppressed groups tend to have serious reservations (what psychologists are fond of calling "mixed feelings") about their collective identities. On the one hand, they feel pride in who they are and what they and people like them have accomplished in the face of hardship, op-pression, indignity, and repeated humiliation. On the other hand (usually without being conscious of it), they often identify with the people who have power over them, taking on some of the attitudes, beliefs, and values of the dominant group, including the latter's negative biases toward their own group.

In the past, for instance, members of minority racial and ethnic groups in the United States often viewed certain characteristics of the dominant white majority as positive. Before the 1960s and the "Black Is Beautiful" movement, social status within the African American community was associated with light skin, straight hair, and white facial features.

After several generations of struggle, American women have won the right to wear trousers, work, and smoke cigarettes—all once considered male "privileges." American men, by contrast, show little or no desire to use lipstick, wear dresses, or carve out careers as full-time homemakers. To this day, to define oneself as a "housewife" or "family nurturer" (traditionally female roles) requires an unusually self-confident person, one willing to risk the condescending label of "soccer mom" to fulfill a function that is not highly valued by our still-patriarchal society.

As a Jewish child growing up in Massachusetts, I learned to behave with appropriate Yankee restraint and moderation. I never spoke in a loud voice, refrained from interrupting others, used only restrained gestures, and expressed only moderate emotions. Although I didn't realize it at the time, I know now that I (or rather, my Creative Self) had made a choice to be accepted by people who probably would have rejected me had I behaved like a "New York kike."

THE CREATED SELF BEGINS TO DEVELOP IN VERY EARLY INFANCY

So far as we can know, the newborn makes little or no distinction between itself and the world around it. It is the world and the world is it. Almost at birth, however, the infant indicates an embryonic awareness of itself as a separate being and shows signs that it relates to its mother or other primary caregiver in a very special, indeed, crucial way.

Within a few months, the infant has developed to the point where it can begin to participate in the looking-glass process. The baby begins then to "see" itself in terms of how others treat it.

From that point on, it embarks on a tremendously complicated task—that of defining its Self in a way that allows it to make sense of the world in which it exists, to minimize pain, control anxiety, achieve some degree of personality continuity, and exert control and predictability in an essentially uncontrollable environment.

THE EMERGING CREATED SELF EXPERIENCES BOTH PLEASURE AND PAIN

From the moment it pops from the womb, the newborn begins to develop behaviors that (1) help it feel comfortable, satisfied, pleased, and unified with the world; and (2) help it avoid discomfort, dissatisfaction, pain, and disharmony with that world. The barely emergent Creative Self is faced with a Herculean task—devising ways, despite its inexperience, to cope with unexpected negative responses and to cushion its immature nervous system from the sudden shock of that negativity. If the infant could put its experience into words, those words might go something like this:

Things are going pretty well around here right now. My belly's full, my diaper's dry, and I feel safe pressed up against this nice, soft being who pats me and makes soft sounds in my ear. What's this? A string of shiny, white, hard things on this soft being. I wonder what would happen if I pulled them—like this? Wow! Look at them go! Falling and rolling around down there in all directions.

Wait! Something's wrong. The soft being is slapping my fingers and making loud, hurtful noises. She's shaking me. She's yelling. Things are starting to feel pretty bad around here. Screaming doesn't help. Maybe if I sucked something—my thumb—I'd feel better. But, no. She's yelling some more and trying to pull my thumb away from my mouth. NO! I need it! It's going to stay put.

What's she saying now? She thinks I'm a stubborn kid. Just like my daddy. But she's smiling, just a little. Maybe, she likes me when I'm stubborn—whatever that means. Things are going okay around here again.

By the time a child has learned to walk, he or she has developed a sophisticated system of "radar," a sixth sense about how to

maintain the goodwill of significant adult caregivers. The following incident, reported by a friend after a family holiday that included her nineteen-month-old granddaughter, shows how
effective toddlers can be at "decoding" messages that might affect
their status within the family and how easily they mold themselves to be the "perfect children" they discern the adults around
them are asking them to be.

My friend was attending a Christmas Day brunch, assisting
her daughter in the kitchen, with the baby toddling around under-
foot, when another relative waltzed into the room, knelt down
next to the little girl, and announced, "Honey, Mr. Brown will be
here today and he will want to swing you. Mr. Brown is an old
man and he really enjoys swinging children, so please try to act as
if you like it."

The child, my friend reported, reacted by "looking horrified,
grabbing her little cheeks with both hands and shaking her
head"—a dramatic expression of her distaste for the heralded
swing by Mr. Brown. "The amazing thing, though, was how she
reacted when Mr. Brown entered the room, grabbed her under the
arms, and began swinging her madly from side to side," she continued. "She grit her teeth, plastered a rigid 'social' smile on her
face, and endured an experience she would quite obviously have
preferred to forgo."

The child was already learning what she had to do to ensure
the approval of important adults.

THE EMERGING CREATED SELF FUNCTIONS TO MINIMIZE PSYCHIC PAIN AND CONTROL ANXIETY

I often compare the Created Self to a tiny, heroic cork bobbing on
the surface of a gigantic Sea of Anxiety. It does its best to remain
dry, stay afloat, and avoid being drenched by waves of fear. As
long as the sea remains fairly calm, all is well. If for any reason,
however, something happens to threaten the real or perceived security of the Self, the sea can become turbulent and the Self (operating almost on automatic pilot) puts into effect its learned
repertoire of defensive maneuvers.

I like the image of the Sea of Anxiety because it describes several important human qualities: the inherent buoyancy of the

True Self; its gallant attempts to transcend the inner torments of humiliation, shame, and guilt that are an inescapable part of being human; and its vulnerability to those feelings when some external event threatens its security and Self importance.

THE CREATED SELF CONSISTS OF MULTIPLE SUB-SELVES

Although most of us can describe ourselves in fairly simple (if incomplete) terms, the Created Self is actually a highly complex amalgam of many Sub-Selves. Your Self, for example, has hundreds of different facets to it, many of which remain latent for long periods at a time and only a few of which are represented by the words and phrases you outlined in exercise 1.

These Sub-Selves spring from many different sources—from the various roles (husband, daughter, employer, mother) we play in life; from special qualities we've learned to admire in others and want to nurture in ourselves (intelligence, humor, obedience, rebellion); or, even, from experiences that conditioned us to avoid certain qualities or ways of relating. A few people have managed to integrate their Sub-Selves to form a well-functioning total mosaic. They carry the same basic qualities with them into their work, play, friendships, community activities, and important relationships. Most of us, however, hobble along with less than perfectly integrated personalities, struggling to bring our conflicting Self definitions into harmony, using enormous amounts of energy to deal with basic confusions over the conflicts between a woman's role as mother, for example, and her role as aspiring business executive.

In a workshop we conducted together several years before she died, Virginia Satir, a wonderfully charismatic teacher of family dynamics, described the personality of a single adult as "the dance of the many Selves." Some of us are less-than-talented dancers. Our many Selves step on one another's toes, kick one another in the shins, and generally get in the way of the dance. Others of us are experts in the art of the dance, executing complicated and ever-changing steps with élan and style. Most dancers, however, get along with simple, repetitive patterns that allow their many Selves to maneuver without tripping on one another.

In a few extreme cases of multiple personality, the Sub-Selves have taken on lives of their own, openly competing with one another for control of the person's consciousness and behavior.

THE EMERGING SELF REFLECTS CONTINUITY AND CONSISTENCY THROUGHOUT LIFE

The adult Self you have created carries many traces of the child you used to be. As Sigmund Freud showed almost a century ago, there's continuity in Self development, with each stage of maturity being based on, and growing out of, the stage that preceded it. Most forms of therapy encourage the patient to look back on his or her childhood to find the seeds of adult behavior. We all know that childhood experiences, especially traumatic ones, are reflected in the adult personality.

Unfortunately, what Freud taught about the relationship between childhood and adult personalities is often misunderstood, with too many of us choosing to blame our problems on how we were treated as children, operating as though we are doomed by past experience to repeat ineffective behavior patterns for the rest of our lives.

The truth is that we are not passive victims of our childhood environments. All of us begin soon after birth to make "choices" about how we will put our Selves together to respond to environmental stimulants. I put the word "choices" in quotation marks because we are rarely aware that we are choosing among possible options—or, even, that there are options. Nevertheless, the variety of options open to even the smallest child for Self formation and Self expression have baffled experts who try to predict how human beings develop. Erik Erikson, a noted psychologist and expert on human development, is just one of many specialists who had to admit defeat in this attempt. He studied well-documented developmental studies of children in Berkeley, California, and predicted how each of these children would fare in terms of mental health as adults. Erikson found, however, that his predictions were surprisingly off the mark. Each child had taken the raw material of his or her childhood and created something unique and unexpected from it—in some cases creating an adult Self that far exceeded Erikson's predictions of the child's potential for adult achievement and happiness.[4]

SOURCES OF SELF CREATION

Like Erikson's subjects, you spent your childhood (and continue to spend much of your adulthood) using your imagination and ingenuity to form and mold the Self you feel you need to be. Like those Berkeley children, you adopted certain possibilities, minimized others, and rejected still others completely. You may argue that you were not aware of making such choices—after all, you were just a child with no clear understanding of even the concept of options and choice. Nevertheless, for a variety of reasons, you chose to travel certain paths, overlook other possibilities, and actively avoid still others. Even without your full awareness, your Creative Self was hard at work making choices on your behalf, just as it does today and will continue to do for the rest of your life.

The sources from which your Creative Self draws much of its raw material are twofold: your inherited temperament, special talents and limitations, and physical and psychological capacities; and your life experiences (especially those that occurred in early childhood) through which your parents, friends, teachers, and associates provide millions of cues, clues, suggestions, prohibitions, injunctions, demands, and expectations for you to follow.

The point here is that Self creation is, as computer-types like to say, an interactive process, with each of us acting on our environments almost as strongly as those environments act on us. Early life experiences can strongly influence the process—but they cannot determine it; they cannot shape a human being as if he or she were a passive lump of clay. The Creative Self is a highly skilled potter, using the qualities of its innate human clay to create a Self that responds ingeniously to the demands placed on it by the world in which it finds itself living.

That potter creates through a complex process of choosing and selecting, sifting and sorting. We choose to cultivate certain of the various potentials with which we are born; we choose to neglect others. We select certain of the cues and clues our parents offer; we ignore a vast number of those cues and clues. I'm not saying that these choices and selections are made in the conscious, deliberate way we might choose a suit of clothes off a rack. On the contrary, our choices as children were made in the heat of intense emotional reaction, suddenly and often accompanied by intense rushes of adrenaline and other mysterious chemical substances into our bloodstreams, carrying such a heat of inevitability that it feels to the child (and to the adult looking back on the experience) as if it happened to us without our consent. But we consented somehow, even if we were not fully aware of having given our consent.

These days, enlightened parents are especially vulnerable to the fear that their human inadequacies will scar their children, that any little lapse from perfection will leave its mark on their offspring, causing them to lead frustrated, unhappy lives. There's a touch of arrogance in this well-intentioned concern: parents simply don't have that kind of single-handed power to create their children's Selves. Parents and other key people merely offer a range of possibilities (a menu, if you will) from which the child is free to choose. And the child does choose—determining for himself or herself who he or she is going to be.

Look back on my friend's story about her granddaughter's encounter with the swinging Mr. Brown. It is quite obvious that the toddler chose to repress her fear and frustration, chose to please the older people by behaving in a way that she understood they would define as "being a good baby." That little story, with its charged emotional elements, speaks eloquently to the power of choice and how early on even the tiniest human beings begin to exercise that power.

The bottom line here is very empowering: you created your Self through the thousands, probably millions, of small decisions you made as a child and continue to make every day. You were and always will be the creator of your Self.

The process of Self creation never stops. You are creating your Self even as you read this, agreeing or disagreeing with each sentence. Chances are, your Creative Self is hard at work, doing its best to fit what you are reading into the matrix of ideas of Self that you carry around in your mind. When what you read fits easily into that matrix, you will find yourself agreeing. But when your mind perceives an idea or impression that shakes that matrix, you may find yourself rejecting the idea, trying to discredit it and its implied attack on who you think you are. It's the old process of sifting and sorting, an inevitable, frustrating, and immensely exciting process of continuous Self creation that will continue until the day you die.

GETTING IN TOUCH WITH YOUR CREATIVE SELF
The first step in opening ourselves to the constant transformational power of the Creative Self is to become aware of that power and how it works. When we remain unaware of that creative power, we erect a formidable barrier to change and growth. We paralyze the Self, casting it in a concrete straitjacket and robbing ourselves of one of the most satisfying experiences available to us as human beings. Change—constant, revitalizing, and rejuvenating change—*is* possible. Change and growth are, in fact, natural processes, inevitable unless hampered by our own refusals to cooperate.

What all this means is that we hold the reins to our lives in our own hands. We are not helpless victims of life, but rather, the creators of our lives. Whenever you feel frustrated, discouraged, helpless, or humiliated, remember that you came equipped into this world with the power to create and re-create your Self. Today, this very minute, your Creative Self is active within you, the source of your energy and creativity. Within your grasp is the power to recognize that source, to coax it out of hiding and put it to work rebuilding or renovating your life to reflect the continuing miracle I believe every human life can be.

The "negative" trade-off (and it really isn't negative at all) is that utilizing this power demands that you accept full responsibility for who you are, that you refuse to blame others, hide behind past life traumas, or relinquish your power to what might feel like overwhelming circumstances.

▣ Exercise 2: How I Created "Me"

1. *Look again at the qualities you listed in your Self description, but this time study those qualities as you would a menu, as options you chose to incorporate into your Self.*

2. *Now think a moment—just a moment—about how those qualities serve you. Remember the experiences, situations, or relationships that stimulated you as a child to consider those qualities important.*

3. *Allow yourself to consider the possibility that you might have chosen to react very differently to each of those stimuli. You could, in other words, have chosen to be a very different person than the person you know so well today.*

In chapter 4 we will explore the high price we pay every day for the choices we made years ago when we decided we had to give up the freedom of childhood to become the adults we are today.

FOUR

The Scrim of Self
(Or How We See through a Filter Darkly)

◫ ◫ ◫

Life is what happens while we're busy making plans.

—Anonymous

The expression "eye of the beholder" describes a phenomenon with which most of us are familiar—the fact that the memories and observations of different individuals exposed to the same event will differ markedly from one another. We inevitably shape what we see and hear, overlooking crucial aspects, sometimes even filling in nonexistent details to make the total picture fit our preconceived ideas.

Usually we treat these distortions as unavoidable errors, proof of our human fallibility, a condition that most of us accept with the same wry resignation with which we accept the inevitability of death and taxes.

What we often fail to recognize is that the concept of our inevitable fallibility (imagine—we are *designed* to be wrong!) is a myth, one that reflects a basic distortion in the way we perceive our world. By clinging to this Myth of Fallibility, we tacitly give credibility to its disempowering corollaries, the first of which is the assumption that there exists a perfect description of the event under discussion, a perfect truth about what happened, a truth that we would all recognize if we weren't so error-prone. The second corollary assumes that there also exists an infallible observer who can describe the True Event (if only he or she would come out of hiding long enough to do so).

The simple act of freeing ourselves from these unexamined beliefs can have an unexpectedly liberating effect on our lives. Seen without the distorting light of the Myth of Fallibility, many of the arguments that take place between human beings become ludicrous exercises in superstition—two or more individuals pleading their cases before an invisible court. "Will the Truth about this event please stand up?" The arguments and the adrenaline flow, tempers flare, and order is disrupted, all in the name of currying favor before a nonexistent, all-knowing judge.

THE WEB OF SHARED EXPERIENCE

Eliminating the Myth of Fallibility and the objective reality the myth implies leaves us with a new multi-reality—a shifting, changing, complex, undefined, fascinating, and often disorienting panorama, a web of reality composed of gossamer threads of human interaction and perception, with each thread cast in a uniquely personal and subjective way by its spinner.

I'm reminded of the web whenever I reminisce with my four adult sons about their childhoods, periods of time which live in each of our memories as distinctly different sets of experiences. Among the most disjointed threads in our family web is an almost mythic account of a cross-country camping trip my wife and I took with the boys when they ranged in age from seven to thirteen. We worked hard on that trip to show the boys all the marvelous sights this country offers and I recall feeling very irritated by their ho-hum attitudes. Each day I grew increasingly annoyed as they sat, mesmerized by comic books or absorbed in board games in the rear of our station wagon. This irritation finally erupted into what I recall as a volcanic tirade on a street corner in San Francisco's bustling Chinatown when, after only a few minutes of sightseeing, one of them asked: "When are we going back to the car?"

I have a crystalline memory of sitting the four of them down the following morning on a bench amidst the quiet grandeur of the redwood trees in Muir Woods north of the city. I can still hear myself apologizing for my outburst, insisting, however, that I remained concerned about their attitude. I can see the youngest boy poking his older brother, urging him to speak for them all.

"Go ahead, Stef," I remember saying to the reluctant spokesman. "You know you can say anything you need to say to me."

After stumbling around a few seconds, our oldest son blurted out: "Well, frankly, Dad, we talked about this last night and we all agreed that we'd never seen such a childish display of emotions!"

Stef's little speech will remain forever highlighted in my memory as one of the defining incidents of my life as a father. My boys, however, consider the story to be an example of my inventive imagination, something that never happened except in my fevered paternal mind. Their memories, likewise, are filled with anecdotes that sound like movie scripts to me, events and conversations that I would swear in court (if I had to) never occurred.

What's important here is not to try to determine who is right or why our versions of our shared pasts differ so markedly. What matters is to recognize that we are *all* right. How each of us remembers—or fails to remember—that afternoon in San Francisco and the ensuing morning in the Muir Woods works for each of us. Our individual reactions to the California trip spring organically from who we are—the complex perceptions, needs, and talents that serve our individual Creative Selves. We all created our own realities, realities based not on some objective set of facts, but on our subjective interpretation of those facts.

Facts and events, seen without the distorting lens of the Myth of Fallibility, are not life. They are just the basic raw materials of life. *Life is the interpretation we choose to give to those events that capture our attention.* This is equally true for what we call memory and for the imaginings that we call the future. Even the most painstaking historian cannot reconstruct past events with any absolute claim to accuracy. History is only a generally accepted version, or "story," of what happened.

It is not surprising, therefore, to find that until recently official historians and those who wrote the histories of major corporations, universities, and other institutions in the United States were, with few exceptions, white, Anglo-Saxon, male Protestants. It is only in recent years that so-called revisionist histories have been written from the viewpoint of those on the lower rungs of caste, class, and gender—that is, African Americans, women, and the native peoples who occupied the continent before Europeans appeared on their scene. Needless to say, their accounts are light-years away from the histories written by those who identify with and are the descendants of the European conquerors of the American continent.

Compared with our contending (and often contentious) per-spectives on the past, our versions of the future engender much less confusion. Time for most of us flows in only one direction—from past to present to future. The events of the past have already happened, giving us the illusion that the past is somehow objec-tively real. Since the future has yet to occur, it feels natural to ac-cept the idea that our thoughts about it are just the best predictions we can make, not a set-in-concrete reality.

THE FUNCTION OF THE MIND

Susanne Langer, an eminent Harvard philosopher, calls the mind an "automatic idea-generating machine," operating whether we will it to or not, whether we happen to be concentrating on a par-ticular problem or simply daydreaming.[1] Just as the lungs auto-matically push air in and out of our bodies, our minds work unceasingly to generate a never-ending stream of ideas. Just as the stomach is rarely entirely quiet, so the mind continues to gen-erate thoughts, images, and other distinctions even when there's no apparent reason for it to do so. As insomniacs and meditators know, it is next to impossible to force the mind to shut down. When denied input from the outside world, the mind will stimu-late itself, creating hallucinatory information to fuel its idea-generating function.

Experienced meditators know that even when they sit for hours staring at a blank wall, their minds continue to work. Uninvited thoughts and feelings, some of them very intense, just "come to mind" and wise meditators soon realize that any effort to turn off the tap of ideas and distinctions is futile. After years of patient practice, they may learn to "disconnect" from those thoughts, recognizing them for what they are—blips on the screen of consciousness, carrying no compelling reality of their own.

Like the stomach's incessant churning, the mind's constant chatter serves a necessary survival function. The mind "digests" experience, breaking it into understandable and, for the most part, manageable chunks. Because the mind creates its distinctions, we can recognize chairs and tables, distinguish between friends and enemies, stick to safe activities and avoid dangers, tell the difference between what we believe to be right and wrong, good and bad, and have no doubt about which way is "up" and which is "down." Without such distinctions, chaos would reign in our lives.

WE ARE ALWAYS RIGHT
The following ancient story, which I've seen attributed variously to Sufi, Buddhist, and Hasidic Jewish sages, illustrates another fundamental truth about the human mind.

> A distraught husband approached a sage and his disciple, and launched into a long tirade about his wife, an unbearable, tormenting woman. The sage waited for the husband to have his say, stroking his beard and nodding sympathetically. When the man finished, the sage said: "You are right, my son, you are right. But what's to be done? Go home and make the best of things." Feeling somewhat better for having had someone listen to him, the man left.
>
> The next day, the man's wife (that unbearable woman) sought out the sage. She, too, was greatly distressed and complained about her husband in an equally bitter and long tirade. Again, the sage listened patiently, stroking his beard and nodding sympathetically. When the woman finished, the sage said: "You are right, my daughter, you are right. But what's to be done? Go home and make the best of things." She, like her husband before her, left feeling somewhat better for having had a sympathetic ear.
>
> The disciple was baffled. "Master," he said, "yesterday the husband complained about the wife and you said, 'You are right.' Today, the wife complained about the husband and you said, 'You are right.' Master, they can't both be right!" Having listened attentively to his disciple, stroking his beard and nodding sympathetically, the sage replied, "You are right."

This ancient parable illustrates a basic psychological truth that is all too often overlooked—that in creating its individual distinctions, a person's mind always puts itself on the right side. In his own mind, the husband was justified in complaining about his wife; in her mind, the wife was right in her complaints against her husband; in his mind, the disciple was right in his protests against this paradox.

Even when we change our minds and adopt another point of view, we take our "rightness" with us, often congratulating ourselves for being able to admit our earlier mistakes. The next time you find yourself telling someone—be it your spouse, child, co-worker, or friend—"You're absolutely wrong," know in your heart of hearts that the one thing you and that other person hold in common is the conviction "I am right." On the wall of my study I have tacked the following quotation attributed to that famous coiner of wise phrases, "Anonymous":

> The world is filled with different people who think they are right.

ON BEING RIGHTEOUS

There is no way to escape this rather remarkable phenomenon: it is quite impossible to be anything but right in one's own mind at any one given moment in time. It is a very basic part of the human condition, one that has played an important role in our survival as a species. Can you imagine a race of creatures in which the individual members attempt to live from the premise that they are wrong?

The problem is not with our innate (and usually healthy) need to insist on our own rightness, but rather with its illogical (and usually unhealthy) corollary: in order for us to be right, someone else has to be wrong. When that corollary comes into play, when we feel compelled to make ourselves right at the expense of proving others wrong, we have a situation that is ripe for conflict. At such times, instead of being content with simply being right (which comes close to being a human birthright), we become righteous. To coin an awful word, one cannot be righteous without making someone else "wrongeous"!

As I've grown older, I've noticed that it's far easier for me to avoid the pitfall of righteousness when I'm feeling mellow, when all's right with my world, when that part of me that doubts my worth is feeling well cared for and quiet. If, however, a situation arises that somehow threatens my Self esteem, my righteousness is apt to erupt in a vigorous defense of my views and an equally righteous effort to prove my "attacker" wrong. Like a fish at the end of a line, my ego is hooked, flopping around with great energy in doomed efforts to set itself free.

CONFIRMERS, CONFORMERS, AND CREATORS
An American fable illustrates our options in determining how we choose to see the events that make up the outer landscape of our lives.

> Three baseball umpires were relaxing after a hot day at the ballpark, quaffing a cold beer and talking shop.
>
> The youngest bragged: "When it comes to balls and strikes, I call 'em like I see 'em."
>
> Not to be outdone, the middle-aged, more experienced man replied: "I call 'em like they is!"
>
> To which the oldest, a veteran nearing retirement, said: "They ain't nuthin' until I call 'em."[2]

Courageous Confirmers are people who, like the youngest umpire, do their best to call 'em like they see 'em, even if others disagree. They know they are human and subject to error, but they have the courage to stand by their convictions. Courageous Confirmers believe that the balls and strikes of life have objective reality of their own, apart from what people say and do. Good citizens and hard workers, they struggle to understand and follow the rules. Insofar as they are able, they obey the regulations that others have set in place, but they are prepared to endure considerable disapproval and even humiliation when their personal convictions make it impossible for them to obey.

Courageous Confirmers are the ulcer-prone among us, those people who, no matter how hard they try, can never feel completely conflict-free. There's a reason for this—they are constantly measuring their performance and convictions against standards set by other people, pleading their case before that nonexistent judge. They can be wonderful people and fine, upstanding citizens, but they have moved very far from the freedom that was theirs before they became wedded to the demands of the Self images they themselves had created.

Infallible Conformers have an advantage over their Confirmer colleagues. In their complete faith in the rightness of their own stances, they are freed of the conflicts and questions that plague the conscientious Confirmer. They are also often blissfully oblivious to the fact that they are slowly alienating everyone around them. At best, they are condescending toward those who don't think as they do; at worst, they are bullies, free to condemn, humiliate, torture—and even kill—those who dare differ from them in any way.

We all know individuals with conformer tendencies—the unreasonable neighbor, the demanding supervisor, the relative who insists on engaging in political arguments at every family gathering. These are people we might prefer to avoid, people who make our lives just a tad more challenging than we really want them to be. They may not be the most likable people on the planet, but they pose none of us any particular threat.

Delinquents, criminals, rebels, and other deviants, on the other hand, are a special subtype of the Infallible Conformer—the Infallible Non-Conformer. Like Courageous Confirmers, they experience the rules and regulations of life as having been set down by others, codified in stone with a life and logic of their own. Unlike Confirmers, however, Non-Conformers find it humiliating to follow rules defined by other people. They reject all rules and those who make, enforce, and obey them. In their places, Non-Conformers substitute their own sets of rules and their own authorities, investing them with an equal degree of infallibility.

Creators are people who, like the veteran baseball umpire, know that life's balls and strikes exist only because they decide to call them. These people are free of the inner conflicts of Confirmers and the outer conflicts of Conformers because they have learned that they are the people who determine their reality based on their chosen interpretation of any given situation.

Recognizing the power they have over their own lives, they create their reality in a way that is affirming and exciting for both themselves and the people around them. As we shall come to understand later, they live in the state I call Appreciation—free of reality-distorting preconceptions and expectations, able to accept each day, each minute, each experience as it comes, open to the spontaneous creativity that is the essence of life.

As I have mentioned before, the idea that there is a substantial gap between external reality and our experience of it has ancient roots, going back to at least the twelfth century. As one author explains, almost a millennium ago, philosophically inclined scholars were questioning the commonsense belief that we can describe the world in a way that is separate from our involvement with and experience of it.[3] The same author presents the following delightful account of how reality becomes personal experience:

> By the time the truths about reality . . . reach our minds they have been through the eyes of a very mortal seer who may have been in need of glasses, and who did not speak our dialect, written down by a scribe who made transcription errors, translated by someone who was not perfectly bilingual, and narrated by a storyteller who got the emphasis all wrong.[4]

PLATO'S CAVE

Plato, the ancient Greek philosopher, said most people behaved as if they lived in a cave with their backs to the entrance. Their reality consisted only of the reflections cast by the fire, flickering and dancing on the cave wall. Plato's cave people spent their lives hypnotized by these dim illusory reflections—much as many of us live our lives mesmerized by the dim reflections of reality that are the mental images we project on our world. The pity is that all they had to do to break the spell was turn around and a whole new, vivid, colorful world would have been waiting just behind them.

Plato's metaphor begins to describe the situation we will be addressing throughout the remainder of this book—the plight of those of us who have forgotten the power of Appreciation to illuminate and transform life. The power of Appreciation is just our modern way of referring to the experience Plato knew was possible, that experience being the ability to perceive the world in constantly new, vivid, and colorful terms. I find the cave story limiting, however, in its implication that utilizing the power of Appreciation is an either/or choice—that we either live in the full glory of reality or we turn our backs on life and hover at the back of a dark cave. One can't see both ways—back into the darkness and out into the bright light of reality—at the same time. But one can make a choice to live with Appreciation as often as possible, allowing it to become a habit that permeates our lives, giving ourselves permission to "regress" to projection without punishment or sanction or discipline. Appreciation is not an either/or kind of thing, but rather a constant redirecting of energy, a conscious decision to change the ingrained habits of a lifetime.

I prefer another analogy, one taken from the tradition of the theater, to describe how we too often allow ourselves to become insulated from life by the ideas and beliefs we create in the process of creating our Selves.

THE ANALOGY OF THE SCRIM

In chapters 2 and 3, I went to some lengths to describe how we sift and select ideas and qualities, looking for attributes to incorporate into our sense of Self to buffer and protect our emerging consciousnesses from the blows of our unpredictable environments. Those buffers are, in effect, pure abstractions that we give the power of reality and allow to serve as barricades between ourselves and the world. They serve their intended purpose well, giving form and structure to our experiences. But they also interfere enormously with our experiences of life, in many cases obliterating the instinctive capacity for Appreciation, absorbing the energies that could be devoted to clarity, joy, energy, and creativity.

Theatrical workers are familiar with a traditional piece of equipment known as the scrim, a transparent curtain that can be painted with scenery and used as a background for the action on stage. When the footlights or spotlights shine on the curtain, it appears opaque and its painted scenery takes on an air of dramatic reality. When the stage lights come on behind the curtain, however, the scrim and its scenery disappear. I like to think of the ideas and concepts that compose your Created Self as the scenery of your life, scenery that you have selected to paint on your personal mental scrim and go to some pains to maintain. To the extent that the lights of consciousness focus on this mental scenery, your scrim appears opaque and those painted-on ideas, attitudes, beliefs, and feelings become your only reality. Sitting psychologically on the audience side of your scrim, you treat your own life like an impersonal drama, something being played out on a rented stage. You've purchased your ticket, but forfeited your right to play the star role. You have, quite literally, traded a badly painted facade for the three-dimensional, Technicolor reality you were born to enjoy.

The analogy of the scrim closely approximates reality as understood by Buddhist monks, people who have been studying human consciousness since before the dawn of Western history. According to Daniel Goleman, a *New York Times* writer and a student of Eastern religious thought and philosophy, the Buddhist model posits at least eight levels (or Jhanas) of consciousness that are available to individuals who are willing, through meditation, to leave Plato's cave, to shift the light of their Creative Selves away from their own creation and back onto the world.[5]

Even at the first, or lowest, Jhana, which the monks refer to as an "access state," practitioners experience an ability to free themselves from unwanted thoughts, focus their concentration at will, and live their lives closer to what Eastern sages considered an undistorted reality. This very lowest "higher" state opens the doors to a procession of higher levels, revealing natural feelings of rapture, happiness, and equanimity. Those who attain the higher levels are able to function at any of the lower levels at will.

GOING BEHIND THE SCRIM

The scrim combines Plato's Western (highly structured, either/or) and Buddhism's Eastern (somewhat formless) models into a many-faceted, but very tangible, possibility that works well for most Western minds.

To understand the concept of the scrim, imagine yourself in a darkened theater, watching a scene in a play that turns out to be the story of your life. Suddenly, the lighting onstage shifts a little, bringing with it a complete transformation of the scenery there. The original scenery, which seemed so solid only seconds ago, disappears and previously hidden parts of the stage are revealed. The scene that you had originally perceived to be taking place around a family dinner table inside an apartment building appears now to be unfolding at a table set in a picnic area of a lovely, manicured park. A whole new reality, and with it a whole new set of dramatic possibilities, appears. The world is so close—just behind

our Self-selected facades—yet so far away, seemingly hidden behind a complex weave of truth, half-truth, denial, illusion, and
fantasy. When you learn to apply that model to your interior life,
you will be able—through the simple act of shifting your inner
lights so you can see through your internal scrims—to perceive
whole new vistas of reality and a broad range of new possibilities.

MORE ABOUT CONFIRMERS, CONFORMERS, AND CREATORS

Confirmers and Conformers live life on a limited stage. Their
worlds lie in front of their painted scrims, which form the boundaries of their experiences and beliefs. For these types, the world as
defined by their scrims is the only reality possible.

Creators, on the other hand, live life on a boundless stage.
Their realities include both what is being enacted in front of the
current scrim and what lies behind that curtain, which they recognize as transparent and amenable to change. They know that
how they experience life depends on how they choose to illuminate events with the light of their own consciousnesses. They
never have to choose between one reality and another because
they recognize (often intuitively) that reality exists on both sides
of their mental curtains. When operating in front of the scrim of
everyday consciousness, they are able to deal Appreciatively with
the illusions that most people treat as life-and-death reality. They
know that behind their chosen scrims lies a boundless reality of
unending richness and deep satisfaction.

Creators, as I have said, choose the lives they live, a way of
being that demands both courage and commitment. Commitment
is necessary to resist the seductive power of the scrim to insinuate
its way between the liver and the life that is being lived, to work
constantly to remain conscious of the mental curtain on which the
scenery of their lives appears. Courage is necessary to be faithful
to the vision of a broader, richer version of reality that they know
is available behind the scrim. I've been privileged to know a few
people who have the commitment and courage to live their lives
behind the scrim. These individuals have all been highly intelligent, competent people, fully aware of the difficulties of life and
the obstacles they face as they strive to meet their goals. They are

not dreamers or starry-eyed idealists, but rather, individuals who are totally committed to bringing the power of Appreciation to each obstacle, to utilize that power to overcome those obstacles, not by dint of will or determination, but with ease and grace.

They also share a common fascination with the totality of what life has to offer and a refusal to waste time or energy defending their Created Selves against real or fancied ridicule or scorn. Perhaps most important, they have all learned that tapping into the power of Appreciation necessitates an acceptance of the tenet that life's dramas are based on interpretations of experience. They understand that we are all the umpires in our own game of life, with full power to call our experiences the way we see them— pleasurable or painful, good or bad, welcome or unwelcome. For all that they share, however, these extraordinary individuals are a diverse lot, including people as different in background and talents as the following:

- Erich Lindemann, a psychoanalyst whose profound positive regard for others, optimism, and ability to involve laypeople in creating an entire community dedicated to the mental health of its citizens helped spark the development of a nationwide revolution in preventive community mental health programs.
- James Rouse, a deeply religious businessman whose compelling vision of caring communities led him to a creative lifetime during which he directed the development of Columbia, Maryland, a planned new city of close to one hundred thousand people; launched a program to rehabilitate inner-city areas; and invested time, money, and energy in creating affordable housing for poor families in many communities around the nation.
- Marlene Williams, a nurse who refuses to see the disease in the people she cares for, preferring to focus her attention on the "wonderfully healthy people who live inside" those illness-racked bodies. With her nonjudgmental, joyous, and transparent manner, she creates a healing presence that I'm sure has helped restore many a patient to glowing good health.

HOW CONFIRMERS AND CONFORMERS SET THEMSELVES UP FOR DISAPPOINTMENT

Several years ago, my wife and I accompanied two other couples on a whale-watching expedition in the Pacific Ocean near San Diego. Our expectations as we set sail were clear—an afternoon spent communing with nature, observing the activities of one of the planet's most dramatic creatures.

We had barely left harbor, however, before a thick shroud of fog encircled our boat. We spent hours straining our eyes and listening attentively for the least evidence of the sea mammals we had contracted to observe. The closest encounter we had with whales occurred late in the afternoon when we heard one surface nearby, breathing heavily through its blowhole, and saw the water swirling as the giant creature passed underneath the surface near our boat. Not once, however, did one of us actually catch sight of a whale.

We headed back to shore, only to have the starter for the boat's motor jam, forcing us to inch our way under sail, blowing our foghorn, listening to the horns of other vessels, and scanning the radar screen to avoid a collision in the fog. We were met at the mouth of the harbor by a friend of the skipper's who towed us, tired, chilled, and soaked by the sea mist, into port.

Viewed from the rigid perspective of either a Conformer or a Confirmer, individuals who accept the scenery as presented by their Self-created scrim of expectation, the day was a disaster. Each couple had wasted the better part of a day and close to one hundred dollars in a vain attempt to see migrating whales. Two of us had been seasick, all of us were wet and tired and more than a little frightened, since we knew very little about navigating in fog.

Envision the same trip, however, from the perspective of a Creator, an individual who is able to move his or her permeable scrim aside to make room for unexpected developments, someone who has rediscovered (or never lost) the spontaneous fascination with life that happy children have. A Creator would begin such a trip with a far broader purpose than whale watching—to experience whatever came along and Appreciate whatever wonderful surprises life onboard had to present.

As the fog descended, a Creator would simply refocus attention, regearing his or her mental lighting to bring his or her companions into bold relief, to discover that they were complex and interesting individuals with fascinating personal histories. A Creator would learn that the skipper was an iconoclast, an independent woman who loved the sea and relished the opportunity to point out the human-made and natural sights of the harbor she knows as well as she knows her own home.

When the motor failed, a Creator would recognize the beginnings of a grand adventure—an opportunity to experience the sea as few landlubbers ever do, complete with pea-soup fog, quacking horns, and the voices of unseen skippers calling greetings from neighboring vessels.

Unlike our fictional Confirmers and Conformers, who would have felt obligated to expend energy on grieving over what "should have been," Creators have the gift of staying in the present, seeing not what should or could or might or would have been, but what *is,* using the energy their colleagues waste in mourning their lost opportunity (the opportunity to enjoy the day as they had painted it beforehand on their mental scrims) to create a whole new set of adventure-filled possibilities.

KEEPING THE SCRIM IN PLACE
Keeping the scrim in place, as all children intuitively know, is hard work, requiring huge investments of energy and a willingness to forgo the wonders that life has to offer at every turn. Keeping the scrim in place is an art form in itself, an endeavor that requires a complete set of learned behaviors.

The first of those learned behaviors is the habit of comparison, of jamming our memory banks with details that become our standard for every new experience. By comparing every new experience with a similar one from our pasts, we can usually manage to drain the wonder from even the most potentially exciting event. Once you start listening to yourself and your companions with the object of minimizing the effects of your mental scrim, you will begin to notice how often we prefer the remembered event to the current one. You will become sensitive to such daily observations as: "This restaurant just doesn't compare to the one we visited last week" or "You really ought to shop at so-and-so's—the prices are better and the proprietor is so much more knowledgeable than the guy who runs this joint" or "The people back home in Omaha [or Texas or Baltimore or Hong Kong] are so much friendlier [or more refined or gracious or outgoing or conscientious] than they are here."

Like all human habits, comparison can serve a useful function, conserving energy by allowing us to select with great efficiency shops, restaurants, movies, friends, and services that meet our needs and preferences. When it becomes an automatic mode of behavior, however, comparison becomes dysfunctional, draining our lives of enjoyment and dampening our abilities to appreciate what the banquet of life puts before us to enjoy.

Another learned behavior that ensures the impermeability of our scrims is our tendency to become indifferent to even the most delightful experience when it is repeated, the human tendency to desensitize the familiar.

I once staffed a weeklong workshop at Columbia University's Conference Center in the palatial Harriman mansion north of New York City. The food for the workshop was catered by a posh service and the menu, which remained constant throughout the week, included a remarkable array of delicious gourmet selections. For the first few days, mealtimes were occasions of delight, with everyone looking forward to the fine fare. By the end of the fourth day, however, more than one participant could be heard to observe, "Oh, no, not the same old menu again."

THE PRICE OF THE SCRIM:
THE DEATH OF WONDER

Small children—human beings whose Creative Selves are still fully functioning—seem to be immune to the effects of comparison and repetition. Unlike adults, they insist on enjoying even the most mundane events in their lives, bringing the full impact of their focused attention and energy to each and every situation. Youngsters approach each experience as a "first," with few of the rigid expectations adults bring to events and situations. What allows children their zestful appreciation of life is the permeability of their scrims, their capacity to see through and beyond their still-thin scrims to the vast reality that lies behind them.

WHY DO WE TAKE OURSELVES SO SERIOUSLY?
Because that entity you call your Self (what we are calling here the Created Self) is no more real than a character in a book or play does not mean that it should be dismissed as trivial or meaningless. A magnificent creation of your mind and imagination, your Created Self is designed to help you achieve value in the eyes of others and to avoid painfully humiliating experiences. Rather than devaluing it as nothing but fiction, you can choose to celebrate the creative talents that have enabled you to design, maintain, and enhance that Self throughout your life. Still, there is no need to take that character any more seriously than you would any character in a novel or play.

The process of moving behind the scrim begins with the recognition that your Created Self exists only because you gave it life and continue to allow and empower its existence, that it has no reality apart from your own creativity. This is a simple recognition with profound implications. Like a watershed change that produces an alteration in the flow of an entire river, this recognition entails a single decision about who you are that affects every aspect of your life.

Moving behind your personal scrim will remove a heavy burden, the burden of fear of what other people might think or say or do. Without this burden, you will have renewed energy—the energy that is too often used for defensive maneuvers designed to forestall humiliation and maintain Self esteem, maneuvers that usually backfire, producing painful results.

No longer having to defend your Created Self, you will become more fully aware of the "made-up" nature of the images that fill your mind. Instead of being frustrated, annoyed, and frightened by life, you will be able to savor the magnificence, beauty, complexity, and delightful absurdity of it all. You will discover that you are able to tune into your inherent ability to bring the feeling of appreciation to bear on whatever life has to offer. In effect, you will once again illuminate life with the fascination and wonder with which you entered the world. You will rediscover the childlike wonder that is every person's birthright . . . the essence of childhood, itself.

This first step is simple, but it is far from automatic or effortless. It can be, like most actions that result in profound change, baffling, confusing, even scary. Only after the change is complete is it possible to look back and see how easy it really was—the change itself was not the least bit difficult; what was difficult was the fear and anxiety we created around the experience of change.

The exercise in the next section will help you begin softening whatever hard-angled attitudes you might have about the process of change.

THE SCRIM AT WORK

As we will see in upcoming chapters, many of the psychological mechanisms that keep our mental scrims locked tightly in place have their origins in childhood efforts to protect the developing Created Self from perceived or real attacks. The scrim is a product of our childhoods, a fabric woven by the embryonic Created Self to filter the full impact of reality, to give it shape and form, often to buffer the immature ego from the more threatening aspects of consciousness.

As with all human adaptations, the scrim promotes our well-being when it functions within the limits within which it is designed to function—as a consciously chosen (preferred) model of reality. Because it is (and was) designed to be malleable, the scrim changes with each subtle alteration in our interior lighting.

▣ Exercise 3: The Scrim at Work

I like to present the following exercise to my workshop participants as an introduction to the scrim and how it affects not simply our actions but the very context within which our actions occur.

Step 1: *Close your eyes, relax, and visualize a television or movie screen. Bring to the screen an image of the moment you entered the room, sat down, and gathered yourself for this activity, including any details you can.*

Open your eyes, look around the room, and notice not what you actually see, but what the experience of seeing is like (that is, how clearly you see the room and its contents, the quality of the lighting, the various perspectives lent by shadow and distance to the objects around you). Make some notes about this experience.

Step 2: *Again, close your eyes, relax, and bring to your mental screen an image of a situation from your life (past or present) in which you ex-perience(d) intense negative feelings, such as anger, disappointment, or jealousy. Experience those feelings now. Get in touch with your anger or other intense negative emotions. Let them be fully present for you right now.*

Let the experience fade from the screen, but retain the intense negative feeling. Open your eyes and bring the feeling with you into the room, look around the room, and notice again the experience of seeing. Make some notes.

Step 3: *Repeat step 2, but this time envision on your mental screen a situation in which you experienced positive feelings such as wonder, fascination, appreciation, joy, or love. Remember a time when you were deeply involved in an experience such as listening to beautiful music, watching a sunset, or enjoying the first raptures of a new love. Give yourself a moment or two to let those feelings "live" for you again, not just in memory, but in the present moment.*

Open your eyes and bring those positive feelings into the room, using them as the background on which your perceptions of your environment are etched. Look around the room, and notice again the experience of see-ing. Make some notes.

Most of my workshop participants report significant differences between the first experience (which establishes a kind of neutral baseline) and the ones that follow. Under step 2 (the lens of negativity) perceptions tend to be less detailed and the room appears darker. Under step 3 (what will be discussed later in the book as the lens of Appreciation) the lighting ap-pears brighter and people and objects stand out more clearly and in a more three-dimensional way.

In chapter 5, we will discuss more fully the power of the "scrim of Self" to operate either as an iron curtain that separates us from our world or as a stage prop for lives of dramatically ex-pressed personal and professional liberation and creativity.

FIVE

The Prison of the Protected Self: The Humiliation Dynamic

◲ ◲ ◲

If life lived with Appreciation is such a glorious experience, why do so many of us choose to live imprisoned by our own mental scrims? Why choose the false (and deadening) security of Plato's cave over the vast vital vistas that are so easily available, that were, in fact, our only realities when we were born? The answer is terribly, sadly simple—we choose confinement because at some level most of us are afraid to live differently, because we have allowed ourselves to be hypnotized into believing that it really is too late to be happy, so we'd better be content with playing it safe.

The following vignettes will begin to illustrate what that fear is about and how it comes to be such an overriding factor in defining the direction and quality of too many lives:

> A project manager in a large aerospace firm is presenting an important project proposal to fellow managers and top brass of his operating division. One of his peers, a brash, outspoken, and often abrasive individual, interrupts the presentation, poking fun at the manager and ridiculing his ideas. Although the presenter is fully prepared, this attack throws him off stride and causes him to be less than effective in presenting his ideas. He feels bitterly humiliated both by the remarks of his colleague and by his own inability to deal with them.
>
> A bright young woman marries in the middle of her junior year in college. She quits school and goes to work so her new husband can finish law school. Once his career is launched,

she gives up a promising job as a merchandising manager to have their first child. Three children later, she finds herself trapped in an impossible marriage with a hard-drinking and increasingly abusive husband. Despite her best efforts to please and placate him, she seems unable to do anything right in his eyes. After a series of episodes in which he hits and ridicules her, she experiences a serious depression, finally entering a private psychiatric hospital for treatment.

The president of Iraq is a charismatic leader of his poverty-stricken, Muslim countrymen and other Muslims throughout the Middle East, who feel they have been humiliated and oppressed by the United States and other Western nations. He builds a formidable military force and invades the monarchy of Kuwait, which his nation has claimed as its own since the territory was divided up in the early 1900s by the colonial powers. Faced with an overwhelming military threat by the United States and a coalition of nations under the aegis of the United Nations, Iraq's president Saddam Hussein is quoted in the media as saying, "Under no circumstances will Iraq allow itself to be humiliated."

In each of these very different scenarios, the protagonists have had their worldviews distorted by the Humiliation Dynamic. Humiliation or the fear of humiliation has so colored their mental scrims that their entire worlds have temporarily (as in the case of the aerospace engineer) or more permanently (in the case of Iraq) become nothing more than stages on which the vicious drama of humiliation is unconsciously and continuously acted out.

PREDISPOSITION TO HUMILIATION

As these cases imply, no one is immune from the pernicious possibilities of humiliation. The protagonists in all three dramas are individuals with no special inborn drive toward humiliation. The engineer was competent and prepared, yet he crumpled under the humiliating assault of his colleague. The young woman started her marriage as a bright and equal partner, yet her inability to protect herself from her husband's humiliating attacks cost her years of productive living. Saddam Hussein is a powerful, respected man in his own and many other countries, yet his fear of humiliation made it impossible for him to respond rationally to the military situation posed by the Gulf War. Fear of humiliation led him to expose his people to the possibility of virtual annihilation rather than "back down" in the face of overwhelming odds.

The point here is that the very process of growth predisposes all but the most fortunate of human beings to the Humiliation Dynamic. In its most formative stages, your Created Self had to deal with a vast array of challenges that made it feel powerless, unappreciated, put down, helpless, and, even, rejected by significant others. Embedded within our sense of Self, therefore, are early childhood experiences, the unconscious memory of which can be triggered by any adult experience that threatens ridicule, scorn, contempt, or rejection. All of us, even the most outwardly powerful, effective, and healthy, carry within ourselves a hidden person—a weak, powerless, and frightened "Humiliated Self" that began taking form when the helpless child we once were realized that it was dependent on others and vulnerable to their approval and power. This internalized "humiliated child" is universally present in all human beings, at the very core of the human personality, complete with intense (and easily activated) feelings of fear, frustration, and impotent rage.

In *The Drama of the Gifted Child*, Alice Miller tells about watching a young couple wander through a park with their two-year-old son. Miller recounts the events from the child's perspective, providing a study in frustration and ambivalence that will sound familiar to even the most well-adjusted adult. The parents had purchased ice-cream bars and were obviously enjoying them as they strolled along the tree-lined pathways. The little boy, however, had no ice cream, a situation that he found most distressing, and he was expressing his dismay by "running alongside the parents and whining." The mother, with affection in her voice and manner, offered the boy a bite of her ice-cream bar because "a whole one is too cold for you." The child persisted in his desire for a whole one for himself, and the father repeated the mother's offer of just one bite. "'No, no,' cried the child," and he ran off, only to return once more with his request for a whole bar. Again, however, only a bite was offered, and when the child tried to take the whole bar, the offer was withdrawn.

The more the child cried, the more it amused his parents. It made them laugh, and they hoped to humor him along with their laughter, too: "Look, it isn't so important, what a fuss you are making." Once the child sat down on the ground and began to throw little stones over his shoulder in his mother's direction, but then he suddenly got up again and looked around anxiously, making sure that his parents were still there. When his father had completely finished his ice cream, he gave the stick to the child and walked on. The little boy licked the wood expectantly, looked at it, threw it away, wanted to pick it up again but did not do so, and a deep sob of loneliness and disappointment shook his little body.[1]

A friend recently recounted to me a story of childhood humiliation that illustrates even more chillingly how routinely, even lovingly, adults unconsciously inflict humiliation on children.

My friend, her daughter, and her seventeen-month-old granddaughter were gathered at the home of a relative, an event that was also attended by the baby's great grandparents. The great-grandfather, whom family members call "Pops," had injured his finger in a woodworking accident and came to the party wearing an enormous splint/bandage contraption. He greeted the child by shoving the finger into her face and saying, "Pops has a boo-boo. Why don't you kiss it?"

The child took one look at Pops's dramatically injured finger and recoiled, adamantly refusing to even look at the object she was being asked to kiss. That little encounter, according to my friend, became quite the topic of conversation among the adults at the gathering, provoking competitive imitations of the child's untutored and unspoiled reaction.

Several days later, my friend was sharing a McDonald's Happy Meal with her granddaughter, enjoying the child's babbled attempts at conversation. Suddenly, the little girl announced, in perfect English and in a voice full of righteous indignation, "GRAMMA, I DID TOO KISS POP BOO-BOO."

My friend's first reaction was amazement at her granddaughter's capacity to utter a complete sentence. Her second reaction was "detached adult amusement" at the little one's precocious ability to rewrite history—since "everyone who was not in a coma throughout the month of July knows that she most definitely did *not* kiss Pops's boo-boo."

It wasn't until later, when my friend had a moment to reflect on that brief conversation, that she realized that the child's assertion showed that she was already beginning to shape her Humiliated Self. She was already feeling put down—over an incident that no one had deliberately used as an instrument of ridicule. As my friend says, "The adults were just having fun with the baby, enjoying her, unconscious of the power they had to wound."

What that little boy and little girl experienced at the hands of their apparently loving parents was humiliation—a deep sense of being made to feel small, of being personally discounted, of having one's personal boundaries invaded and ignored, of being ridiculed, scorned, and treated with contempt. The inevitably humiliating power differential between child and adult creates gnawing insecurity in the dependent young person and plays a major role in the process of shaping one's Self concept. Like a pearl, the Created Self is made up of the internalized deposits of myriad interactions with parents, brothers and sisters, other family members, friends, teachers, and acquaintances, both real and imagined. In this process, actual or potential ridicule, scorn, and contempt play an important—often unconscious—part. As children, we all experienced unconsciously humiliating treatment, if only for isolated moments, but moments that probably stand out as if highlighted with Magic Marker in our memories. Experiences such as these are the foundation on which we build the almost universal aversion to humiliation that dictates so much of our behavior as adults.

The Humiliation Dynamic, then, is woven into the very fabric of the scrim on which we paint the opaque images of ourselves and through which we view our relationships with other people and the larger world. The Humiliation Dynamic is so much a part of who we are that it forms a virtually indelible thread that runs through all aspects of our lives and is especially strong in the psychologies of individuals from deprived or distorted backgrounds or among the members of minorities who have experienced humiliation as part of their communal lives. It can kick into action at any moment in adult life, causing even the most effective individuals to suddenly feel hamstrung and unable to respond effectively to what is going on around them. Even the possibility of minor humiliation can raise the unrecognized specter of those awful, degrading feelings we all had as children when we were put down, excluded, teased unmercifully, or in one of thousands of other ways exposed to ridicule and contempt.

The Humiliated Self can be stubbornly unforgiving, even when it remains unconscious of the real source of its grievance. Severely humiliated individuals are quite capable of holding grudges for an entire lifetime, nursing self-destructive complaints against parents, former teachers, and ex-bosses long after the offending parties are dead and gone.

FEAR OF HUMILIATION

The fear of humiliation (and the defense mechanisms that fear keeps in place) is almost as pernicious an influence on human behavior as the actual experience of humiliation itself. It's hard to overestimate the extent to which the desire to avoid humiliation affects how people think and what they do. To escape their fear, people will go to unbelievable extremes—including murder and suicide. Even pacifists have been known to don uniforms and march off to fight wars they can't condone to avoid the risk of being humiliated as cowards or traitors. You don't have to be a victim of humiliation to develop an overwhelming desire to avoid it. Merely participating in or observing someone else's humiliation is quite enough to restimulate the hidden, humiliated child we all carry inside.

THE HUMILIATION DYNAMIC AS A
FORCE FOR EVIL

It is no exaggeration to say that when we deal with humiliation, we are dealing not only with psychological and cultural issues, but also with evil itself. Among the disastrous results of the Humiliation Dynamic are mental illness, overpowering rage that erupts into violent crimes, suicide, international terrorism, and the tension, grudges, and disputes that repeatedly erupt into war. So far-reaching and so vast are the dehumanizing consequences of humiliation that the Humiliation Dynamic may well qualify as a powerful force for evil in human affairs.

Carl Goldberg, who has made a life study of the dark side of human consciousness, says, "Evil involves treating another person without respect for that person's humanity."[2] If we accept this definition of evil, it follows that to deliberately inflict humiliation on other human beings is to behave evilly. Not only are we treating them as dangerous, beneath contempt, or in some other way as deserving of our scorn; under some circumstances we are also at risk of creating intense bitterness, grudges, and the burning desire for revenge. In other words, those we humiliate may seek to get back at us, or they may humiliate or inflict violence against people who have not directly offended them. It can be argued, for example, that when we inflict humiliating treatment on convicted offenders, we create a vicious cycle of evil. That is, we make it more likely that once free, they will take their revenge by inflicting further evil on others. When it comes to humiliation, "evil begets evil."

Many explanations have been offered as to why people engage in evil, inhuman acts against other people. Why do people become serial killers? What personal and social forces combine to create a malevolent bureaucrat such as Adolph Eichmann in Nazi Germany? Why did highly educated Nazi physicians engage in sadistic medical experiments on helpless, living human beings? What leads everyday people to "run amok," "go postal," and kill co-workers or classmates before turning their guns on themselves? Why do so many people in positions of authority become brutal bosses who seize every opportunity they can to humiliate those who report to them?

We don't really know what leads any particular individual to become malevolent. Nevertheless, we all have our pet theories on the subject. For some it is a breakdown in moral authority among the leaders of the world; for others it's as simple as the need to return to a simple, fundamental belief in God's moral order. Psychologists have offered their own explanations, such as the need to overcome one's fear of death; our ability to keep separate, tightly divided compartments in our minds that enable torturers to have "ordinary" loving family ties even as they inflict horrendous physical and psychological suffering on their victims; and a deeply flawed, self-admiring, narcissistic personality that makes it impossible for the person to recognize, let alone acknowledge, his or her own malevolence.

I lean toward those who believe, from their clinical studies of serial killers and others, that there is a developmental pathway down which those who inflict psychological and physical harm on others travel. Those who humiliate others have been deeply and repeatedly debased, ridiculed, and scorned as small children, most usually by their parents. Like every other human being, such children must try to make sense out of what's happening to them. Why are they being subjected to such awful misery? Very often, parents and others offer a simple explanation. "You are a bad person—not just a naughty child but a hopelessly bad human being. You were born bad. And nothing we can do will change that situation. Nevertheless, we will continue to do our best." That best, as it turns out, is to continue to deride, berate, and punish the hopelessly bad child in a noble effort to be good parents in the face of overwhelming odds. Under such circumstances, many children grow up deeply torn in their views of themselves. On the one hand, they want to feel and be normal human beings, who behave in ways that are acceptable to themselves and others. On the other hand, they have adopted an underlying view of themselves as hopelessly flawed individuals, capable of unpardonable sins. It is no surprise that so many of those children are driven to behave in malevolent ways toward others and, at the same time, often blame others—especially their victims—for what they do.

To uncover foul memories of humiliating events in one's life can be excruciatingly uncomfortable—forcing us to face, in effect, our own potentials for "evil"—but such memories also can be most enlightening, even liberating. Memories of humiliations that I myself suffered, observed, and inflicted have helped me to unearth rich personal insights and to arrive at valuable hunches regarding the Humiliation Dynamic itself. I was amazed, first of all, to discover the extent to which the fear of being humiliated had affected my life. Among other events, I recalled that as a child I found little solace in the supposedly comforting saying offered by my teachers and other adults: "Sticks and stones may break my bones, but names will never hurt me." My own experiences and observations of others' reactions to the taunts of their peers had taught me that some names burned with the intense fire of ridicule, scorn, derision, and contempt. They were, indeed, personally hurtful and represented major threats to being accepted by one's peers. As a teenager, I remained inhibited and ignorant about sex because the fear that my sexual longings would make me an object of scorn kept me from discussing the subject with friends and family. Later, when I was a young professional, the fear of humiliating stage fright kept me for many years from giving talks and making presentations on topics with which I was completely familiar.

HUMILIATION IN LITERATURE

Literature offers incredibly rich veins of insights about humiliation. Writers have shaped entire novels and plays around themes of ridicule, contempt, and scorn. The Humiliation Dynamic, which forms the basis of so much interpersonal and intergroup conflict, offers a treasure trove of possibilities for dramatists and novelists.

Virtually every character in Katherine Anne Porter's outstanding novel *Ship of Fools* (which later became a movie) is either a humiliated victim or someone who, driven by the fear of humiliation, heaps contempt on those perceived as inferior—Jews, physically disabled individuals, and the poor people crowded into the steerage section of the vessel.

Graham Greene's novel *Doctor Fischer of Geneva* also plumbs the depths of humiliation. Dr. Fischer, the wealthy protagonist, has been humiliated by his wife's desertion. As a kind of heartbroken revenge, he is driven to humiliate a circle of acquaintances, who fawn over him and put up with his torments because they are greedy for the gifts and attention he lavishes on them. Expressing his inner despair with biting humor, Fischer justifies his behavior by maintaining that God, Himself, relishes the humiliation of humans. Here's what the devout Catholic author has Dr. Fischer say about the Deity:

> [H]e can only be greedy for our humiliation, and that greed how could he ever exhaust? It's bottomless. The world grows more and more miserable while he twists the endless screw, though he gives us presents—for a universal suicide would defeat his purpose—to alleviate the humiliations we suffer. A cancer of the rectum, a streaming cold, incontinence.[3]

Sleuth, written by British playwright Anthony Shaffer and made into a popular film some years back, is a riveting study of the violence that results from the deliberate use of humiliation by two rivals. One of the protagonists says, "The shortest way to a man's heart is humiliation. You soon find what he's made of."

The theme of humiliation also gave Mark Twain, that engaging, white-haired, cigar-smoking, impish treasure of American letters, many convenient pegs on which to hang his biting humor. From a wonderful collection of his sayings,[4] I offer the following insightful commentaries on the Humiliation Dynamic:

> There it is: it doesn't make any difference who we are or what we are, there's always somebody to look down on.
>
> —*3000 Years Among the Microbes*

> There is no character, howsoever good and fine, but it can be destroyed by ridicule, howsoever poor and witless. Observe the ass, for instance: his character is about perfect, he is the choicest spirit among all the humbler animals, yet see what ridicule has brought him to. Instead of feeling complimented when we are called an ass, we are left in doubt.
>
> —*Pudd'nhead Wilson*

> Each man is afraid of his neighbor's disapproval—a thing which, to the general run of the human race, is more dreaded than wolves and death.
>
> —*The United States of Lyncherdom*

> Each boy has one or two sensitive spots and if you can find out where they are located you have only to touch them and you can scorch him as with fire.
>
> —*Autobiography*

CONSPIRACY OF SILENCE
Our inability to deal with humiliation is compounded by an unspoken taboo against putting the experience into words. Even psychologists and other professionals in the mental health field have, for the most part, avoided discussing humiliation and its effects on those subjected to it. With rare exceptions, leading personality

theorists have been silent on the subject of humiliation as a major factor in shaping human behavior.

In our culture—and in many societies—to admit that one is feeling humiliated is even worse than humiliation itself. Victims of humiliation find it easier to express rage, to seek revenge on those who have tormented them, or simply to accept themselves as inadequate, inferior, unworthy of care and respect—deserving, in other words, of the humiliation they have suffered. A few victims may tell their families or friends how angry they felt, how unfairly treated, and how misguided, depraved, racist, or downright evil are those who humiliated them. They are far less apt to acknowledge to themselves, let alone to others, "I felt deeply hurt and humiliated." To admit humiliation is to admit weakness, to pile one humiliation on top of another, and to make oneself vulnerable for further humiliation.

The same conspiracy of silence surrounds the fear of being humiliated. We're far more apt to use excuses—"I don't have time." "I don't really care to get involved." "I'm too lazy."—than to say straight out, "I don't want to run the risk of being humiliated."

Newspaper reporter Matthew Brelis put it quite simply in a feature article on the Columbine High School massacre in Littleton, Colorado, where two high school students used homemade bombs and automatic weapons to kill as many of their fellow students and teachers as possible before killing themselves:

> One hallmark of humiliation is the difficulty we have talking about it, or sometimes even acknowledging it. We can talk about the embarrassing time we tripped, or didn't zip up our pants. We can acknowledge guilt by confessing it, apologizing, and moving on. . . . But not so with humiliation, which is something people have great difficulty in expressing.[5]

William Ian Miller, law professor and author of *Humiliation and Other Essays on Honor, Social Discomfort, and Violence,* maintains that to confess to feeling or being humiliated is virtually unthinkable. The things that humiliate us, he maintains, we will never reveal to anyone.[6] Humiliation leaves a bitter taste in the mouth. Metaphorically, you might even say that it corrodes the soul, eating away at the sacred essence of one's being, threatening to destroy one's basic sense of being a valued person in the world.

Hardly anyone glories in being considered weak, inferior, damaged, or otherwise less than other people. For most of us it feels better to bottle up such feelings of humiliation and hide them somewhere in the recesses of our awareness.

If it is so difficult to acknowledge *occasional* humiliations, what do people do who face repeated humiliations at others' hands by virtue of their gender, race, sexual orientation, social class, or other so-called social stigma? For these individuals, humiliation may occur at any moment as they go about their daily lives. What happens if they speak from the heart about what it's like to be put down, treated with contempt, or made to feel invisible?

THE VULNERABILITY OF
SUPPRESSED HUMILIATION

Many years ago a colleague and I traveled from New York to Washington, D.C., on the Metroliner. We had been conducting a three-day workshop on group dynamics. It had been a satisfying but challenging experience and we were winding down, basking in a job well done, and enjoying a new level of intimacy and friendship. It was during the height of the Civil Rights Movement and our talk turned to our experiences as minority members of society—I, a Jew; he, an African American. He told me of the almost daily humiliations he experienced: the slurs, insults, and sneers from unexpected sources; slow and inferior service from clerks and food service personnel; patronizing comments from white colleagues about his achievements as a Negro. It was a long and dreary list.

When we arrived at Union Station, he hurried ahead of me, eager to catch a cab to his home in Northeast D.C. where his wife and children, whom he hadn't seen for almost a week, were awaiting his arrival. I gathered my bags and followed more slowly to the entrance of the station. When I walked outside, my friend was standing alone, looking distraught. He rushed up to me and shouted, "Do you see what I mean? Do you see? This is what I meant!" It turned out that he'd not been able to find a cab to drive him to his home. Driver after driver had turned him down, with one excuse or another. I got a cab and drove with him to his home before going on to my destination. As we rode together, he said, "I really lost it. I don't usually let it get to me this way. But talking

with you on the train about how it felt somehow left me more vulnerable. I shouldn't have let down my guard."

Because we so seldom allow ourselves to talk about our humiliations, the negative feelings tend to get stored within us, like
corrosive material bottled up in a container. Long after they have
occurred, humiliating experiences remain unexpressed, sometimes even unacknowledged, eating away at our vitality, confi-
dence, and capacity to enjoy life.

When we break the conspiracy of silence that surrounds the
Humiliation Dynamic, it soon becomes clear that humiliation and
the fear of it encase and cling to most of us almost as closely as a
second skin. If you want direct confirmation of how completely
people wrap themselves in the cloak of humiliation, I suggest that
in the next few days you conduct your own study. Pay attention
to people's conversations about the hurts they've endured at the
hands of others. Notice what gets under your skin. And take a
look at the many different ways in which affronted individuals
and collective egos are regularly reflected in the news. I expect
you'll be as fascinated as I was to discover how frequently people
embroider their lives with stories of real and imagined slights and
insults.

The fear of losing peer approval, which in childhood is second
only to the fear of losing a parent, extends for most of us into our
adult years. Few of us lose our sensitivity to the subtle change in
facial expression, the telling glance, or a certain tone of voice that
signals that we've been found wanting by someone we would
like to impress.

Bullying and denigration of family members and bosses are
experiences that almost everyone with whom I've talked is familiar. Often, horrendous instances of individual and collective humiliations at the hands of supervisors and peers are described by
respondents in a wide variety of work settings. Being berated in
public by one's boss is an amazingly common occurrence, reported so frequently that it stands in my mind as the prototype of
humiliation in the world of work. Management consultant Harvey
Hornstein, in his book *Brutal Bosses and Their Prey*, reports that he
found humiliation in all types and sizes of organizations—large
corporations, small retail outlets, business firms, government
agencies, nonprofit organizations.[7] None is exempt.

Today the classic image of the child with dunce cap seated sullenly in the corner of the schoolroom has been replaced by searing memories of other indignities, such as being falsely accused of cheating, publicly chided for daydreaming in class, made to read a personal note to a friend aloud, labeled lazy and held up as a bad example to other pupils, and called on to recite even though it was obvious one wasn't prepared.

Take a moment to reflect on humiliations you've suffered. Ask yourself, "What was it like to feel humiliated?" Then, as you read the following paragraphs, compare your experience with what others whom I interviewed have had to say and notice to what extent you are already familiar with the reactions of victims of humiliation.

In my study most individuals report an initial reaction of confusion, paralysis, and helplessness when they are confronted by a humiliating experience. More than one person described this initial gut response as "feeling small" or wiped out. In the classic Erich von Stroheim movie *Greed*, an enraged, humiliated character eloquently sums up this feeling when he angrily exclaims, "He can't make small of me!"

The second common denominator in reactions to humiliation is the physical component, the sense of being punched in the gut, stabbed in the heart, or hit in the solar plexus.

The third shared reaction is rage, accompanied by flushing and a desire to disappear "into the woodwork."

Perhaps most striking is the fact that most victims report that, instead of putting the unpleasant experience out of their minds as quickly as possible, they dwell on it, embellish it, keep it fresh in their memories for years, even decades, after it has passed.

In chapter 6, we'll take a closer look at these elements and how they impact our sense of Self, our interactions with other people, and our community, national, and international lives.

SIX

The Elements of Humiliation: The Dance of Disgrace

◻ ◻ ◻

Psychologists and counselors are apt to point out that it is necessary for a victim of humiliation to define an incident as humiliating in order to experience it as such. That's true. But humiliation is not a solitary experience, defined by the victim alone. The Humiliation Dynamic, rather, involves a bitter embrace, the psychic interlocking of three sets of players—the humiliator, the victim, and the witness—in a patterned dance of disgrace.

COMPONENTS OF HUMILIATION

If you have passed middle age, you may recall the old Charles Atlas advertisements, cartoons that appeared on the back of comic books and magazines aimed at the young male readers who comprised the major market for the Atlas bodybuilding course. The story line featured a ninety-pound weakling on the beach with his beautiful girlfriend. A powerful two-hundred-pound bully mocks the hero, kicks sand in his face, and leaves him the object of scorn in the eyes of the girl. The entire scenario played on the vulnerability of young men to physical and sexual humiliation.

Despite its rather obvious manipulation of the young male psyche, the cartoon was highly effective in attracting adherents to the Charles Atlas regime. It remains, even today, an equally effective illustration of the essential humiliation triangle: the humiliating bully, the hapless victim, and the witness, a lovely girl, who not only witnesses the demeaning of her male friend, but also eventually even participates in it.

In all circumstances in which humiliation plays a central role, these same three prototypical players collude to produce the psychological traumas of the Humiliation Dynamic. Let's examine each of those traumatic components.

Feeling Demeaned

It is no coincidence that the root word for humiliation is the same as that for "humus," which refers to the earth. The image is of having one's face forced to the ground, to be made to "eat dirt." To use even more earthy expressions, common when I was in the Army, a person who is helpless to cope, forced to placate his or her oppressors, is being made to "eat shit" and may be accurately described as wearing a "shit-eating grin." Clearly, the connotation is of dirtying one's countenance in the eyes of others.

Feeling Excluded

Humiliation threatens personal integrity and wholeness. The humiliated person feels he or she doesn't belong, that he or she is inferior to those who choose, for whatever reason, to exclude him or her, perhaps to behave as if he or she doesn't even exist.

Women, people of color, individuals with disabilities, members of religious and other minorities all experience humiliation when their ideas and potential contributions are ignored, unacknowledged, or unrecognized.

Loss of Face

To be humiliated is to suffer damage to our sense of who we are. Americans tend to think that loss of face is an Asian, rather than a Western, preoccupation. The fear of losing face is, however, alive and active in U.S. society. We simply describe the experience differently—substituting words like "hurt feelings" and "wounded pride" to express the same emotionally deadening experience.

The real difference between Western and Eastern culture is that in the West, loss of face is often denied, repressed, and ignored. In the cultures of the East, however, the powerful effects of loss of face are understood and acknowledged and society is organized to avoid those consequences whenever possible. For Westerners, loss of face is an individual matter. The humiliation is seen almost entirely as belonging to the person. In China, however, face exists for the family, within the context of familial relationships, a valuable commodity to be gained or lost by the actions of individual family members. Membership in a Chinese family involves both a common destiny and acceptance of joint responsibility for ensuring the family's place in society.

In the West, we pay lip service to the concept of individualism, insisting that loss of face (when it occurs at all) occurs only at the individual, not at the family, level. Counselors who work with families with an alcoholic parent or other member point out that, contrary to the professed belief, the family as a whole often experiences profound feelings of degradation as a result of the behavior of the alcoholic member. Even while locked into destructive patterns of denying the impact of the illness (or even the illness itself), family members suffer severe private fears about the possibilities (and realities) of being humiliated in public by the very behavior they deny.

Violation

The humiliated person may endure the subjective experience of feeling figuratively undressed, naked, and exposed. Tom Wolfe describes this experience in his best-selling novel *The Bonfire of the Vanities*, when his hero, Sherman McCoy, is charged with killing a young African American in a hit-and-run accident. The incident hits the newspapers as a racial cause célèbre with strong political overtones.

> [O]ne's self is not a mere cavity open to the outside world but has suddenly become an amusement park to which everybody . . . come[s] scampering, skipping and screaming, nerves a-tingle, loins aflame, ready for anything, all you've got, laughs, tears, moans, giddy thrills, horrors, whatever, the gorier the merrier. [That is the state of] the mind of a person at the center of a scandal in the last quarter of the twentieth century.[1]

Few people, fortunately, ever experience the full fury of public humiliation as Wolfe describes it. But we've all been singed by the fires—enough, at least, that we can identify with the psychic pain endured by McCoy and other victims of public degradation. As I've written elsewhere:

> Whether one has experienced it or not, it's possible to know in one's bones what it was like to be McCoy or, for that matter, what it would have been like to be a Jew publicly reviled in Nazi Germany, to be a victim of China's Cultural Revolution paraded through the streets wearing ludicrous hats and insulting placards to the jeers of the Red Guards, to incur the unspeakable degradation of standing in chains in a slave market in the old South, or to experience the bitter, helpless outrage of a rape victim who is accused in open court of "asking for it."[2]

COLLECTIVE HUMILIATION

Humiliation can too often be a collective phenomenon, an experience shared by entire groups within society. I was raised a Jew in a largely Christian community and I share with many others of my heritage a special sensitivity to possible discrimination, slights, and insults that might be directed against people "like" me.

Similarly, African Americans are bitterly aware of the emphasis the nightly television news broadcasts put on young black men being arrested and incarcerated for drug-related crimes. Very few white people feel compelled to wonder why the media choose to concentrate on black criminal exploits, while virtually ignoring the many legal and legitimate contributions black Americans have made to our society.

Nations, too, are deeply affected by the Humiliation Dynamic. Leaders and citizens will do almost anything to avoid national humiliation, including risking their very national existence on the brink of global nuclear warfare. The pervasive influence of our need, as nations, to avoid humiliation and avenge humiliation when it does occur can actually dictate foreign policy, even when that policy flies in the face of rational national interest.

Remember for a moment the emotions you or someone you know experienced when you saw the television news coverage of the disastrous attempt by the Carter administration to free

American hostages in Iran through a helicopter strike. Remember, too, the similar emotions you felt when just months earlier you witnessed the live coverage of the takeover of the American embassy in Teheran, when our embassy staff members were marched through crowds of laughing, jeering Iranian demonstrators, humiliated before the eyes of the entire world.

Our inability to deal effectively with a small, underdeveloped nation hit our national psyche like a bombshell, with explosive aftershocks to our sense of national well-being and prestige. According to many political analysts, the ensuing rage reverberated in a change of administrations and such symbolic efforts to restore national morale as the invasion of the tiny island of Grenada and the overthrow of General Manuel Noriega in Panama.

It is my conviction that the dynamic of humiliation is the single-most important factor in sparking and fanning the flames of conflict between individuals, groups, and, even, entire nations, with the offended parties maintaining vendettas that bridge lifetimes, handed down like precious heirlooms from one generation to the next.

THE PREHISTORIC ORIGINS OF HUMILIATION

There is every reason to believe that human beings are predisposed to being caught up in the Humiliation Dynamic. It is always possible, though hardly provable, that we inherit the tendency to choose one side of the humiliation triangle, being either one of those who humiliate, one of those who are humiliated, or one of those who validate the process by witnessing the humiliation. I believe that our predisposition to humiliating behavior is an inevitable result of the many years during which human infants cannot avoid being made to feel small, inferior, and impotent. The Humiliation Dynamic is very likely to be one of the unfortunate by-products of the fact that human infants remain dependent on their parents for survival for far-longer periods of time than any other creature. The chances are, therefore, that infant cave dwellers in prehistoric times were as likely as children of the twenty-first century to develop what I refer to as the Humiliated Self.

Certainly, even the most cursory examination of recorded human history reveals times beyond counting when parents inflicted the most awful humiliations on small children; when rulers raped their subjects' wives and treated them in all manner of ways as inferior beings; when conquered peoples were enslaved and subjected to endless indignities.

According to one scholar, there is abundant evidence that the Humiliation Dynamic was already alive and well among the Sumerians, the earliest civilization known to have invented writing. Clay tablets written at least three thousand years before the Christian Era reveal a society in which those high in prestige despised poverty, kings lorded it over their subjects, and a favorite sport was something called the "contest," during which rivals engaged in public verbal disputes replete with such appellations as "dolt," "numbskull," "illiterate," and "windbag."[3]

WHAT'S IN A NAME?

Name-calling is one of the most common ways to inflict humiliation, both on individuals and entire groups. Expressions of contempt—"nigger," "kike," "fairy," "wop," "wog," "Chink," "Jap," "welfare queen"—are weapons used to demean those who are viewed as fair game for verbal abuse. Although many people use such terms casually and with little thought, given the right circumstances these terms become horribly dehumanizing for both those who label and those who are labeled. Derogatory labels have the power to turn human beings into despised, subhuman objects who, in the minds of those who use such labels, become fair game for physical abuse, degrading treatment, torture, and murder.

In his enlightening book *The Language of Oppression*, Haig Bosmajiian describes how derogatory labels have been used over the centuries—and are still used today—as instruments of control and subjugation. Roman slaves, for example, were seen as nameless cattle until purchased by masters who gave them names. We reenact that ancient drama of abasement today in our treatment of prisoners, assigning them numbers and addressing them by their first names as marks of their lower status.

Bosmajiian points out that those in power assign demeaning names and derogatory labels to exercise control over their victims. Name-calling, in other words, is a political act that, under certain circumstances, has dire consequences for those who are labeled. He says:

The names, labels, and phrases employed to "identify" a people may in the end determine their survival. In addition to their given names, Jews in Nazi Germany were required to take the stereotypic name of Israel for males and Sarah for females. A Nazi party manual referred to Jews, Poles, and Russians as "two-legged lice, putrid vermin which good Aryans must squash like roaches on a dirty wall."[4]

HUMILIATION IN U.S. SOCIETY

Our highly competitive society is virtually saturated with humiliation. At an early age, we learn that there are winners and losers in life. Even in the supposedly nurturing bosom of our families, we notice that love is often conditional, given out as a reward for good behavior, replaced by rebukes and punishments when our behavior falls short of some arbitrary standard. The acceptance of some form of humiliating disparagement as a weapon in the parental disciplinary armamentarium is commonplace. The intermittent guerilla warfare called sibling rivalry, which in our society is so common as to be considered normal, often consists of humiliating insults, disparaging remarks, and demeaning practical jokes.

In school, young people find themselves compared with others, being graded up or down for their behavior as well as for their academic accomplishments. Even on the playground (*especially* on the playground) children discover that acceptance and recognition is never something that can be taken for granted, given to each child as his or her natural right. Many of us received our initiation into the Humiliation Dynamic at recess, when we were supposed to be having fun but were all too often learning to avoid the ritual childhood chants of scorn, and experiencing firsthand the wounding power of the pointing finger of contempt.

IS THERE A POSITIVE USE FOR HUMILIATION?

The Humiliation Dynamic does occasionally produce positive results. The success of well-known public figures sometimes appears to have turned on their single-minded commitment to overcoming humiliations in their lives, including those who have sought revenge against people who have humiliated them and also including those who followed the path of forgiveness. An example of the tempering effect of a lifetime of humiliation is cited in journalist Matthew Brelis's article on the Columbine High School tragedy. He quotes the pastor of a church in Boston who, preaching on Columbine and humiliation, said:

> "Look at Nelson Mandela. Apartheid was an ironclad system of humiliation which required the degradation of people and he was able to harness the energy out of that for change without rancor."[5]

We often fail to recognize, however, the cost these individuals may have paid in terms of personal happiness and effectiveness for their narrowly defined victories. We have no way of predicting the achievements of which these usually exceptionally talented individuals might have been capable had they not been saddled with the emotional burden that the humiliation-prone carry.

In more traditional societies, both physical pain and humiliation were incorporated into rituals that helped children make the transition to adulthood. Those rituals, however, were carefully orchestrated and controlled events, with all participants aware of their ultimate purpose—the integration of a new generation of adults into the community, not the exclusion or diminution of any among that generation.

Only vestiges of such controlled use of humiliation remain in our individualistic, competitive society. The hazing rituals of sororities and fraternities come to mind. Werner Erhardt used humiliation liberally in his well-known personal growth workshops (which he called est), repeatedly deriding participants as "ass holes" and requiring them to submit to such indignities as not being able to go to the toilet when they felt the need to do so. The movie *Full Metal Jacket* depicts in a stark and uncompromising way how Marine recruits are subjected to many humiliating degradations that have as their final aim transforming them from undisciplined teenagers into gung-ho leathernecks. Aaron Lazare, dean of the University of Massachusetts Medical School, documented the fact that medical education abounds with instances of personal put-downs and ridicule directed by faculty and supervisors toward medical students and residents.[6]

What's amazing about these practices is that they often appear to work. Adherents of Erhardt insist that their experiences in est were transformational, changing their lives and their relationships, making them more effective and positive forces in the world. Marine loyalty to boot camp sergeants is legendary. And very few physicians feel compelled to criticize the education that enables them to go about their healing work; most, in fact, consider the humiliating aspects of their educational experience necessary to forging the discipline required of a medical practitioner.

Various forms of degradation have been part of the criminal justice system for hundreds of years. Public displays—such as the stocks, pillory, and ducking stool—were common in colonial days in this country and elsewhere. Other publicly humiliating practices included wearing special garments or signs, such as the fabled scarlet letter for adultery, hand branding, and visible mutilation of the body. Today judges are reported to be imposing humiliating punishments on convicted offenders, such as drunk drivers, who are required to put warning stickers on their bumpers; patrons of prostitutes, whose pictures are published in the daily newspaper; and child molesters, who must display warning signs on their lawns.

What is missing in these commentaries on the benefits of humiliation is an accounting of the costs (in terms of human happiness and creativity) at which these benefits are attained. It is also possible that degrading punishments are counterproductive. Rather than discouraging criminal behavior, they may even create conditions that lead to its increase. Such practices as public displays, branding, and making offenders wear signs that proclaim their offenses were designed to let people know the kind of person they were dealing with. That is precisely why, according to one criminologist, they probably "further encouraged illegal behavior because the public was reluctant to allow the offender back in the mainstream of the society."[7]

HUMILIATION IN THE WORKPLACE
Humiliating practices are common in all but the most enlightened work settings. As a consultant to large government, business, and

nonprofit organizations, I have been impressed by the creativity bosses exhibit in finding direct and indirect ways to humiliate employees. Humiliation is not limited to public criticisms, intemperate tirades, and withholding earned recognition and rewards. It also shows up in the humiliating everyday physical and social arrangements that, in order to uphold the status hierarchy, literally are designed to keep people in their places.

Scott Adams's *Dilbert* cartoon strip has established a large following because of the often savage humor with which it reveals the many absurdities of organizational life. In *The Dilbert Principle*, Adams devotes an entire chapter to the various ways in which humiliating arrangements are used to keep employees in their places. Among the more obvious are the use of cubicles for those who are not managers, various other differences in sizes and type of work space, and differences in style and quality of office furnishings. Adams points out that cubicles "serve as a constant reminder of the employee's marginal value to the company."[8] He likens them to cattle pens, cardboard boxes, babies' playpens, and prison cells. Most of us are familiar with the "name on the door and the rug on the floor" as a sign of one's importance to the organization. You may be as surprised as I was, however, to discover that, in the name of efficiency, some organizations have taken to assigning lower-status workers to different cubicles as they arrive each day, the message clearly being that you don't count enough even to have a small patch of territory in this place that you can call "home."

According to Adams, even employee recognition programs (widely touted by progressive managers and management consultants) have their humiliating downside. To be eligible for your organization's "employee of the month award," he points out, is to be a low-status hired hand, an inhabitant of one of the lowest organizational realms. To receive a "certificate of appreciation," which presumably you can hang on the wall of your office, signals that you have risen to the ranks of salaried middle management. You have arrived as an executive member of the highest caste in the organization, Adams concludes, when you are no longer eligible for any of the organization's employee recognition programs.

Hazing at Work

Management consultant Natasha Josefowitz found that teasing, cruel tricks, and other forms of hazing of newcomers are common in many work situations. She likens such hazing to tribal degradation ceremonies designed to test youngsters before admitting them to the rights, privileges, and responsibilities of adulthood and defines hazing in the workplace as serving the threefold purpose of "teaching novices their place in the . . . pecking order; teasing the newcomers . . . to see whether their personality fits in . . . ; and, finally, testing the rookies for . . . competence, loyalty and reliability."[9]

My observations are that almost everyone has experienced humiliation in his or her work. A random sampling of remarks recorded in my notes over the years includes the following:

- My boss bawled me out in front of co-workers.
- I spent hours preparing a report and my boss ripped it to shreds when I presented it at a staff meeting.
- Although I believe I have valuable skills and knowledge to contribute to the project, I'm not consulted when important decisions are made.
- I overheard my boss bad-mouthing my ability, qualifications, and job performance to another manager.
- My boss repeatedly makes end runs around me to tell my subordinates what to do.
- At staff meetings, our boss picks out a different staff member for "target-of-the-week" treatment, ripping to shreds an action or a decision made by the victim.
- Soon after I started work, I learned that the fact that I'm a black female was the major reason I was interviewed and hired.
- As someone who assists a senior executive at high-level meetings, I feel undervalued by the other executives who see me as a flunky and aren't aware of my skills and the important work I do.
- Our work unit always gets the leftovers. Our work area is crowded, dirty, noisy, and in many other ways inferior in comparison with what others in the organization have.

The experience is so universal that it would appear that humiliation in all its guises and the fear that humiliation generates have a substantial impact on workplace behavior, often inhibiting the quality and quantity of production on the job and significantly reducing the quality of life for workers.

Individuals who have been humiliated by their bosses report that the bitterness persists for years after the event. In the weeks and months following the injury, they find themselves preoccupied with thoughts of what they could have done or said at the time to protect themselves and of what they might do now to avenge the insult. For most, their enthusiasm for their work vanishes. Many operate as if they've retired at full pay, doing only enough to avoid being fired.

Their loyalty to the firm or work unit plummets, with many finding other employment as soon as possible. To protect themselves from further humiliation, victims learn to be less frank and forthcoming than they were before the incident occurred. The increased fear, tension, and defensiveness cause victims to take less initiative and make more mistakes.

SOCIALLY SANCTIONED "CRIPPLING"
Clearly, the costs of humiliation as a socializing mechanism in modern society vastly outweigh its benefits. Even those who survive humiliation (graduates of medical schools, boot camps, and est training weekends) and emerge with a new group identity may be crippled in ways that are never defined. Victims usually find lifelong significance in the sheer fact of having gained acceptance within the ranks of their former tormentors, looking down on those who have not undergone the same ordeal, viewing them as somehow less valuable as human beings, individuals who deserve to be scorned and derided as they were prior to their "initiation." Unknowingly, they also incorporate into their psyches an intense fear of humiliation, a fear that often manifests itself in an inability to accept and deal with even legitimate criticism.

Victims also tend to develop a rigid sense of hierarchy, a device to protect themselves from humiliation—at least from those who are defined as being in an inferior social position. Bosses, for example, rarely take kindly to criticism from subordinates; parents have difficulty responding to negative feedback from their children; and teachers are seldom totally open to corrective input from their students. Psychoanalyst Karen Horney puts it quite simply when she writes about those whose Self esteem depends on feeling superior to others: "Criticism from people of lower status is the ultimate humiliation."[10]

Humiliation, in its more extreme forms, is a factor in many, if not most, clinically recognized emotional and social disorders. I've found it cited as a causative factor in juvenile delinquency, depression, serial and mass murders, paranoia, sadomasochism, generalized and social anxiety disorders, spousal and child abuse, and suicide. Humiliation as a device of social control exacts, in other words, a high—although as yet not totally computed—social cost, a cost that we pay every day in lost productivity and crime, not to mention sheer human suffering.

Humiliation in Everyday Life
We live in what Jungian analyst Helen Luke describes as a society obsessed with "the gradings of money, academic prowess, I.Q.'s and A's, B's and C's in every department of life."[11] In such an environment, almost everyone is destined to experience failure at one time or another.

For some, failure is the stuff of everyday life and fear of humiliation is their driving force. They live in fear of the contempt that might be rained down on them if they become unemployed or suffer a demotion, divorce, or other loss of social status. These people (who may be a majority in our culture) never have the time or encouragement to overcome and eradicate from their scrims the insecurities engendered during the uneasy and often unsupported adolescent transition. These are the people who project their own fear of humiliation on others, quick to heap contempt on people who differ from them because of caste, class, religion, gender, age, physical disability, or sexual orientation. Until we eliminate the fear these individuals endure for their own safety from humiliation, our efforts to create a humiliation-free culture will be limited to doing what is "politically correct." We will not have the psychological freedom necessary for truly humane action.

Given the unconscious humiliation that I believe is built into the very process of human growth and development, I doubt that it is possible to create a completely humiliation-free society. But the society we have created is one that emphasizes the value of humiliation, ignoring its costs in terms of what could be accomplished by members of a culture that encourages cooperation among Self-assured, loving, happy, and caring human beings. In the ideal society, no one would live in the shadow of others' contempt should they be unemployed or fail to achieve. Insecurities having to do with the transition from child to adult would be minimized by understanding, supportive peers as well as grown-ups. It would be possible to talk about those insecurities and to acknowledge the fear of scorn and derision from one's peers. The tyranny of one's peers would be no more. In short, the Humiliation Dynamic would no longer flourish in the fertile soil of differences of caste, class, religion, gender, age, physical abilities, sexual orientation, or other stigmatizing characteristics. This version of an ideal world may well be as unrealizable as all such utopian visions have turned out to be in the past. Nonetheless, like all such visions, it sets a useful direction by motivating us to move ourselves away from destructively paranoid relationships and toward interactions based on Appreciative knowing. However short we may fall in specific instances, in the long run, I submit, it is a useful vision that will guide us in worthwhile directions.

No doubt, meanwhile, we will continue to long for a life free of all oppression, degradation, and personal humiliation. Garrison Keillor's *Prairie Home Companion* portrays tongue in cheek a mythic town in which "all the women are strong, all the men are good looking, and all the children are above average." Despite the fact that the residents of Lake Wobegon face the same gnawing concerns, frustrations, and problems with which the rest of us deal—and then some—Keillor has the happy ability to bring out into the open and talk about everyday humiliations similar to those we've all experienced. And he does so in a lovingly humorous way that imparts a warm and even welcome glow to life's frustrations and belittlements.

Humiliation in Public Life

When individuals who have been nurtured in a culture of humiliation act collectively, the results can be disastrous. It is almost commonplace to attribute Adolf Hitler's rise to power in 1933 to the fact that he embodied and expressed the humiliation and impotent fury experienced by the German people in the face of the reparations and reprisals imposed by the victorious Allies following World War I. In addition, Hitler's rise also occurred in the midst of the depression, which had hit those in the lower middle class especially hard. It was this group who supported him most strongly because either they had already slid into the poverty-stricken lower class, which they considered to be a humiliating disgrace, or they feared they were about to be degraded by losing what shaky social and economic status they had. Hitler and his followers promised patriotic Germans a rebirth of national pride and power; they promised the mass of economically marginal Germans an end to downward social mobility, unemployment, and homelessness. These experiences are among the most potent stimuli of shame and a key to the politics of violence.

Other examples abound:

- Many pundits say the Chinese Communist revolution was fueled by years of humiliating gunboat diplomacy and economic exploitation of China by the European powers and the United States.
- Intergroup strife in the United States, Lebanon, the former Yugoslavia, Ireland, South Africa, Somalia, Angola, Cypress, the former Soviet Union, and elsewhere often reflects deep-seated grudges held by people who feel they have been humiliated at the hands of hated oppressors.
- Middle Eastern terrorists (or revolutionary patriots, depending on your point of view) often speak of their activities in terms that reveal their sense of having been humiliated by the rest of the world.
- Former President Richard Nixon reported, in the November 20, 1989, issue of *Time* magazine, a conversation he had had with leaders of the Chinese democracy movement following the Tiananmen Square massacre. The following quote from that article reveals how the fear of humiliation

can impact international affairs: "One top Chinese leader told me that any colleague who humiliated China in the world community by acting contrite did not deserve to be in office. Contrition may be an attractive characteristic in soap opera stars, but not in leaders of great nations such as China."

HUMILIATED FURY

Dramatist William Congreve wrote three centuries ago: "Heaven has no rage like love to hatred turned; nor hell a fury like a woman scorned." Those lines pinpoint the most powerful and potentially destructive "hot spot" of the Humiliation Dynamic. Whoever we are—man or woman, young or old—our reactions to the Humiliation Dynamic share the characteristic called "humiliated fury," rage either turned against oneself as victim or directed outward against one's tormentors or both.

Turned inward, humiliated fury becomes depression and despair, as it did in the case of the young wife described at the beginning of chapter 5. The resulting Self hatred renders victims incapable of meeting their own most basic needs and drains them of any energy they might once have had to love and care for others. The desire to escape or override humiliation motivates the behavior of many alcoholics and drug addicts, who are willing to destroy themselves physically and psychologically rather than deal with the unbearable pain of past humiliations or face the possibility of similar humiliation in the future.

Turned outward, humiliated fury can take the form of vengeful fantasies, paranoia, or cruelty. Those who are driven by such fury almost literally consume themselves and others with their rage. When those responsible for their plight are unavailable, it is not uncommon for people driven by their Humiliated Selves to vent their rage on anyone who is available—a child, an employee, an entire nation. Sometimes this fury is exacerbated by the fact that no one person or group can be held accountable for their situation.

Tragic results occur when two parties—be they individuals, groups, nations, or other communities—become locked in reciprocal humiliated fury. Examples in our own time are the so-called troubles between Irish Catholics and Protestants, the ongoing Arab-Israeli dispute over national sovereignty in the former Palestine, the massacres in Rwanda, the well-entrenched intercommunal dispute between Turkish and Greek Cypriots, and the bitter conflicts between Serbs, Bosnians, and Croats in the former Yugoslavia. These intercommunal disputes are rooted in generations—in some cases hundreds of years—of grudges having to do with what each party to the conflict interprets as humiliating defeats, exploitation, and oppression at the hands of the other. The humiliated fury and the desire for revenge are passed down through mythic accounts of past injustices, betrayals, and glorious defeats and victories. They are part of each individual's collective identity. The flame of humiliated fury fires up the thirst for revenge, making it possible for neighbors to slaughter neighbors, freedom fighters to bomb defenseless civilians, and regimes to view ethnic cleansing as a matter of policy.

Turned outward, humiliated fury solves nothing, only creating additional victims, often innocent ones, as so often happens in war, civil strife, personal and family vendettas, and terrorism.

In either case, those whose energies are consumed by humiliated fury are absorbed in themselves and their causes, wrapped in wounded pride, and shielded by their individual or collective righteousness. They are the very epitome of egoistic Self importance.

In chapter 7, we will review the dire effects unexplored and unexorcized humiliation can have on the mental health and happiness of the individual—how, in other words, humiliation can fester until it results in the very death of the Creative Self, leaving only a shell of humanity, a zombie incapable of feeling the wondrous emotions that underlie and support the Psychology of Appreciation.

SEVEN

How Humiliation Kills the Creative Self

▣ ▣ ▣

Most attempts to cope with humiliation are physically and emotionally destructive, both to the victims of humiliation and to those around them. Frozen in a state of impotence, humiliated victims waste energy in attempts to get revenge or withdraw into a world of fantasized revenge. Their mental scrim becomes rigid, making it impossible for them to escape their pain-filled lives and blinding them to the world of options that lies behind the humiliation that forms the totality of their mental scenery. Any degree of humiliation (as we all know) lends rigidity to the Created Self, making it less willing to risk change and adventure, and more intent on protecting the individual from real or imagined assaults from the outside world. People who are exposed to high levels of humiliation during their formative years (or who, for whatever reason, come into the world poorly equipped to deal with humiliation) can be prone to the variety of soul-killing (and socially unproductive) conditions described in the following pages.

MORTIFICATION

Extreme and persistent physical violence, insults, put-downs, ridicule, and degradation leave some humiliated victims in what James Gilligan, former director of the Center for the Study of Violence at Harvard Medical School, calls a state of mortification. In medicine the term "mortification" refers to the death or decay of one part of the body while the rest remains alive. To be emotionally mortified means to be walking around, engaged in everyday activities at school or work, alive in body and mind but dead in the spirit that animates most of us and leads us to value the gift of life. According to Gilligan:

> Violence to the body causes the death of the self because it is so inescapably humiliating. When we cannot fend off, undo, or escape from such overwhelmingly unloving acts, when we cannot protect ourselves from them, whether by violent or nonviolent means, something gets killed within us—our souls are murdered.[1]

As Gilligan uses the word, "mortification" has a double meaning: the death of the Self and the cause of that death. Basing his views on many years of work with murderers, he says that "those who kill have been 'murdered' themselves, or else fear that they are about to be destroyed, and so they kill for what appears to them as self-defense."[2] Violence, he says, "is the ultimate humiliation, one that cuts so deep it can kill the soul even when it does not kill the body."[3] Without exception, he reports, the violent acts committed by the offenders with whom he worked were triggered by the experience of feeling disrespected, ridiculed, or otherwise humiliated. In his view, even capital punishment will not deter those who have been mortified from murder and other violent acts designed to prevent or undo what for them is unendurable disrespect.[4]

A tragic example of the consequences of mortification was the Columbine High School disaster in Littleton, Colorado. Here's what journalist Matthew Brelis wrote about what had been going on in the lives of the two students who carried out the massacre:

> [S]everal students of the clique to which the seventeen and eighteen-year-olds belonged have detailed a litany of abuse that some members of the so-called Trenchcoat Mafia suffered at the hands of the more popular, powerful jocks. There were constant taunts, they say, ranging from "dirt-bag" to "faggot," physical abuse such as being slammed up against lockers, pelted with rocks and sodas, and forced to bus the jocks' trays in the cafeteria.[5]

Caste differences in many societies, including our own, consign whole groups of people to mortified lives of repeated insult and degradation. The caste system in India is an obvious example. The caste system in the United States, which is less obvious and more complex, appears to be based on a combination of factors, including poverty, social class, and race. To be poor in this country usually means to be made to feel inferior. To be on the low end of the totem pole of material goods is inherently humiliating.

According to Brelis, "The very fact that the words 'low' and 'status' are used to describe these differences . . . tells us which population groups in our society are more exposed to experiences of shaming. Who would not feel ashamed and inferior if described as 'lower class' or of 'lower status.'"[6] Despite tax breaks for the wealthy and other economic policies that create growing disparities in wealth between rich and poor, a humiliating myth shared by many Americans holds that if people are poor, it is their own fault. Despite local educational systems that often provide inferior education to poor people, many of us would like to believe that if they really wanted to, those in poverty could lift themselves up by their own bootstraps. We blame poor people themselves for the fact that the rate of violence in the United States is greater than the rate of violence in any other developed country and that such violence is primarily committed by poor people against other poor people.

The racial caste system in the United States is primarily directed against those of African descent. One of the humiliating myths of such racism is that, compared with other races, African Americans are innately stupid. We institutionalize the caste system and perpetuate the mortifying myth by depriving many lower-income black children of the education that would enable them to realize their true intellectual potential. An ironic tragedy is that some young African Americans, to avoid being disrespected by their peers for selling out to the white society that humiliates them, deliberately downplay their intelligence and do not take advantage of whatever educational opportunities are available to them.

HUMILIATION AND MENTAL ILLNESS

Given the widespread nature of the Humiliation Dynamic and its powerfully corrosive effect on people's lives, I am fascinated by the fact that it was not identified and carefully studied by earlier generations of psychologists and other mental health professionals. Sigmund Freud frequently mentioned the humiliations he experienced as a Jewish physician attempting to establish himself within professional circles. Freud, like the rest of us, had his emotional blind spots. Despite careful and courageous lifelong study of his dreams and fantasies, he remained unaware of the Humiliation Dynamic in his own life and could not discern the powerful effects it was having on himself and his patients. From one of his most difficult and instructive patients—a man named Schreber—Freud gleaned much of his understanding of paranoia as the projection of unacceptable wishes or impulses onto the external world. Schreber, a judge, had delusions that people were accusing him of homosexuality and that homosexual advances were being made toward him. Freud concluded that at the root of paranoia was the fear of the paranoid person's own unacceptable impulses. What Freud did not discern, according to Willard Gaylin, author of *Feelings: Our Vital Signs,* was the judge's fear of the humiliation that would result if his homosexual proclivities were exposed to public view. In a typically complex—some might say convoluted—Freudian interpretation, Gaylin focuses on Schreber's belief that God Himself was trying to reduce him to being a homosexual and thereby humiliate him. That belief served two purposes: first, it freed him from having to face his own guilt about his homosexuality; second, it shielded him from the contempt and derision of his friends and associates.[7] In the years following Freud's breakthrough work, guilt and shame have received enormous amounts of attention as causes of emotional difficulty. By comparison, the Humiliation Dynamic is given only passing mention. In the *Dictionary of Psychology* published in 1968, "guilt" and "shame" are listed along with hundreds of other psychological terms; "humiliation" does not appear, even though I have come to believe it is responsible for even more human misery and dysfunction than guilt and shame.

Dysfunctional Relationships

The exception to the general neglect of humiliation as a subject of psychological study can be found in the richly revealing and often underrated work of Karen Horney, who points out that humiliation plays an important part in what she refers to as "basic anxiety." In recent years Horney's work has provided welcome psychological groundwork for feminist scholars. According to one such scholar, humiliation is at the core of Horney's observations about the relations between men and women in our society.[8]

One of Freud's most controversial ideas is that little girls feel basically inferior to little boys by virtue of the fact that boys have penises and girls do not. Freud called it "female penis envy." It's likely that when he came up with the idea of penis envy, Freud was more than a little biased by what later writers on the subject have pointed out was the firm conviction among members of his generation that women were inherently inferior to men and, therefore, that their proper place in society was to be subordinate to their male partners.

Horney is adamant about challenging Freud's concept of penis envy and countered with one of her own, the male's fear of humiliating rejection at the hands of a woman. Horney goes on to say that, in effect, relationships between men and women are driven in large measure by the fear of humiliation: men's fear that their puny penises will be ridiculed and rejected by women; women's fear of humiliating disappointments at the hands of men whose Self esteem rests on their assumption that women are somehow essentially inferior.

The powerful influence of the Humiliation Dynamic on male-female relationships makes satisfying, long-lasting ties between men and women extremely difficult, with a majority of marriages ending in divorce or deteriorating into sterile, even destructive relationships. As I put it in an article written several years ago:

> [T]he proverbial "battle of the sexes" is fueled by a volatile mixture of past and anticipated rejections, belittlements, and other humiliations, which can gradually saturate into both partners in a relationship and, when sparked by financial or

other frictions—as so often happens—explodes into serious psychological and physical abuse.[9]

Specific Mental Disorders

Although humiliation is accorded little or no attention in theories of personal development and psychopathology, the Humiliation Dynamic is often cited in academic work as a given in the development of a wide range of conditions, including delinquent behavior, neurotic depression, mass murders, paranoia, sadomasochism, various anxiety disorders, spousal and child abuse, and suicide.

Juvenile Delinquency

Erik Erikson, a foremost artist among personality theorists, uses the following words to describe a typical pattern of how a boy develops into a delinquent youth:

> Gifted, ambitious, proud, he is at the same time possessed by wild drives, is immature in his social ideas, unsure of his ideals, and morbidly suggestible. During a period of rapid growth and strong aggressiveness he suffers a severe humiliation. He disavows his primitive tendencies and attempts to adjust abruptly to his neighbor's standards. This personality, however, is not ready to sustain the change; he "over adjusts." . . . Adjustment becomes self-debasement. . . . The adolescent finds that he has relinquished his old self without gaining a new one in his adjustment to the conflicting demands of his environment. As he begins to mistrust them he mistrusts the values which he has just begun to share with them. At this point he meets a leader and a gang who proclaim that the adolescent is always right, that aggression is good, that conscience is an affliction, adjustment a crime.[10]

Having pinpointed humiliation as a major factor, however, Erikson does not tell us the nature of the "severe humiliation" suffered by the predelinquent. Neither does he incorporate humiliation into his basic theory of personality development. Nevertheless, it's clear that Erikson recognizes that the delinquent adolescent he describes has been held in contempt for exhibiting values and behaviors that he later embraces in defiance of conventional standards.

In my cursory review of the literature on male delinquency, I found that Erikson was not alone. Humiliation is mentioned as a factor among boys with severe learning disorders who later turn to delinquency. After studying fifty such boys, one delinquency expert concluded that humiliations associated with repeated failures to learn and keep up with classmates over many years contributed to the boys' feelings of vulnerability and low Self esteem, which were then expressed as antisocial impulsiveness.[11]

Depression

While delinquency directs aggression outward against the world, depression turns aggression *inward* against oneself. Here again, the Humiliation Dynamic is implicated. Helen Lewis is a pioneer in the study of what she considers to be a family of shame-related emotions, including humiliation. Depressed people with whom she worked often suffered from the added burden of feeling humiliated because, in comparison with family members and friends, they were trapped in a morass of hopelessness. These depressed individuals were snared in what she calls the "feeling trap" of humiliated fury. According to Lewis:

> Depressed patients are in a chronic state of shame proneness, if only because they are depressed and helpless to get out of it. But although they are in a humiliated state—a state, incidentally, usually accompanied by quick fury—they are not at all conscious of being angry at anyone.[12]

Sadomasochism

When people are sexually aroused by being subjected to pain, we call it masochism; when people are sexually aroused by inflicting pain on others, we call is sadism. Sadomasochists find sexual pleasure in both. Sadomasochism comes in many forms and degrees. On one extreme are sadists who find pleasure in torturing helpless, nonconsenting victims and masochists who are turned on when they goad others to inflict pain on them. On the other extreme are sexual relationships between consenting adults in which partners engage in bondage, whipping, and other sado-masochistic activities, taking care not to do permanent bodily harm and using prearranged signals that enable them to control the discomfort.

In addition to physical pain, many sadomasochists also revel in psychological debasement. In fact, noted psychoanalyst and author Erich Fromm defines a sadist as "a person with an intense desire to control, hurt, humiliate another person." And Karen Horney refers to "the repeated tendency to subjugate, dominate, disparage, deprecate, humiliate, berate, blame, defeat, and cruelly criticize others."[13] Notice that for both Fromm and Horney sadism does not necessarily involve the mixture of pain with sexual pleasure. In view of the fact that the tendency to "cruelly criticize others" to their faces or to third parties is so prevalent, we might conclude that the desire to humiliate is a widespread human characteristic.

For those who delight in torturing others, there very likely is an element of displaced psychological revenge. Horney, for example, refers to "vindictive sadists" whose cruelty is fed by "bitter envy arising from repressed self-contempt and discontent."[14]

On the flip side of sadism is masochism. Psychological masochists—or as they are now labeled "Self-defeating" individuals—have been so deeply humiliated by events in their lives that they expect to fail and often find pleasure in being painfully abused and rejected. They become expert at finding ways to place themselves in harm's way, physically and emotionally. The life of a severely Self-defeating person is one of constant or repeated misery, anxiety, and humiliation. Jill Montgomery, a psychotherapist who specializes in working with Self-defeating patients, says, "A masochistic life is one of seemingly endless, prolonged, self-inflicted *suffering and humiliation.* [italics added] These patients feel that they suffer from life, that they are untreatable, and yet in desperation demand our help, while simultaneously clinging to pain."[15]

Generalized Social Anxiety

Of all psychiatric ailments, generalized anxiety disorder is the one that psychologists and psychiatrists agree has the fear of humiliation at its core. Unlike stage fright, which for most people is a temporary, more-or-less intense dread of performing before an audience or speaking up in a large group, those suffering from generalized anxiety disorder have a deep and abiding fear of exposing themselves to public scorn and ridicule. Not only do they feel ill equipped to ward off such ridicule, but also deep inside themselves they feel that they deserve it and that others have a right to amuse themselves at their expense.

For some the anxiety is so great that the individual feels compelled to avoid public situations altogether. Those suffering from such "social phobia" fear that they will behave in ways that are embarrassing and humiliating. In severe cases, the fear of humiliation is so great that patients are unable to leave the confines of their own dwellings.

As I have pointed out elsewhere:

> The generalized anxiety associated with the fear of humiliation is itself a cause of shame and humiliation. In a kind of vicious cycle . . . sufferers, anxious about being exposed to public scrutiny and possible ridicule, experience an inner sense of humiliation because of their very vulnerability to social anxiety, which, they believe, makes them fundamentally flawed in others' eyes. In effect, they arrange for themselves the awful humiliation that they so desperately wish to avoid.[16]

Suicide

People kill themselves for many reasons, including severe depression; loss of a loved one; pain, loss of mobility, paralysis, and other suffering associated with terminal illness; and despair over business failure, job loss, and other economic disasters. With few exceptions, suicide is an act of desperation. More often than is generally realized, those who commit suicide are driven by humiliation. They are taking the only way they see to escape from the failure to meet others' expectations or their own expectations of themselves. The epidemic of suicide following the Wall Street crash of 1929 exemplifies this dynamic. Suddenly wiped out by the failure of the stock market, hitherto wealthy men jumped from skyscrapers or used other means to take their own lives because they could not stand the idea that they must otherwise face the world as failures. Many other examples come to mind, including newspaper reports of elementary schoolchildren in this country and elsewhere who kill themselves after failing exams, the comparatively high rate of suicide among gay and lesbian teenagers, and statistics showing that unemployed men take their own lives far more often than those who are employed.

It would appear that for many people a fate to be feared worse than death is the humiliation of public exposure as a failure. According to Larry Gernsbacher, an expert on suicide, many who are prone to take their own lives hold an inner conviction that they must be without flaw—perfect and powerful. This inner ideal—about which they are often unaware—makes them prone to overwhelming humiliation and despair.[17] Gernsbacher reports that people differ markedly in how they try to deal with their fantasized ideal of themselves. How they do so leads them to play out different roles in the Humiliation Dynamic.

There are those—a disproportionate number of which are women in our society—who give up on power altogether. They do their best to placate those around them by being innocently sweet and putting others' needs before their own. Taken to an extreme, these people become the humiliated victims of others' exploitation and abuse. If pushed to the extreme, they can turn their humiliated fury against themselves and take their own lives.

Another type—in our society they are disproportionately men—try to realize their fantasized ideal of themselves by gaining total mastery of their lives via control over others. When it comes to the Humiliation Dynamic, such persons are apt to be the ones who inflict humiliation on the ones they dominate. These are also the ones who, triggered by financial failure, exposure of wrongdoing, or other personal disaster, are prone to suicide.

Finally, there are those who glorify absolute freedom and Self sufficiency. They avoid close personal relationships because life as they know it is absurd and without meaning. Their sense of personal humiliation from experiences in their early years is profound. Although they go through the motions of living, they are observers of life. In the Humiliation Dynamic, they are ideal witnesses of the humiliations that people inflict on one another. For them life is ridiculous. It is humiliating merely to be alive and in the world. Suicide is the solution when the feelings of despair and meaninglessness become overwhelming.

In less extreme cases, most of us react to our fear of humiliation with self-protective maneuvers that keep us from speaking frankly, revealing ourselves fully even to intimate family members and friends, acknowledging inner doubts and uncertainties (and asking for help in handling those fears), trying out new behaviors, and developing interests and talents that remain unexpressed throughout our lives. The result is what Henry David Thoreau called "lives of quiet desperation," lives characterized by the conviction that it is better to be unrecognized and unfulfilled than it is to run the risk of failing, of exposing ourselves to ridicule, of learning through our Self examinations that we are truly deserving of the contempt we so fear.

Amount of Damage

We have already seen that in the broad canvas of human affairs, from the individual to the international, the Humiliation Dynamic causes an incredible amount of damage. Far more than either guilt or shame, we see how it can be implicated in doing damage to the human spirit in ways that lead to murder, war, intercommunal conflicts that affect the lives of one generation after another, and horrible acts of genocide.

Most of us grow into adulthood carrying a twofold burden of shame about ways we've treated others and of guilt about violating, both in thought and behavior, the codes of conduct that we have adopted as our own. For perhaps 10 percent of us, these burdens become emotionally intolerable and lead to alcoholism, drug abuse, neurosis, or some other form of disabling emotional disorder. The rest of us bear those burdens in ways that do little overt harm to ourselves and others—but very definitely detract from our ability to enjoy life.

In terms of its effects on all our lives, however, the Humiliation Dynamic is far more pervasive and destructive than either shame or guilt. The more I have studied humiliation, the more I have come to understand that humiliation is an experience no one escapes. Everyone endures humiliation at some point in his or her life. And everyone—with the possible exception of saints, Buddhist monks, and others who live their lives in a state of spiritual grace—is motivated by fear of humiliation and the desire to avoid another such experience if at all possible—and sometimes at all costs.

Age of First Exposure

As discussed in chapter 5, years before they are developmentally ready to feel shame and guilt, infants and small children experience humiliation, the sense of being small in comparison with more powerful adults and older siblings. They know the bite of ridicule, being laughed at, and not taken seriously. And they know the awful sense of being disregarded and made to feel invisible. This is an almost prototypic experience. That is, it comes with the territory of being a small member of the human species that requires years of adult care and guidance in order to make it into adulthood.

Shame comes later. The infant can feel powerless almost from birth on. It cannot experience shame until it knows the difference between itself and those around it. Only when children reach the point of knowing themselves as separate, unique individuals to whom others react in terms of whether what they do is "okay" or "not okay" can they know shame. The capacity for guilt comes last—when the child finally reaches the developmental point at which he or she can make judgments about what is "good" and what is "bad" behavior. At that point, the child has a measure against which to assess his or her own impulses and actions.

The sequence, then, is humiliation, shame, and, finally, guilt. About two years before being capable of knowing shame, the very small child must in some way incorporate experiences of feeling powerless, ridiculed, and ignored—that is, humiliated. The burden of shame allows the child to blame himself or herself. By feeling ashamed, the child takes some responsibility for the negative reactions others have to what he or she says and does. Several more years of development must occur, however, before the child adopts others' negative reactions and develops what Freud called the superego, roughly equivalent to what most people refer to as conscience.

The point is—humiliation occurs so early (when the child is still unable to speak and has few tools to deal with his or her environment) that it leaves its victims virtually defenseless. Humiliation, in other words, is an insidious and silent soul-killer, one we all must confront and defeat before we can hope to begin our voyage on the wondrous waters of Appreciation.

▣ Exercise 4: Getting to Know Your Humiliated Self

This exercise is offered to help you take stock of your "enemy within" and begin to free yourself from its clutches.

As we have seen, all of us are restricted to some extent in our freedom to Appreciate life by the effects of the Humiliation Dynamic. The following quiz was compiled by my colleague Linda Hartling to help individuals measure how susceptible they are to the energy and enjoyment-killing effects of humiliation. For each question, circle the number that best describes your response.

	Not at All				*Extremely*

1. Throughout your life, how seriously have you felt harmed by being:

(a) excluded? 1 2 3 4 5

(b) put down? 1 2 3 4 5

(c) ridiculed? 1 2 3 4 5

(d) discounted? 1 2 3 4 5

(e) cruelly criticized? 1 2 3 4 5

(f) called names or referred to in derogatory
   terms? 1 2 3 4 5

2. At this point in your life, how much do you fear being:

(g) ridiculed? 1 2 3 4 5

(h) put down? 1 2 3 4 5

(i) laughed at? 1 2 3 4 5

(j) cruelly criticized? 1 2 3 4 5

(k) made to feel like an outsider? 1 2 3 4 5

3. At this point in your life, how concerned are you about being:

(l) teased? 1 2 3 4 5

(m) discounted as a person? 1 2 3 4 5

(n) made to feel small or insignificant? 1 2 3 4 5

4. How worried are you about being:

(o) viewed by others as inadequate? 1 2 3 4 5

Scoring: The purpose of this test is not to compare you with other people, but simply to provide you with information about how you react to potentially humiliating experiences. You might find it useful, however, as a personal measure of the impact of humiliation in your life, to know how participants in Dr. Hartling's sample survey responded. According to Dr. Hartling, the mean (average) score, based on a sample of the 247 respondents, was 37; the standard deviation was 13. She suggests using the following scale to rate how relatively important the Humiliation Dynamic may be in determining how you live your life:

Low
A score of 24 or less indicates significantly fewer internal feelings of humiliation.

Moderate
A moderate score is between 25 and 49.

High
A score of 50 or higher indicates significantly greater internal feelings of humiliation.

In chapter 8, we will examine how our efforts to avoid humiliation often "boomerang" back to us, creating situations we'd rather not experience in our lives—situations and experiences that serve only to further isolate us from the spontaneous delight possible when we decide to live by the tenets of the Psychology of Appreciation.

EIGHT

The Prison of the Disowned Self: Boomeranging (Or How We Get Hit By What We Thought We Threw Away)

▣ ▣ ▣

> The game of life is a game of boomerangs. Our thoughts, deeds and words return to us sooner or later, with astounding accuracy.[1]
>
> —Florence Scovel Shinn, spiritual guide
> and author of *The Game of Life*

My study of the Humiliation Dynamic led me into a years-long quest to understand a paradoxical corollary of that dynamic—the phenomenon through which we all seem to attract experiences and circumstances that we emphatically want to avoid, usually because we associate them in our minds with some form of humiliation. The following examination of a common experience provides an almost classic example of the type of behavior I began to observe on a daily basis in myself, my colleagues, and my friends, relatives, and clients.

Imagine yourself at a cocktail party or other informal social gathering. You have just arrived and are in that preliminary process of "scouting" the place, trying to determine whom you know, where you fit, and how you can best enjoy your time at the gathering. You notice a group of acquaintances, people you admire, at one end of the room and approach them, hovering around the perimeter of the circle, waiting for an opportunity to join the conversation. You listen carefully, discouraged to discover that they are discussing a topic about which you know very little but about which you have a great deal of curiosity. You wait in vain for somebody to say something to which you can respond knowledgeably. The conversation continues at a level you consider to be just slightly over your head. What would be your response to such a situation? Would you:

A. Continue to listen, hoping against hope for an opportunity to shine?
B. Swallow hard and ask a question carefully phrased to hide as much of your ignorance as possible under the situation?
C. Ask the questions that come up for you, exerting little or no effort to hide your ignorance?

If you answered either A or B, you are among the probable majority of individuals who allow their fear of humiliation to limit the freedom with which they can live their everyday lives. When I began to explore my reluctance to reveal myself in similar situations, I learned a lot about my priorities: it was more important to me to avoid any possibility that I might be condescended to, laughed at, or ridiculed (especially by individuals I admired) than it was to reclaim the spontaneous power of my Creative Self. I was forced to admit that the fear of humiliation was a significant factor in my daily life (an admission that had its own power to humiliate, considering that I had devoted the better part of my working life to promoting mental health in other people).

As I examined my reactions more closely, I learned something even more interesting. I realized that my reluctance to reveal my ignorance by asking questions was working, not to make me appear less ignorant, but to ensure that my ignorance would remain forever in place. I was, in other words, getting exactly what I was trying to avoid. My clumsy attempts to hide my lack of information reminded me of a cartoon character trying to dispose of an Australian boomerang by throwing it into the air—away it would spin, only to circle around and hit the luckless character on the back of the head.

I had discovered a basic truism: *Whenever we try to "throw away" (by renouncing, denying, or avoiding) unacceptable parts of our psyches, they always return to us and impact our lives, usually in ways that we least expect, always in ways we find less than productive.*

As I expanded my observations, I became convinced that this kind of psychic "boomeranging"—often undertaken to protect us from a real or imagined humiliation—is reaching epidemic proportions in this country. Across the land, people like those in the following vignettes are desperately trying to rid themselves of unwanted qualities, habits, or attitudes by simply tossing them away, disowning them, keeping them hidden even from themselves. The results of their valiant efforts are that those parts they most want to get rid of keep coming back to haunt them—in such psychologically ingenious forms as projection (giving our unacceptable parts away to others), rationalization (devising elaborate justifications for actions we consider unacceptable), and suppression (an attempt to hide our True Selves from others).

The vignettes in this chapter are offered simply to show how broad ranging and ingenious is the boomerang's capacity to wreak havoc in our lives.

SHE DIDN'T WANT TO BOTHER ANYBODY

I had just conducted a workshop on boomeranging at a professional conference and was attending a lecture given by a well-known and highly respected speaker. The meeting room was long and narrow, with the entrance located behind and to the right of the speaker, who was using a flip chart to illustrate his talk. The speaker was warming to his task, intent on presenting his ideas in the most interesting way possible, and the audience was responding, engrossed, nodding its collective head each time the speaker made another interesting point.

In the middle of all this, the door to the room creaked open and a friend of mine appeared. She crept into the room and, instead of walking boldly in front of the speaker to find a seat, chose to sit meekly on the floor in the entrance, behind the speaker where she could not see his flip charts. She had managed to position herself so she was in full view of everyone in the room—except the speaker.

I beckoned discreetly to her, encouraging her to take a seat near me. Other colleagues around the room joined in, signaling that seats were available near them. The speaker showed signs of increasing discomfort, finally craning his neck and noticing my friend crouched in the doorway. Without skipping a beat, he moved to where my friend lurked and invited her to come on in and join the crowd. She walked sheepishly down the aisle, eyes cast low, with the entire room watching her. As she sat down next to me, she muttered, "I didn't want to disturb anybody."

I thought to myself: "There it is again! Boomerang! She got exactly what she didn't want."

I asked myself later what my friend could have done to avoid creating a distraction in that lecture room. After all, she was as quiet as a person can be and it wasn't her fault the room was arranged so that it was impossible to enter without being in full view of the audience. The answer is so simple that it seems invisible! *All she had to do was quit worrying about creating a distraction.* All she had to do was walk into the room, move quickly and purposefully down the aisle, and take a seat. If she had chosen that course of action, she might have created at worst a flicker of disturbance. The meeting would have proceeded with hardly an interruption, perhaps none at all.

It was, in other words, her very concern about "bothering" people that led her to choose a course of action that was almost guaranteed to attract attention. The very act of focusing on what she did not want caused it to come into fruition. It appears, then, that one way to avoid the boomerang backlash is to focus on the positive—*focus your attention on those aspects of your life, your psyche, or your current situation that you do want, rather than on those aspects you would prefer to throw away.*

HE WAS AFRAID HE WOULD STUTTER
This vignette illustrates how boomeranging can distort not just isolated situations, but entire lives.

A nine-year-old boy noticed that he had difficulty pronouncing certain sounds. Fearful of being labeled a stutterer (or worse, a "sissy" with a lisp), he began to avoid those words in which the "difficult" sounds appear. When he had to use those words, his fear of ridicule caused him to tense up and stammer.

Years later, as an adult who had endured decades of social discomfort and wasted megawatts of energy to hide his Self-inflicted stuttering, he sought help from a remedial speech teacher. After three sessions, the teacher helped him become aware of how his chosen childhood belief that he might be a stutterer and his fear of humiliation had combined to create his apparent speech disorder. Once he was able to believe that fear was the root cause of his problem, his speech improved. His Self-imposed stutter disappeared.

MATCHED SETS OF BOOMERANGS

Boomerangs can be even more pernicious when, as often happens, they occur in matched sets, with two or more parties cooperating to ensure that everyone gets exactly what he or she does not want. Here's an example of matched sets at work.

A junior member of a company-wide task force charged with developing a new line of products was having difficulty understanding how to accomplish a certain assignment. Rather than ask for help, he chose to muddle through on his own. The head of his task force, he told himself, was too busy to be bothered with such a minor matter. Besides, he did not want to give the boss any reason to think he didn't know exactly what he was doing.

As the weeks went by, it became more and more apparent that the young man could not deal with the assignment on his own, a fact that came to the leader's attention only after the young man made several costly mistakes that required a great deal of time and attention to unravel. The leader was very upset, complaining to me (his consultant), "I can't understand this. How can such a bright, promising person be so stupid?"

As we investigated the situation, it became clear that several factors had conspired to ensure the boomerang effect:

- The leader was a hard-driving individual who was great at dealing with the big picture but hated details.
- He set demanding performance standards for himself and others and boasted about giving team members a free hand as long as they produced results.
- The junior task force member had an outstanding academic record but no job experience. He was totally focused on proving himself in the "real world," on avoiding even the possibility of appearing less than miraculously competent.

This situation presented a setup for boomeranging—two individuals predisposed by temperament and circumstance to behave in ways that were almost guaranteed to produce exactly what neither wanted. As often happens in families, organizations, and other complex settings, both men failed to achieve their shared objective (which in this case was the smooth accomplishment of their common task). The younger man, who wanted neither to bother his boss nor to appear incompetent, ended up so irritating his superior that he was almost fired for poor performance. The older man, who wanted neither to be bothered by details nor to discourage outstanding performance, ended up with a frustrated staff member whose work was below standard and the prospect of investing large amounts of time and energy on a relatively small, but vital, detail of the overall project.

Fortunately, the team leader was quick to understand how he and his subordinate had boomeranged, thereby sharing responsibility for the undesirable situation. Instead of acting on his initial impulse to fire the younger man, he accepted his role as mentor, initiating a close and productive work relationship. The young man responded by developing into a highly valued, performance-oriented member of the team.

A key point here, again, is that this matched-set boomerang could have been short-circuited had either man recognized earlier the value of focusing on the positive, rather than on the negative, aspects of his desired outcome. The younger man, for example, would have been in a much better position had he been able to recognize that asking for assistance was a move toward accomplishing his assignment, rather than an admission of weakness. The older man learned that spending a few moments every day checking the details of his operation would save him endless hours of rechecking (and perhaps correcting) those same hated details later.

I am convinced that in each of these cases of boomeranging, the experience of humiliation or the fear of humiliation was involved. Although I can't claim to be able to read anyone else's mind, I think it is safe to assume that my friend who arrived late to the lecture was motivated by her desire to avoid the (probably subtle) mockery or professional derision of her more punctual colleagues. Our stuttering friend was, most likely, haunted by specters of his comrades laughing at his peculiar speech. The common adult fear of humiliating failure or incompetence might have motivated the task force leader and his subordinate in their reluctance to address the realities of their work situation.

BOOMERANGING IN PUBLIC LIFE

Boomeranging takes on world-shaking potency when it appears in the public realm, creating situations that not only shape but also sometimes distort history.

In his autobiography, former Secretary of State Dean Rusk describes two important instances of international boomeranging following World War II.[2] The first involved Charles de Gaulle's failure to achieve a leadership role for France in the postwar world. The second resulted in the rearming of America as a response to Joseph Stalin's aggressive efforts to ensure the security of the Soviet Union.

General de Gaulle, according to Rusk, was deeply and understandably affected by his country's humiliating collapse in the face of the Nazi onslaught at the beginning of the war. He was sensitive to even the most minor slight toward France and insisted in numerous, often petty, ways that his country be treated by its Western allies with respect verging on deference. The leaders of the other Western nations came to regard the French leader as a man driven to arrogant extremes by his desire to restore French honor, especially after he began to insist that France be the voice for all of Western Europe.

The Western allies perceived the French leader's refusal to cooperate on minor matters as an obstacle to their efforts to present a common front to the Soviet Union. In the end, de Gaulle's actions produced results that were just the opposite of the ones he so desperately wanted. Here's how Rusk sums up what happened:

> Ironically, had President de Gaulle thrown himself into the leadership of the European movement and promoted transatlantic cooperation, he would have become the spokesman for Western Europe. But the very tactics that he adopted to build up the position and prestige of France frustrated his central purpose. Rather quickly, the Kennedy administration reached a point where we simply did not care what de Gaulle

thought except on those matters over which he held a veto. We learned to proceed without him.[3]

Rusk contends that Stalin played diplomatic and military hardball following World War II to establish the Soviet Union's unchallenged sphere of influence in Eastern Europe, create a secure situation for his country, and move toward a position of dominance in the world. His actions, however, fueled a chain of reactions that fed into his worst fears about the threat the United States and its allies posed to the Soviet Union. Faced with Stalin's aggressive attitudes and actions, the United States began in the early 1950s to rebuild the military power that it had almost completely scrapped after the defeat of Germany and Japan. Rusk writes:

> [F]rom the Soviet point of view, Joseph Stalin made a great mistake at the end of World War II. If Stalin had invested ten years in genuine peaceful coexistence, he would have faced a disarmed and isolationist America. But instead, he embarked upon adventures which forced the United States to rearm and play a greater role in world affairs.[4]

The role of matched sets of boomerangs in each case is paramount. The more the other Western leaders ignored what de Gaulle had to say, the more his humiliated pride operated to fuel his fierce efforts to create a position for France as leader of the alliance. The more vigorously he pursued France's interests, the more the other leaders ignored him. And, on and on in an escalating boomerang war.

Likewise, the more the United States and its allies worked to create a defensive shield against Stalin, the more the Soviets felt the need to increase their own power position. The more militant the Soviets grew, the faster the West rearmed. The result was the incredibly costly Cold War from which neither side would back down for fear of humiliating defeat.

Again, what stands out in these scenarios is that neither party got what it wanted, but rather, the opposite. Each party got exactly what it was putting so much energy into preventing. And, as is usually the case in boomeranging, each party managed to remain blissfully unaware of how its behavior was contributing to the escalating efforts and diminishing returns.

BOOMERANGING IS BLIND

As Peter Senge, a noted expert on organizational behavior, points out in *The Fifth Discipline*, the dynamics of boomeranging require the person involved to be unaware of what is happening. He cites the example of a brilliant CEO who bemoans the fact that his underlings lack both vision and forceful leadership, qualities that the CEO has in abundance. Senge observes that the CEO is so good at expressing his views that people feel intimidated by him and have learned not to challenge his views.[5] Thus, without realizing that he is doing so, the CEO creates the compliance he deplores and, in so doing, ensures the absence of what he knows his organization needs: "real leaders." Senge suggests that the CEO is caught up in a defensive strategy of intimidating other people so that they won't confront his thinking. "If the CEO saw his strategy presented in such bald terms, he would almost certainly disavow it." He concludes: "The fact that it remains hidden to him keeps it operative."[6]

From Senge's account, I conclude that the frustrated CEO's defensiveness originated in his fear of humiliation. His Achilles' heel may well have been that, despite his brilliance, he lived in constant fear of the ridicule that might come his way if others found flaws in his reasoning about what his company needed in order to flourish.

I suspect that the fear of being shown up in some way is at the bottom of most, if not all, instances of boomeranging. From a very different culture that of Communist China—comes the following telling account of boomeranging grounded in fear of humiliation. William Hinton, a noted expert on China, describes with some humor the rigid behavior of a woman from the Chinese foreign ministry who traveled with his party in visits to out-of-the-way villages:

> Lin T'ung combined reverence for rank, especially her own, with political rigidity. Her appetite for dogmatism rivaled her appetite for fish, and the opinions she held at any given moment tended to be absolute. . . . What mattered was her interpretation of the Party line at the moment and she held to it tenaciously, as if the slightest adjustment, the slightest doubt, had the capacity to throw her whole world outlook into question. I suspect that her outward certainty concealed an inner

uncertainty. The less secure she felt about a position the more dogmatically she asserted it. Others said of Lin T'ung, *"She is so afraid to be wrong, that she is wrong!"* [italics added] But that, of course, she would not admit, even to herself.[7]

BOOMERANGING IN POPULAR LITERATURE

Newspaper stories, magazine articles, and even comic strips abound with instances of boomeranging. The following paragraphs feature a few instances I've collected.

Boomeranging is one of the main themes of *Cathy,* the comic strip by Cathy Guisewite. In strip after strip, Cathy vows not to overeat, not to buy clothes a size too small, not to compete with her mother—of whom she is a carbon copy—or not to behave in some other ingrained Cathy-like way. But, often because of her resolve to mend her ways, the pressure builds up and she ends up gorging herself with ice cream and cookies, stuffing herself into new dresses that are about to burst at the seams, and attempting yet again (and failing yet again) to outdo her mother.

In a typical sequence, Cathy gobbles one cookie after another while preparing for a Thanksgiving Day visit with her parents. She always overeats, she says, when she goes to see her mother because she is determined to show that *her* weight-loss plan works better than her mother's. "The more determined I am to prove that *I* have conquered the family eating problem, the more I eat." In this particular strip, Guisewite also neatly illustrates that boomeranging often comes in matched sets. The last panel shows Cathy and her mother, both equally overweight. Cathy says, "I'm home, Mother." To which Mother responds with a beatific smile, "I believe we have a tie this year, dear."

In an article entitled "The Coup Plotters" in the January 6, 1992, issue of *Time* magazine, journalist George Church describes the boomerang that resulted when a group of high-level, hard-line Communists failed in their effort to overthrow the government of Soviet President Mikhail Gorbachev in order to maintain the Communist system. He points out that Soviet citizens' outrage at the coup hastened the demise of the Soviet Communist system. Church writes:

> To fail so totally as to bring about the exact opposite of what you want—that calls for more than run-of-the-mill incompetence. It

requires a kind of perverse genius that will make the Moscow Plotters memorable long after the state they betrayed has faded into history.[8]

Washington Post columnist William Raspberry brings the boomeranging process much closer to home in his column of September 1, 1995. Writing about the controversial O. J. Simpson trial, Raspberry refers to "Mark Fuhrman, the racist cop whose demonstrably false testimony has thrown the trial of the century into disarray."

The columnist outlines Fuhrman's boomerang as follows.

1. The Los Angeles detective hates black people because he believes they have certain characteristics that he rejects: dishonesty, cheating, and criminality.
2. In his zeal to make sure that criminals are punished, he has, when necessary, manufactured evidence.
3. It is obvious that Fuhrman is convinced that O. J. is guilty.
4. By his own admission, the detective has made himself vulnerable to the charge that he manufactured evidence in order to nail O. J. If true, he himself has become dishonest, a cheat, and a criminal.
5. In his very zeal to make sure that O. J. is punished for his crime, Fuhrman may have contributed to the situation wherein a person he *knows* to be guilty is aquitted.[9]

"Wouldn't it be ironic," Raspberry writes, "if this hater of black people should turn out to be this black man's rescuer?"

But Raspberry cuts much closer to the bone than simply pointing out how Fuhrman's race hatred may have led to the acquittal of O. J., the very opposite of the result that the detective was eager to bring about. Without using the term itself, he turns the controversy about Fuhrman into a parable that teaches how prone we all are to boomeranging by becoming what we hate.

As examples, he cites, on the one hand, "good kids" in the inner city who own handguns in order to protect themselves against arrogant menaces, only to end up becoming arrogant menaces themselves; and, on the other hand, how easy it is for mild-mannered, peace-loving people like his readers to work up a thirst for violent revenge against bullies, lawbreakers, and policemen-gone-wrong. Peace loving you may be, Raspberry says, but note how often you opt for vengeance—in your thoughts, if not your behavior—thereby becoming like those you hate.

JUST LOOK AROUND YOU

We don't have to go to large, complex corporations, the vast international political scene, or sensational trials to find examples of boomeranging. Once you begin looking and listening, you're sure to find many instances in your own family and in the stories of good-intentions-gone-wrong with which you and your friends entertain one another. A common intergenerational boomerang has to do with how parents treat their children.

Years ago when I was a graduate student at the University of California, I conducted parent education classes for the city of Richmond's adult education program. In group after group, I found young mothers who were upset and angry with themselves because they'd discovered that they were treating their children in the very same ways their parents had treated them, even though they'd vowed as children never to inflict such awful treatment on their own offspring. I didn't call it boomeranging back then, even though the term would have fit perfectly. How many young parents have been chagrined to discover that, without realizing it, they've become just like their parents in ways they thought they'd totally rejected as children? From my experience with successive generations of parents—not to mention my experience parenting my own children—I've discovered that it's more the rule than the exception. When it comes to parenting, intergenerational boomeranging takes on epidemic proportions.

I suspect that boomeranging is central in most, if not all, sustained disputes—international, national, organizational, familial, and personal. As differences escalate into head-on disagreement, and disagreement threatens to become open conflict, opportunities for clear, unambiguous exchange of ideas and concerns rarely occur. Each side blames the other for causing the dispute. Neither side wants what's happening, yet neither is prepared to understand and accept its part in creating the very difficulties it insists it wants to avoid. Typically, as the situation deepens, the sides withdraw from one another, becoming more committed to what they do not want to happen and more deeply entrenched in their conviction of their own righteousness.

Many of life's most melodramatic and often tragic boomerangs have their origins in the darker, more tempestuous emotions—such as envy and jealousy—that so often lie just under the surface of the love, pride, and other positive feelings we treasure in our relationships with others. Fiction writers are very aware of this fact. More than one short story has been written, for example, about the jealous lover whose repeated unjustified accusations of infidelity finally drive his or her beloved into the arms of a less possessive mate. And when you look for them, you spot little gems of boomeranging in your favorite novels. Here's one from Frank Norris's wonderful novel *McTeague*. Early in the novel he introduces Augustine, an elderly French woman, who prepares meals for a San Francisco woman named Trina and her family. Augustine provides a classic caricature of someone who, because of her desperate efforts to avoid disturbing others, ends up disturbing them very much:

> Augustine cooked well, but she was otherwise undesirable, and Trina lost patience with her at every moment. The old French woman's most marked characteristic was her timidity. Trina could scarcely address her a simple direction without Augustine quailing and shrinking: a reproof, however gentle, threw her into an agony of confusion; while Trina's anger promptly reduced her to a state of nervous collapse, wherein she lost all power of speech, while her head began to bob and nod with an uncontrollable twitching of the muscles, much like the oscillations of the head of a toy donkey. Her timidity was exasperating, her very presence in the room unstrung the nerves, while her morbid eagerness to avoid offense only served to develop in her a clumsiness that was at times beyond belief.[10]

HOW I LEARNED TO SPOT A BOOMERANG

Over the years I have become convinced that the very ubiquity of the boomeranging phenomenon is what makes it so difficult to see. It occurs so often and so consistently that it has become as invisible as the air we breathe. It is simply there, a mysterious force that (like the gremlins and elves of folktales) can be depended on to waylay our best-laid plans. The following personal experience made me aware of how susceptible we all are to boomeranging and illustrates how easy it is to set oneself up as a victim.

I was attending a workshop that focused on the use of non-verbal movement to explore the polar opposites (groupings such as right brain/left brain, shy/outgoing, right/wrong) that occur regularly in human interactions. Our specific objective was to explore mechanisms for bringing opposites together in a workable, functioning, integrated manner.

At one point, we were asked to participate in an active two-part exercise. During the first part we were to move in a totally balanced way, preplanning every movement in advance. During the second part we were to operate in the opposite mode—moving in a totally random, unplanned, spontaneous manner.

I was delighted with the first part of the exercise. Preplanned, balanced movement came naturally to me. I moved with grace and dignity and splendor, developing a new appreciation for the impact and importance of ceremonial occasions, with all their pomp and circumstance.

The second part presented a not very pleasant surprise. I let myself go as completely as I knew how, but my efforts at spontaneous movement degenerated until I was flopping and reeling around the room, caroming off walls, objects, and people. Within only a few minutes (perhaps only seconds, but it seemed longer), I was feeling nauseous, disoriented, and anxious. Panicked, I grabbed a colleague's leg and hung on for dear life.

Later, as we discussed our experiences, I saw that my reaction to the second part of that rather simple exercise represented boomeranging in full tilt. I remembered how I felt when I was four-teen—six feet tall, weighing only 134 pounds, not very athletic, and terrified of being ridiculed for being so awkward and ungainly. It was back then (at a time when my childhood experiences were definitely less-than-completely "happy") that I took an unconscious vow to be "cool," to compensate for my gangly physique by behaving at all times in my most dignified manner. By the time I attended that workshop, I had grown out of the gangly stage, but not my emphasis on dignity. I won't go so far as to say that, at the age of thirty, I acted like a stuffy old man, but I suspect it would have been accurate to describe me as just a tad uptight.

I realized during the course of the post-exercise discussion that I held myself so upright and straight and moved so carefully and with such restraint that I had, literally, disciplined my muscles to the point where it was impossible for me to move fluidly and with genuine, unpremeditated grace. My body was boomeranging on me—giving me, in spontaneous situations, exactly the lack of grace I'd so studiously worked to avoid.

I discovered that if I wanted to be graceful, I was going to have to allow myself to run the risk of feeling and appearing ridiculous. I began to experiment with behavior that, at least in my own mind, appeared silly. I expressed spontaneous enthusiasm at formal gatherings. I practiced moving to music on dance floors and *a cappella* in other public places. I began to discard my limited conventional wardrobe, which expressed my formerly carefully controlled tastes, in favor of more conspicuous clothing. Through all this, I began to see that the more relaxed I was, the more graceful and truly dignified and balanced I came to be. Now that I was not desperately trying to throw my awkwardness away from me, it no longer mattered how I moved, or what I wore, or at what level of vocal volume I chose to express myself. The less I cared how I appeared, the more I could be what I wanted to be—graceful, spontaneous, and immune to ridicule.

I learned another important lesson from that workshop, namely this: being ridiculous is not a static condition, some tangible state that sneaks up and overwhelms its victim. Rather, it's a judgment, one made by the Self or others and imposed from the outside. What I learned, in other words, is that the state of being ridiculous exists only in the eye of the beholder. To paraphrase our veteran umpire, "It ain't nuthin' til I call it." With that recognition, I was able to add appearing ridiculous to the permeable parts of my mental scrim—it was no longer inextricably woven into the fabric of my life; instead, it changed and moved and disappeared as I moderated my interior lighting.

You have probably noticed that many men in this society are uptight about being or seeming ridiculous. Their image of acceptable masculinity is generally stiff and linear, demanding a semi-military bearing, emphatic gestures, and limited facial expressions. Their demeanor rules out graceful movements and gestures that in any way seem "feminine." Those men who, like myself, learn that violating this masculine image no longer matters often find they are not ridiculed and rejected. As the following story suggests, just the opposite sometimes happens:

> About fifteen years ago, my wife and I conducted a residential workshop on personal and organizational power. A man in his early thirties showed up wearing one earring, a red bandana, leather pants, and a Harley Davidson T-shirt. Even in our very informal group of participants, he stood out as exotic, possibly even menacing. Imagine our surprise when it turned out that he was a first sergeant in the U.S. Army.
>
> Toward the end of the second day, some of the participants felt comfortable enough to ask why a senior enlisted man like himself dressed in a way that reminded them of a cross between a drag queen and a Hell's Angel. The sergeant explained that five years before he had decided to take up skiing. In a class with other novices (both men and women), he noticed how much more quickly the women learned to negotiate the beginner's slope than did the men. He watched how gracefully and naturally the women moved their hips and the rest of their bodies, swaying and balancing themselves far more easily than the men, who seemed stiff and even rigid. He decided to imitate the women, allowing his hips to sway and his body to bend in more graceful curves. Sure enough! Like the women, he was able to master the beginner's slope very quickly.
>
> From that moment on, he said, he decided he would no longer be "confined" (his word) by norms of what it means to be "a man." If he wanted to wear a bandana on his head, why not do so? If he felt like having his ears pierced and adorning them with earrings, so be it. "But how do you get away with it in the Army?" they asked. "Simple," he said, "when I'm on duty, I wear the costume of a macho first sergeant. When I'm off post, I dress and behave in ways that please me." He paused a moment and then grinned at the men in the group. "You guys should know," he told them, "that since I've allowed myself to be graceful and dress the way I want, I've become far more attractive to women!"

HOW HUMILIATION GIVES
BIRTH TO BOOMERANGING

As I indicated at the beginning of this chapter, boomeranging and the Humiliation Dynamic are intrinsically intertwined. The scenario goes something like this: individually or collectively, we experience some form of humiliation at the hands of parents, teachers, bullies, rivals, bosses, socially sanctioned oppressors, or others. To avoid repeating that experience, we incorporate certain qualities and characteristics into our Selves, attaching our identities to those qualities and attitudes because we believe they will protect us from humiliation. We label those qualities and attitudes "Me" and make them important components of our definitions of our Selves.

To be complete, however, a definition must say both what something is and what it is not. For every "this" there must be a "that." The idea of "up" has no meaning without "down." "Good" cannot exist without "bad." Similarly, every idea in our heads about who we are has its opposite side that defines who we are not—who we will not, under punishment of possible humiliation, give ourselves permission to be. Let's say, for example, that the "Me" you value can be described as *bright, fair, caring,* and *flexible.* The opposite "Not-Me" qualities, which you devalue and disown, might be characterized by such descriptive words as *stupid, biased, cold,* and *rigid.* Both the Me and the Not Me are essential to your Self definition; you probably invest essentially equal amounts of energy distancing yourself from the Not Me qualities as you invest in expressing your Me's.

The Not Me, in other words, is more than an abstract concept. It is a powerful psychic phenomenon that exercises considerable negative influence on how you live your life. We use copious amounts of energy in repressing or rejecting our Not-Me qualities. And, by refusing to acknowledge our Not Me's, we place unnecessary and sometimes crippling limits on how we can use our remaining energy.

Perhaps the most deleterious effect of the Not Me is associated with our need to find someone to "hold" the qualities we refuse to own in our Selves. For you to continue to exhibit your wonderful, warm, and loving qualities, it is essential for you to identify people who are less wonderful, warm, and loving. The Me/Not-Me dichotomy also holds sway in defining the identity of groups. Suppose we belong to a group that we believe is loyal, trustworthy, heroic, reverent, and noble. To balance this positive "We," we need at least one other despised group who, in our minds, is the very opposite: disloyal, treacherous, cowardly, irreverent, and base.

WHY "NOT ME" KEEPS COMING BACK

The essence of the boomeranging dynamic is that we are haunted by an unconscious compulsion to feel and behave in ways that we consciously reject. No matter how hard we try, no matter how vigorously we denounce certain qualities and attitudes, no matter how adamantly we reject them when we see them in other people, those attributes we "throw away" seem destined, like boomerangs, to return to complicate our lives, usually in disguised and unexpected ways.

In actual fact, the characteristics we reject never really leave our hands. They continue to exist in our minds—to ask them to leave and never return is like entreating someone not to think about a pink elephant. The more we try to repress them, the more energy we feed them.

Psychologists have long been fascinated with the boomeranging process. Freud himself spoke of the "return of the repressed," referring to his observations of how hidden emotions and impulses—even those his patients found totally unacceptable—found expression in their lives, in disguised and highly dysfunctional ways. Carl Jung, an early colleague of Freud's, pointed out that each positive quality we value in ourselves is paired in our minds (albeit unconsciously) with a psychologically negative opposite quality. He used the image of the Shadow to refer to such rejected personal qualities because, like the shadows cast by our bodies, they follow us around whether we choose to acknowledge them or not.

Freud and Jung worked primarily with emotionally disturbed individuals. As the study of human behavior progresses, however, we are learning that boomeranging is neither a "symptom" of mental illness nor a deeply buried psychological mechanism. It is a pervasive part of "normal" everyday life, so pervasive, in fact, that references to the phenomenon are beginning to appear in such popular publications as *Reader's Digest*. The April 1988 issue of that magazine (on page 11) carried the following warning by Peg Bracken under the headline "Never Say Never": "You may have noticed, as I have, that if you ever find yourself declaring emphatically and unequivocally that you will never do some one particular thing, chances are good that this is precisely what you will one day find yourself doing."[11]

Linked as it is to the Humiliation Dynamic, boomeranging represents the most insidious and powerful motivator of dysfunctional and destructive human behavior, serving as the hidden trigger for projection, rationalization, Self blame, and other less-than-productive defense mechanisms.

That very link to the Humiliation Dynamic, however, holds the key for finding a way to disengage the boomerang's power over human life. Boomeranging, quite simply, occurs because people—individually and collectively—take themselves so seriously. Defending our Self importance becomes, for many of us, more important than life itself. Even extinction of the Self through suicide or death on the battlefield can seem preferable to enduring threats to our Self esteem, whether those threats are addressed to us individually, as members of a religious or other group, or as citizens of a nation. At the very least, most of us are prepared to boomerang our way through life, throwing away unacceptable Not Me's and blithely ignoring the fact that, inevitably, we all get what we throw away.

The real answer to the dilemmas posed by the Humiliation Dynamic and its boomeranging companion lies in learning to live with Appreciation, in moving behind the scrims that we hold so tightly in place, utilizing our native power to create and define our own lives. The next step in that process of Self reclamation might be to complete exercise 5. It is a two-part exercise: the first part is designed to help you begin to recognize your Not Me—the psychological entity that sets you up, time and time again, to attract what you most want to throw away; the second part is designed to help you reclaim the Not Me as a valuable part of who you are.

◨ Exercise 5: Reclaiming the "Not Me"
Part 1: Recognizing the "Not Me"

1. Turn again to the chart on page 23 that contains your Self description and the outline of experiences that might have motivated your choices.

2. In the middle column (labeled "Not Me") write a word or phrase that you consider to be the opposite of each of the adjectives you listed in the left-hand column (labeled "Me").

Caution: Avoid using "not" in front of a word to form its opposite. The opposite of "modest" isn't "not modest" or even "immodest." A the-saurus lists a variety of antonyms for "modest," such as "boastful," "shameless," and "show off." Choose the word that comes closest to defining your Not Me.

3. Read your list of Not Me's aloud to yourself or to a friend or partner. Then consider what type of person you would be if your list were re-versed so your Not Me's were Me's and your Me's were Not Me's. The chances are that you would be less than enamored of such a person. Most of us prefer our Me qualities to our Not Me's. With the exception of an occasional positive quality that we may be striving to achieve, our Not Me's usually are loaded with unpleasant, inadequate, or immoral impli-cations.

Part 2: Reclaiming the "Not Me"

In the right-hand column (labeled "Also Me"), next to each of the nega-tive Not Me's write a different word or phrase that basically means the same thing but has a positive connotation or at least a neutral one. Because the negative labels are so firmly planted in your mind, you may find this task difficult. If so, get suggestions from others or use a the-saurus. To help you get started, here are some examples:

Not Me	Also Me
Selfish	Thrifty
Dumb	Deliberate or methodical
Unfeeling	Matter-of-fact
Passive	Calm

Read your list of Also Me's aloud to yourself or to a friend or partner and consider how it feels to be both your Me and your Also Me. Chances are that what you have listed as Also Me's are far more acceptable than the put-downs you listed as Not Me's. In certain situations each of these qualities probably stands you in good stead.

I am going to end chapter 8 with this disconcerting thought: what you have defined up until now as negative Not Me's are as much a part of you as the positive Me's, those qualities you admire and nurture in yourself. In many ways, you are the person you've spent your entire life trying not to be. In exercise 5, you took an important step in the important task of claiming those disowned qualities as your own.[12] In upcoming chapters, we will explore ways to utilize this bad news to transform your life and open vast new vistas of opportunity and choice.

NINE

Ego-Hooking: Boomeranging Gone Wild

◨   ◨   ◨

> Anybody who wishes to do so can get all, and indeed more
> than all, the mortification he wants out of the incidents of ordi-
> nary, day-to-day living, without ever resorting to harsh bodily
> penance.[1]
>
> —Aldous Huxley, philospher and critic

The prospect of reading a whole chapter about what happens
when boomeranging goes wild might feel like cruel and unusual
punishment, especially in light of Mr. Huxley's reminder of how
easy it is to find mortification in the course of everyday living,
without searching it out in books.

The purposes of this chapter, however, are completely positive—
to detail in slow motion how our psychological equipment co-
operates under the spell of Self importance to produce mortification
and to introduce the idea that it is possible to short-circuit this
seemingly automatic response. This chapter, in short, is presented
in the spirit of empowerment, a few pages full of ideas and techniques to produce a freer, more zestful, and productive life, a few
pages about how we grown-ups cooperate in having our childhood potentials continually stolen from us.

I have taken some poetic and professional license with the
term "ego," as it appears in this chapter. For most psychologists,
"ego" is a technical term that refers to that part of the personality
that analyzes information, makes decisions, and initiates action.
No value judgment is attached to the use of the word in the
strictly professional sense. In the next few pages, I will be using

the word as it commonly occurs in everyday speech, as a shorthand term for feelings of Self importance, as in "John has a big ego," meaning he seems to place an inordinate amount of emphasis on his pride.

THE EGO-HOOKING PROCESS

Ego-hooking includes those everyday phenomena through which we "normal" people find ways to become needlessly upset.[2] When our egos are hooked, our inner umpires scream out "disaster," "misery," "doom and gloom," eliciting responses that are filled with debilitating negativity, narrowing the range of choice available to us in creating our lives. When our egos are hooked, we waste energy, blind ourselves to behavioral options, overlook vital information, engage in sloppy analysis, make poor (to rotten) decisions, find ourselves enmeshed in unproductive conflicts, and generally display an amazing array of highly creative ways to limit our ability to deal effectively with people and situations.

All ego-hooking encounters follow the same basic pattern and all are amenable to short-circuiting at any point in the pattern. The tricky part is that most ego-hooking incidents develop very quickly, in units of time most accurately measured in nanoseconds.

1. The pattern begins with an event—something as simple as an unexpected encounter with another driver in traffic or a spouse's offhand comment.
2. Our senses (alerted to the possibility of danger) begin collecting information, often faster than our minds can process it.
3. The overloaded mind tries to sort the information, relying on its past programming to determine what it all means and to select a proper course of action in response to that Self-generated meaning.
4. The mind (which is committed, remember, to making sure we are always right in a world in which to be wrong feels fatal) generates a story to justify and rationalize the (possibly less-than-edifying) actions we selected in step 3.

Step 1 on the Road to Humiliation: An Event Occurs
The essential factor to remember when analyzing the events that generate ego-hooking is that an event is just an event, nothing more, until the mind becomes engaged and invites the ego in to do its dirty work. As the third umpire says, "It ain't nuthin' til I call it."

For illustrative purposes, let's say:

> I'm driving down the freeway when another car zips past me, barely missing my left fender as it cuts back into the lane in front of me.

Again, notice that the event itself is value-free. There is nothing inherent in the series of actions described above that dictates any specific emotional or behavioral response. Some people might react with anger or a desire for revenge. For a few, it might even be an occasion for an explosion of road rage. Others might simply be surprised, slow down, and resolve to drive with greater caution. There are those who would be concerned for the other driver's safety. Some might primarily find themselves wondering about what was causing the driver's recklessness and poor judgment. And no doubt some might ignore the event altogether, preferring instead to continue to think about whatever was on their minds before the incident took place. It's probably safe to say that men would have a greater tendency than women to react with anger, experience the incident as a personal challenge, and think about some way to get revenge.

Step 2: The Senses Start Shoving Data In
Almost simultaneously with the event, the senses start collecting information about what has happened, feeding it to the brain for processing. In the case of the encounter on the freeway:

- My eyes convey data about the size, shape, and color of the object that suddenly appears ahead of me, triggering my brain to begin calculating the distance between my car and this stranger.
- My ears detect the sounds of squealing tires, roaring engines, and high-speed air currents.

- My olfactory apparatus sends signals to my brain about exhaust fumes, burning rubber, and, perhaps, my own nervous perspiration.
- The nerves in my skin become super-sensitive to the feel of the hard, cold metal of the steering wheel in my white-knuckled hands.
- My inner-sensing devices tell me something's going on: my stomach feels hollow, my chest feels too small, my head throbs slightly from the sudden onrush of blood.

Within seconds of my first realization that something unexpected had happened on the freeway, I begin to experience an overwhelming onslaught of new data from my sensory organs, a complex endeavor made even trickier by the nature of the human sensory process. Under the best of circumstances our senses are limited, prohibiting us, for instance, from hearing the high frequencies dogs hear or detecting motion with the accuracy of frogs. We are incapable of seeing the sound and light waves that carry radio and television messages or of detecting X rays and other forms of radiation.

In the types of circumstances that lend themselves to ego-hooking, our limited sensory apparatus has to contend with a sudden flood of unexpected information, an activity that restricts still further our range of sensitivity. We are forced, by the sheer quantity of data vying for attention, to be selective in what we choose to perceive. We simply cannot respond to all the stimuli.

The design and function of our sensory apparatus force us to deal at all times with a distorted picture of reality. Situations of high-ego-hooking potential tend to redouble this basic human limitation by narrowing our field of focus, shuttering our line of sensation to the tunnel that involves the event that has captured our attention.

Let's examine how these limitations affected my view of that freeway encounter:

Because of the sudden demands being made on my sensory apparatus by the rush of data relating to the intruder ahead of me, I lose contact for the moment with other aspects of my physical environment—aspects that, only moments before the event, had been my major focus of attention.

I no longer hear the Bach concerto issuing from my tape player. My eyes are suddenly blinded to the fall colors of the trees that line the road. I can no longer feel the cool rush of air on my cheek from the open window. And, most amazing of all, I've forgotten entirely the faint gnaw of hunger that just moments ago had me scanning the roadside for a place to stop for lunch.

Step 3: The Mind Tries to Sort It All Out

By step 3, we are in a situation in which we feel called on, under great pressure and with limited information, to make a decision. We rise to the occasion by using the complex vehicle psychologists call "perception."

Perception, in its most general definition, is the process by which our minds organize sensory data into understandable patterns, taking limited raw material and molding it into more-or-less intelligible, more-or-less useful information that enables us to make more-or-less rational decisions and choose more-or-less effective courses of behavior.

Behavioral scientists are still debating the basic components of perception and how those components work together to produce mental patterns. But it is fairly well agreed that an individual's perceptive mechanism is greatly influenced by past experience; by beliefs, values, and attitudes; and by the individual's current physical and emotional condition and health.

Past Experience

Past experience influences perception in two basic ways.

First, it serves as the standard whereby we judge current experience. We learn from experience, for example, what a chair is and how to use it. On the basis of that experience, we are able to recognize chairs whenever we see them, even those designed in ways we have never encountered before.

Second, past experience shapes perception through the various unconscious decisions we make in the course of developing our sense of Self. In chapter 8, I recounted how as a result of my experience as a gangly youth, I perceived all spontaneity as a risk to my dignity, a risk that I avoided by redoubling my efforts to appear controlled, balanced, and dignified, no matter what the cost.

In terms of the freeway incident:

My past experience with drivers who pass me emphasizes the fact that they can be discourteous, dangerous, even malevolent. Some of them were even menaces to the public health.

I also have an active repository of memories involving myself as the hero—weaving in and out of traffic, passing car after car. I know that being on the interstate fast track can be a very satisfying, even heady, experience. "Eat my dust, Turkey," or words to that effect, are stored in the inner sanctum of my mind. My Humiliated Self will go to any length to maintain my personal status as a hero and avoid any associations with those dust-eating turkeys.

The application of past experience to this situation brings me to a state of quite definite ego arousal.

Beliefs, Values, and Attitudes

While past experience allows us to *recognize* a chair, it is our values and attitudes about chairdom that determine our *reactions* to particular chairs. If our belief system happens to include the conviction that kitchen chairs belong only in kitchens, we will be unlikely to react happily to the sight of a kitchen chair being used to seat guests in the living room. If that same system of beliefs tells us that chairs are for sitting in, and only for sitting in, we will probably avoid using a chair as a coffee table or to store papers in need of filing.

Beliefs, values, and attitudes may or may not be valid, but they influence to a greater or lesser degree how an individual perceives his or her reality.

My beliefs, values, and attitudes about driving behavior and etiquette include a conviction that I know the rules of the road. I take pride in my ability to apply those rules. It is also clear to me that the other driver has committed an offense against both society-at-large and me, as an individual.

The Perceiver's Condition

If I'm happy with my life—if my gut is full and my other physical and emotional needs are being met—I will unconsciously let this sense of satisfaction spill over onto the events of my life, affecting positively how I evaluate their impact on my overall well-being. If one or more of my needs is not being met, my perceptions may (no! *will*) reflect an overriding sense of deprivation and my physical and my emotional landscape will take on a murky, overcast aspect.

> Let's assume that at the time of my encounter I'm on my way to lunch after a busy, stressful morning. My general emotional and physical state, in other words, is such that I am not predisposed to behave magnanimously toward the other driver, judging him as careless, stupid, and, possibly, actively malevolent.

Step 4: Creating My Story

As we have seen, reality is a subjective phenomenon, created by the mind on an *ad hoc* basis from bits and pieces of information, with the frontispiece being that chunk of data that happens (through sheer force of physical or emotional circumstance) to stand in boldest relief.

The process through which the psyche generates a story to explain the data mirrors the very process through which it went about selecting the data. Like the earlier process, the story-generating (or explanation) process contains emotional, judgmental, and Self-image components, usually arranged in such a way as to protect the ego from any and all perceived attack.

The Emotional Components

Over the years, psychologists have devised many ways to classify and describe the vast range of human emotion. Some of those classification schemas are nothing more than long laundry lists of terms expressing subtle nuances and shades of feeling. Others are complex matrices relating feeling states to broader emotional patterns. For our purposes, I have chosen to rely on a simple system from Eric Berne's transactional analysis[3] that divides emotion into two broad categories: (1) the positive feeling states, which all derive in some way from the emotion of love; and (2) the negative feeling states, which include four basic emotional responses— fear, anger, hurt, and desire or wanting (the sense that something basic to our welfare is lacking or inadequately supplied).

If the mind perceives the preponderance of data as harmless, it calls an "all clear" and responds with one or more pleasurable feelings, such as love, happiness, or contentment.

If, however, the mind interprets the data to mean that one is under attack, exposed to some degree of physical or psychological danger, it chooses from its repertoire of negative emotions to attach to the event.

My ego's response to the freeway incident was overwhelmingly negative. I was frightened, an emotion that generated the following "lead paragraph" for my story about what had happened to me. Notice how the story encompasses my sense of humiliation and vulnerability:

> That careless, stupid person has endangered me. He thinks I'm nobody, someone he can whisk past, ignore at will and whim. I could have been killed. How dare he? Driving in a world potholed with people like him is risky. I'm vulnerable as long as there are idiots like him loose on the road. Someone— preferably me—ought to show him what happens to guys who act that way.

By this time (approximately 3.5 milliseconds into the event), my mind was beginning to bestow this routine encounter with heroic, dramatic attributes. Notice how I've let this event take on a life of its own, a life infused with intensity, charged with the kind of excitement that is guaranteed to attract and hold my total attention, distracting me at least temporarily from all other thoughts and considerations. We humans habitually fashion the self-generated stories we create around our everyday adventures to include the emotional stuff that is the basis of all great drama.

The Judgmental Components

I am now ready to pass judgment, selecting a hero and a villain for my tale. My mind fans through its storehouse of memories, selecting those experiences that can help me pin a label on this most recent event. Nothing subtle is going on: judgment involves only gross either/or polarities, such as "good/bad," "moral/immoral," "right/wrong," and "fair/unfair." We are all remarkably talented at judgment. We may be limited by our lack of information, restricted by our overstressed sensory equipment, handicapped by an ego-mind designed to see danger and alert us to it—but none of that matters now. We have a snap judgment to make. Mine went something like this:

> That jerk is dangerous. He could have gotten us both killed. He's a menace. He's definitely wrong. And I am very definitely right.

The Self-Image Components

The final step, in which we create what might be called the climax of the story, involves the ego's need to preserve and protect a sense of Self importance and Self esteem. In writing the final paragraph to a personal story, the ego asks the simple questions "Am I okay?" or "Am I not okay?" first posed by Berne in his transactional analysis model.

The answer to those questions depends almost entirely on whether or not the situation, as perceived, has aroused the Humiliated Self. If not, chances are that the ego has not been hooked and we will be able to relax and take the situation in stride. If, however, the situation has activated the Humiliated Self, the ego cries out to be soothed. Our tension level rises and whatever unconscious mechanisms we use to protect and preserve our wounded Self esteem lock into gear. Our energies are devoted almost entirely to finding a way to "fix" this intolerable situation. Here's a very broadly translated version of how my ego went about letting me know there was repair work to be done:

> How can I be okay? I've just been humiliated in front of all these other drivers. I hope you aren't planning to let him get away with this. If anyone saw this, they'd think you were the biggest wimp east of the Mississippi.
>
> Hurry up. He's trying to get away. Catch up with him and give him a taste of his own medicine. Scowl, shake a fist, give him the finger. Do something to make us feel better. Show him that you're not weak.

THE COSTS OF EGO-HOOKING

Depending on how violated the Humiliated Self feels, it can be a matter of seconds, minutes, hours, days, weeks, or even years before the ego-hooking process finally subsides. Until that subsidence occurs, enormous amounts of energy will be consumed, wasted in activities designed to shore up Self esteem and calm the Humiliated Self. Ego-hooked individuals often indulge in fantasies of revenge and imagine conversations in which they come out Big Winners, vanquishing and humiliating the individual or group whom they feel have "done 'em wrong."

For hours, I rehearsed what I might have done and what I could have said to my opponent—if only I'd gotten the chance:

> Boy, I wish I'd gotten his license plate number so I could report him to the Department of Motor Vehicles. I could have forced him over to the side of the road and explained to him, in the spirit of sweet reason, what a jerk he is, what a menace he is, what a waste of human protoplasm he is. Wait until I tell my friends about this.

▣ Exercise 6: A Personal Look at Ego-Hooking

For this exercise, you will need to recall an event that triggered an ego-hooked response in you. Take a moment or two to bring the event to the front of your consciousness, to reexperience the sensations and feelings you experienced when the event occurred.

Step 1: Something Happens

Describe your nothing-but-an-event below, eliminating all emotion or value-laden words. Just give us the facts, nothing but the facts.

_____

_____

_____

_____

_____

_____

Step 2: The Senses Get Involved

• *I saw* _____

• *I heard* _____

• *My skin felt* _____

• *My body reacted by* _____

I reacted to the onslaught of information by filtering out information, as follows:

• *I no longer saw* _____

• *I no longer heard* _____

• *I no longer smelled* _____

• *My body reacted by* _____

Step 3: Perception Takes Over

• *Those experiences from my past that determined what data was available during my drama included* _____

_____

• *The filter of beliefs, values, and attitudes through which the data had to pass included* _____

_____

• *How were you feeling physically and emotionally at the time of your incident?* _____

_____

Step 4: Creating Your Story

Write your "lead paragraph."

_____

_____

_____

_____

_____

• *Make a few notes about your judgment of the situation.*

_____

_____

• *Describe how your ego let you know it felt threatened by the event.*

_____

_____

• *How did you waste emotional/physical energy trying to salve your Humiliated Self?* _____

_____

• *What productive, creative, and pleasurable things could you have been doing with that wasted energy?* _____

_____

Ego-hooking wastes huge amounts of individual and collective energy, takes time and attention away from worthwhile endeavors (sometimes scuttling them entirely), distracts us from goals we want to achieve in our personal, social, and work lives, and contributes nothing but confusion to the problem-solving process. Worst of all, as any issue of your daily newspaper quickly reveals, ego-hooking is susceptible to escalation in a way that often results in misery, destruction, even death. Consider, for example, the many newspaper and television accounts of drivers beaten or killed by other motorists whose egos were hooked by offenses no more serious than the near-fender-bender that so outraged my personal sense of justice.

Ego-hooking, in other words, is bad news, benefiting nobody but (possibly) the editors of those scandal sheets we all pretend we aren't reading in the supermarket checkout line.

The good news is that ego-hooking, and its power to alienate us from the simple Appreciative powers of childhood, can be prevented. In chapter 10, we'll find out how.

TEN

How to "Hook-Proof" Your Ego

□　□　□

To reiterate the warning at the end of chapter 9: ego-hooking is bad news! It never helps anybody. Nothing of long-term utility or beauty has ever been achieved by anyone operating from the ego-hooked state.

You may find yourself eager to disagree with me, your mind abounding with examples of social and political activists who have channeled their hurt and outrage into constructive social change, who have expressed their anger in efforts to ameliorate the inequities and injustices that plague humankind.

I won't (can't) argue with anyone who tells me that the world is replete with upsetting injustices, that corporations can act in ways that show little concern for the welfare of their employees or the general public, that governmental officials can be guilty of incompetence, indifference, even downright corruption. I agree that these matters deserve, even demand, our informed concern and attention.

Coupling that concern and attention, however, with the anger or outrage that characterizes the ego-hooked state will do little to correct the problems besetting our modern world or to create an environment that encourages individuals to reclaim the power of their Creative Selves. At best, the opportunity to express such feelings in a socially acceptable way offers the so-called concerned citizen a cathartic outlet. How good it feels to blow off the steam of righteous indignation! How impressive we sound when we hold forth on our positions against all evil and for everything that is good! Such expressions, however, almost always generate more conflict than cooperation, draining vital energy desperately needed to resolve the challenges confronting our families, communities, and nations. Expressing outrage, anger, or frustration over a social problem—no matter how eloquently the expression is framed—is usually only a thinly veiled attempt to maintain, defend, or restore one's individual sense of Self importance. It is *not* the same as getting to work on the problem.

Everything we know about such successful and revered engineers of social change as Mahatma Gandhi and Martin Luther King Jr. suggests that those men seldom, if ever, succumbed to the ego-hooking temptation. They wasted little energy on what other people thought of them. They had almost no personal investment in righteously defaming or humiliating their opposition. The vast majority of their energy was free and their perceptions of reality were basically clear, undistorted by their mental scrims, enabling them to deal creatively with the problems and opportunities that presented themselves, *as* they presented themselves.

I am convinced that the true champions of human progress (the ones we celebrate in our history books as well as the "ordinary" men and women who work quietly and effectively behind the scenes) have been individuals who knew how to short-circuit the ego-hooking process, perhaps using techniques similar to the ones described below.

TURNING OFF THE TAPE

I have found that it is possible, with conscious effort, discipline, and practice, to abort most ego-hooking episodes-in-process. When the ego-hooking process begins, it feels as if a tape recorder has been turned on in my brain, sending me into automatic response—dictating the outraged reactions of my Humiliated Self, a Self that is totally focused on restoring my damaged Self esteem. If I allow the tape to continue playing, I am abdicating my innate right of choice, preferring to respond like a pre-programmed robot, even down to my facial expressions and body movements.

In the brief moment after the recording clicks on, while my Creative Self is still in control, I can often interrupt the scenario by asking myself, "Is this what I really want to do or say right now? Do I want what is about to happen in my life?" The answer is almost always a resounding *no!*

If you want to reduce the frequency and severity of ego-hooking episodes in your life, you might begin to become familiar with the personal signals warning that activated your tape recorder. The specific signals differ as widely as individuals do, but all signals focus around the presence of negative feelings. Such emotions as hurt, anger, fear, or frustration are sure signs that an ego-hooking episode is either under way or about to start, that your sensitive Humiliated Self has been tweaked by a threatening perception and is gearing up its defenses.

▣ Exercise 7: Turning Off the Tape

On the lines below, note those points at which you might have noticed the warning flags of ego-hooking, the points at which you could have decided to say no and turned off the tape. Begin by thinking about a specific ego-hooking event, possibly the one you used in exercise 6.

Step 1—When My Event Occurred: _____

_____

Step 2—When My Senses Got In on the Act: _____

_____

Step 3—When My Mind Started Sorting the Data: _____

_____

Step 4—When I Created My Story: _____

_____

THE BOOMERANGING CONNECTION I:
PEOPLE WE LOVE TO HATE

Hidden deep in the recesses of most ego-hooking episodes is our old friend, the Boomeranging Dynamic. As we saw in chapter 8, boomeranging reflects those parts of our Selves that we have chosen to disown, those aspects of the total Self that our Humiliated Selves view as dangerous or destructive to our sense of Self importance and Self esteem.

When I look closely (and objectively) at my freeway incident, for example, it quickly becomes apparent that my aversion to being seen as a wimp has its roots—like so many of my idiosyncracies— in my awkward adolescence, when I saw *myself* as a wimp, the proverbial ninety-pound weakling on the beach of life. Much of my early adult life was dedicated to boomeranging efforts to prove that I was as tough as any other guy on the road, disowning any hint of physical incompetence in myself—and loathing it when I saw it in those around me. The instant the other driver pulled over in front of me, my Humiliated Self was awakened from its delicate half-sleep, drowsily making connections between this latest event and all those earlier adolescent events I've worked so hard to disown. I was angry at the other driver, not only because he was creating a nuisance for me on the road, but also because he was exhibiting a kind of incompetence that I hate in myself. For that particular moment in time, this unknown "other driver" embodied for me a huge chunk of my disowned self—and I simply "couldn't stand" him.

"Big deal," you may be saying. "So I don't like people who exhibit qualities I don't like to see in myself. So they make me angry. How's this information going to change my life?"

That information, my friend, is *not* going to change your life. What will change your life—by reducing the amount of time you spend in a state of ego-hooked impotence—is the recognition that it is *not* the quality in the other person that we don't like. What we don't like, what indeed frightens us and drives us into the ego-hooked state, is the mirror that person holds up to us, a mirror that reveals to us the worst of all horrors, the possibility of who we might become "if only" we didn't strive as hard as we do to be the wonderful people we are, repressing and suppressing any hint of inadequacy.

Your life will change as you realize that it is safe to quit striving. You already *are* the wonderful person you need to be, and nothing that obnoxious "other" person can do will change that fact. Your Humiliated Self is safe, protected. First, nobody knows who you "might have been" except you. And second, who you have become is not the awful person you fear you might have been.

This is a critical concept. Once comprehended and accepted, it initiates a shift in the way you see the world. Life becomes less a battleground and more something that is closer to a wonderland of possibility. The truth is, the war is over. The struggle you waged against your fear of humiliation ended long ago, and you won. You became the person you are. You've already overcome the qualities you're seeing in others that you don't like to see in yourself, so you can quit fighting against them and send your soldiers home. They're not needed anymore.

As you become conscious of the effect your disowned qualities have when you see them reflected in other people, you will probably begin to delve a little deeper into those closeted parts. The simple willingness to allow the light of consciousness to shine on those secret places will do wonders, reempowering you in situations that once rendered you ego-hooked and powerless. You may find that anger and judgment are simply outdated and purposeless strategies for keeping your Disowned Self locked away. When you let it out, become willing to look at it openly, you will find that the qualities of the Disowned Self that you fear are quite likely not really yours. Those qualities can, however, teach you a lot about who you really have become.

▣ Exercise 8: The People We Love to Hate

This exercise will help you identify the ego-hooking qualities of the Disowned Self that you dislike in others.

Use the space below to identify the three or four "hottest" individuals in your life, the qualities you find so unacceptable in them, and the disowned aspects of your own personality (or your experience) that those qualities call forth in you. On the line marked "Ego-Hooking Event," outline how those disowned qualities showed up in an encounter with that personality, creating a situation you found less than pleasant.

1. Name (or Alias): _____

"Hot" Quality: _____

Disowned Aspect: _____

Ego-Hooking Event: _____

2. Name (or Alias): _____

"Hot" Quality: _____

Disowned Aspect: _____

Ego-Hooking Event: _____

3. Name (or Alias): _____

"Hot" Quality: _____

Disowned Aspect: _____

Ego-Hooking Event: _____

4. Name (or Alias): _____

"Hot" Quality: _____

Disowned Aspect: _____

Ego-Hooking Event: _____

To complete your experiential examination of the boomeranging/ ego-hooking connection, review your responses in the Me/Not Me columns of the chart on page 23.

You will probably discover that your Not Me's match very closely those disowned qualities that so annoy you in the people you simply "can't stand," those individuals who seem to possess uncanny talents for involving you in ego-hooking scenarios.

THE BOOMERANGING CONNECTION II:
SITUATIONS WE LOVE TO HATE

Another indication that we are stuck in a boomeranging/ego-hooking cycle is the recurrence of similar-but-different unpleasant situations in our lives. It is as if we are human magnets, who, despite our best efforts not to do so, attract to ourselves over and over again certain kinds of difficult circumstances or people. Examples of such unpleasant recurrences among people I know include a friend with a genius for running into unusually rude and incompetent sales clerks in major department stores, a colleague whose three unfortunate marriages to men who turned out to have serious drinking problems ended in divorce, a neighbor whose apparently talented son routinely encounters last-minute emergencies that leave him unprepared for important examinations, and a relative who rarely finds a competent boss who understands and makes good use of her skills. Not being their therapist, I can't prove it beyond a shadow of a doubt. Nevertheless, it is easy to see that very likely each of these human magnets, without intending to do so, contributes in a boomeranging way to the presence in his or her life of these undesirable, dysfunctional experiences.

It is not so easy, however, to see how we all fall at some time or the other under the unconscious domination of "the repeat performance." What happens, as I outlined in chapter 8, is that our Humiliated Selves become fixated on what we *don't* want, paying so much attention to the possible negative outcomes of any given experience that we have no energy left to devote to the positive activities that would contribute to the achievement of what we *do* want. The very energy I gave in my younger years to appearing dignified and "cool" contributed to many, many situations in which I ended up feeling decidedly undignified and uncool—ego-hooking situations that I had, indeed, created for myself through my determination to disown the real, not-always-so-dignified me. I suspect my colleague who disrupted that long-ago lecture through her very determination *not* to disrupt it has experienced many similar situations, circumstances in which she brought unsought, and mystifying, attention to herself.

Again, inoculating yourself against such recurrent ego-hooking is simple—stop worrying about what you don't want and start looking forward to what you do want. The solution, when faced with yet another incident of "déjà vu all over again," is to become conscious of what your Humiliated Self needs so desperately to avoid. Recognize it, accept the fact that you are already what you have been so afraid of being, then refocus the energy you have been devoting to Self protection into the much more rewarding and creative activities of Self expression.

FROM THE OTHER SIDE OF THE WORLD:
WISDOM TO STAY UNHOOKED BY
Buddhist monks, individuals who devote their lives to activities designed to encourage transcendence of the personal ego, practice a form of meditation called "mindfulness." To be mindful means to perform a given activity (usually a very common, routine activity such as walking or chopping wood or eating) with carefully focused attention, absorbing every iota of data that the sensory equipment has to convey about the experience, as rapt in concen-

tration as a child at play. A monk who is practicing mindful walking, for example, feels each muscle of his legs and feet as it contracts and releases, senses his body sway in balance with each step, connects with the contours of the earth as they change beneath his feet, smells the air as he moves through it, observes the changing landscape as he passes. A mindful monk would never become involved in an ego-hooking episode simply because he would be too busy paying attention to what *he* was doing to invest much energy in the unsettling aspects of his environment, using the inherent limitations of his sensory apparatus to protect himself from unnecessary distress.

Had I been driving mindfully that day on the freeway, my ego-hooking experience would have been aborted at the beginning of step 2, when my senses began generating thousands of bytes of data about what was going on. I would have been so involved in *my* experience that I would have had little surplus attention or energy to devote to what the other guy was doing wrong. I would have noted the other driver's behavior, then released what I had noticed to turn my full attention to the activity of driving, in which I was totally absorbed.

The purpose of the mindfulness meditation is to train monks to live totally in the present moment, savoring each second of present time for what it has to offer without comparing it to any similar moment in the past or any possible moment in the future. Had I been operating fully in the present moment, I would not have harkened to the wails of my Humiliated Self, the Self who believes I am still the awkward adolescent boy I was for five short years more than a half-century ago.

Buddhist monks spend hours of each day in contemplation with the ultimate goal of achieving absolute equanimity. Most of us cannot (and don't want to) devote our lives to that single-minded pursuit. We can, however, take a few moments from the hustle of our daily routines to remind ourselves to *pay attention.* I invite you to pause at least once a day to focus on your senses, to make a mental list of the data being streamed at you. Just make a list—what you see, how your body feels, what you hear and smell. Don't interpret the data. Don't create a story around it. Just observe the data. Then let it go and continue your day.

REMEMBER—IT REALLY *IS* UP TO YOU

Paradoxical as it may seem, your memory can be your most effective ally in your campaign to overcome the effects of ego-hooking. I'm not talking here about the selective memory that recalls every put-down you experienced during your childhood or adolescence or every insult you absorbed from that son-of-a-gun for whom you used to work. Not *that* memory, the one that feeds your Humiliated Self and seems intent on keeping you in a state of more-or-less-constant ego-hooked agitation.

The memory that is your friend and ally is the one that recalls your Creative Self, the one that remembers, as we discussed in chapter 8, that you have the miraculous power to create yourself and define your experience of the world. The Creative Self understands that this power is always at work—for good or for ill. It is this memory that is short-circuited when the tape recorder clicks on, sending you messages from your Humiliated Self that an attack is under way, messages that insist that you have lost control, that the world is a dangerous place and you have no choice but to prepare for war.

◨ **Exercise 9: Lightening Up**

From the field of neurolinguistic programming comes an experiment that may help illustrate the benefits of dissolving the weightiness we bring to many situations.

For this experiment, you will need to select an event in your life that involved other people and about which you have strong, unresolved feelings of anger, embarrassment, frustration, or loss. You may select the same experience that served as the basis for your personal analysis of the ego-hooking process in exercise 6. When you have finished this experiment, you will probably feel much more in touch with your "storyteller," another name for the Creative Self.

Step 1: *Review the event in your mind until it is clear in your memory from beginning to end.*

Step 2: *Divide the event, as a playwright would, into three parts or acts. You may divide each act, if you choose, into one or more scenes.*

Act 1 includes enough action and information to show how the individuals related to one another and how the situation began.

Act 2 develops the plot and begins the action moving toward a climax.

Act 3 usually includes a climax and shows the situation being resolved—or simply brought to an end.

Step 3: *Using this structure, describe the event to yourself as if it were a play in three acts. Be sure to provide information about the emotions of the key actors and include dialogue as part of the action of the play.*

Step 4: *Start over, telling yourself the story of the event in scrambled order, being careful to avoid beginning with act 1 or ending with act 3. Let both the dialogue and the emotions develop in any way that seems appropriate under these changed circumstances.*

Step 5: *Tell yourself the story a third time—this time in the correct order, beginning with act 1, but as you do so close your eyes and visualize what happened. Imagine each of the scenes in the most vivid color possible, such as canary yellow, bright orange, or flaming red.*

Step 6: *Now, as you tell yourself the story for the last time, set it to music—something loud, lively, and brassy, like "Stars and Stripes Forever," "Roll Out the Barrel," or a circus march complete with calliope.*

Step 7: *Finally, check how you are feeling about the event and yourself at this point. How weighty does it seem now? How serious is it to you? Are your feelings still heavy and negative—or have they lightened up considerably?*

Has your view of the situation changed in any other way? Do you have a different perspective about it and what it all means in your life? Did breaking the mold of negativity help you see the situation more clearly and perhaps understand better both what happened and what you might do differently next time?

PAUSE

You have just challenged your Creative Self—the storytelling aspect of your psyche that shaped and colored your experience of your remembered event when it originally occurred—to see the event anew, divested of the negative emotions that you have laid on it. By participating in the retelling of your own "story," you may have just created a new, lighter, and, possibly, happier history for yourself.

Your Creative Self knows that you always have a choice, a

whole range of choices, every second of every day. There is choice, too, throughout the ego-hooking process, choice about what you choose to perceive, about what messages from your inner psyche you choose to hear, about how you choose to interpret those perceptions and messages in creating the stories you weave to give structure and meaning to the isolated events of your life.

Exercising that power of choice requires only a decision to do so and a determination to live that decision every day, knowing that in that decision lies the revitalization of all the facilities your Creative Self had to give up to produce the Created Self who lives your life. Sounds simple. And it really *is* simple. The *decision* to change is easy. But acting on that decision, actually bringing the desired change to manifestation in your life, can seem overwhelmingly complex. In chapter 11, we will look at factors that make change appear so complicated and examine techniques for dealing with those complexities.

ELEVEN

The Psychology of Appreciation

□　□　□

I'll admit, things aren't looking too good for the Creative Self right now. In the last eight or so chapters, we've barraged that most essential, basic, pure, free, and adaptable part of the human psyche with a whole armamentarium of joy-killing weapons - humiliation, confusion, preconceptions and prejudices, boredom, tedium, repetition, habit. It's a wonder, you may be thinking, that any of us manage to enjoy any moments of unprogrammed joy and delight at all, what with all the grime and clutter we have allowed to become woven into our scrims as the years went by. It's amazing that the collective childlike Creative Self hasn't simply drawn a final, polluted breath and expired, victim of our suffocating adult insistence on seeing the world dimly, through the ego scrims we created when only half-conscious to protect ourselves from a threatening world.

It is, indeed, one of the most wonderful wonders of the human experience, this ability of the Creative Self to remain viable in a world that seems intent on burying it alive under miles of culturally dictated ego debris. But, somehow, the Creative Self survives — occasionally even breaking free for a few (often shocking and sudden) moments of Appreciative joy — assuring us that we are still the delighted, eager, creative, and fascinating children we once were, before the various layers of the Created Self had a chance to distort and sully our worldviews.

We may be carrying several dozen pounds of unnecessary psychic fat, invented ways of being that prevent us from joining fully and joyfully in the ever-changing game of life, forcing us to choose instead to be sidelined, hypnotized into the belief that our ego-hooked, boomeranging, humiliation-avoiding Created Selves are the real stars of the game. But the good news—the really *great* news that is my whole reason for writing this book—is that all we have to do to reclaim our joy-filled and joy-finding Creative Selves is to make a simple decision. That decision is to begin to live Appreciatively, stripping away everything that gets between our True Selves and a full, complete, immediate connection with life.

Appreciation, as I have learned to define it, is nothing more than the delight, fascination, and wonder that we experience simply because we are alive, without attaching judgment or value to the events that go into making up each day. Appreciation cannot help but be present at any event or relationship that we experience directly, without interpretation of any sort, without remembering to play umpire to the game of our own lives. Appreciation is the state that gives the Creative Self room to breathe, to begin to express itself in the unrestricted manner of a child at play.

THE GIFTS OF APPRECIATION

As any adult who has ever watched a child at play knows, Appreciation—simple and childlike as it is—is a powerful and intensely illuminating way to experience life. With Appreciation comes a variety of gifts, subjects that have fascinated sages, philosophers, and religious leaders throughout the ages. These gifts include the following:

- **Clarity:** an intensity, brightness, and vividness that make even the familiar and timeworn seem brand-new

- **Joy:** a collection of positive feelings of wonder, ecstasy, and delight in life; a sense that "all is well"

- **Creativity:** a sure intuitive grasp of situations, a "knowingness" that allows us to cut through complexity to see immediately what needs to be done

- **Energy:** vitality, a strong sense of emotional well-being, an absence of stress that allows us to focus our mental, physical, and emotional resources on whatever task or situation lies immediately before us

As I mentioned a few paragraphs ago, the first step toward re-claiming the birthright of the Creative Self is easy—a simple deci-sion to begin living Appreciatively, behind the scrim of illusion that is the Created Self. The second step is much harder than the first, for it requires us to be willing to *let go of everything* we have come to think of as our "Selves." Love that sweet, caring person you have created your Self to be? Let her go; refuse to believe that she is "who you are" for an instant longer. Really feel secure and pleased with the financial success you've acquired over the years? Release it; let it go—pretend it has all disappeared and you are left with nothing but the "real" you, the person you were be-fore the money started rolling in. Let it go and realize that you can still be "you" without it. Still holding a grudge against that great aunt who used to make you eat peas, even though she *knew* how much you hated them? Forget the grudge—just release it and no-tice how much lighter, clearer, and more energetic your body and your life feel without it. It doesn't matter whether the qualities, memories, skills, values, or relationships by which you have learned to define your Self are positive or negative ones—they *all* have to go, at least in terms of the importance you attach to them. In fact, the *more* important a quality or skill seems, the more it adds to your sense of status, success, or importance, the more es-sential it is that you learn to live as if you had never acquired it.

What we're talking about here—this process of learning to loosen your ego's hold on everything you consider essential to your sense of Self—is one of the most frightening endeavors a per-son can undertake. Nothing is easy about it. Nor is there any guide for undertaking the process or any way of measuring how success-ful you are or how much ground you have gained in your inward journey back to your Creative Self. I am asking you (metaphorically, of course) to toss your Self into the void of "Selflessness," without any assurances or restraints. I am asking you, not to adapt a new science or skill, but to begin practicing a seamless, formless art form, one that is different for every human being who pursues it.

I can't tell you how to do it, but I can assure you that, as you practice the art of Appreciation, you will slowly develop an acute sense for when you are "backsliding." You will begin to notice, for example, when you are immersed in a negative state. Wildly negative feelings such as anger and panic will begin to feel down-right painful—and unnecessary. Mildly negative states such as ir-ritation will also lose their charm. You will begin to want to leave those states behind—by releasing your attachment to whatever illusory part of your Self has been offended—as soon as possible, so you can return to the more productive, freer, happier, and all-round more gratifying state of Appreciation.

The next few sections of this chapter are devoted to case stud-ies of how adults (normal adults, just like you and me) have used Appreciation to transform even the most challenging tasks into joyous, creative, life-affirming enterprises.

CLARITY—THE MYSTERIOUS CASE OF THE CEO WHO TURNED LOVE INSIDE OUT

One of my favorite examples of how Appreciation clarifies seem-ingly complex situations occurred years ago when the CEO of a prestigious financial institution asked me to help resolve the bitter infighting that had developed among the members of his executive committee. These three trusted, handpicked, and hand-groomed lieutenants were frustrating their boss's efforts to mold them into a team, refusing to speak with one another and taking every op-portunity to complain about one another to him.

The executive, a man who prided himself on his integrity and who was revered in his field as an elder statesman, was baffled. "I respect all my employees, especially these three," he said. "I had envisioned a team with each of these ambitious and talented young people playing a key role. I've done everything I know to nurture in them qualities of leadership and cooperation. I've worked to become close to each of them and to their families. What could possibly be wrong? Why is there so much tension on my executive committee?"

There was a time when I would have devoted hours (maybe months) of painstaking analysis to developing an understanding of this seemingly complex problem. I've learned, however, to view my organizational clients and their problems through the clarifying lens of Appreciation. It took, therefore, only brief con-versations with each of the three younger people—who were all quick to express their admiration, affection, and gratitude for their boss—to determine exactly what the problem was.

"I consider Mr. X to be my mentor, my guide, a veritable father figure," explained one. "But he plays favorites. He will forget a commitment to me if one of the others happens to catch his ear."

His colleague put it this way: "I love the man, but I don't trust him. It's not that he wants to create an atmosphere of distrust; he's just a sucker for people who know how to pressure him at the right moment and in the right style. It's a setup for political intrigue."

I asked the logical question: "Why don't you all just tell your boss when you feel he is treating you unfairly?"

"I can't," each one replied in his or her individual style. "I care about him too much. Integrity is so important to him. He would feel deeply hurt to learn that I think he has been unfair. The best I can do is complain about my colleagues and hope he'll get the hint and change how he deals with all of us."

When the time came for me to reflect on the information I had gathered, I immersed myself in Appreciation, clearing myself of preconceived ideas and theories so I could see the situation as it really was, with no one person to blame, but with everyone co-operating to keep the problem locked firmly in place.

I wrapped myself in Appreciation for the ingenuity of my clients as they gathered for my second visit, a joint meeting with the CEO and his three lieutenants. I spoke with great Appreciation about their frankness and their willingness to talk about the pain they had experienced. I described the admiration and affection that the three younger employees had for their boss, their image of him as the caring, guiding father of their (slightly dysfunctional) work family. I let myself dwell Appreciatively on the sense I had during my conversation with the boss that he was a man of high integrity, deeply committed to the well-being of each of the younger people. What I did, in effect, was mirror to my clients their own picture of who they all wanted to be, a picture illuminated and brought to life by my own Appreciation of their fine human characteristics and professional skills.

Then, I went on to detail the fears the younger people had expressed about hurting the boss. I spoke of how they dreaded the prospect of making him feel less than revered by insinuating they thought he had treated them in any way that was not totally fair and productive.

"It's this very affection that lies at the root of our problem," I explained. "It is impossible to guarantee that one will act fairly unless others feel free to tell it like it is when they feel they're being treated unfairly. The way things stand now 'father' is at risk of being hurt by the discovery that he's acting unfairly because the members of his work family are afraid to hurt him by telling him their truth."

The irony here is that it was the CEO's deep commitment to fairness and integrity (rather than his flagrant disregard for these qualities) and his protégés' affection and respect (rather than their lack of these fine and positive emotions) that were working together to keep these four people (who basically cared very much for one another) locked into their painful situation.

To use language we explored earlier in this book, I was telling the group that the CEO's discomfort with his Not Me had created a "boomerang" situation. With the collusion of his subordinates, he had managed to establish a predicament in which he got exactly what he did not want. To be accused of being unfair would activate his Humiliated Self. Realizing this, his subordinates held back the feedback the CEO needed to live up to his own ideal. The upshot was that the employees were becoming convinced their chief was both uncaring and unfair—the last judgment he would want them to make.

Bringing the power of Appreciation to this situation enabled me to speak in ways the members of the group could hear and accept. As I put into words what all four had been thinking and feeling, I invited them to join me in marveling at the ingenious, complex, and often dysfunctional webs we humans weave for ourselves. I suggested they discuss with one another what they wanted to do about the situation. After a long moment of shocked silence, the CEO said he understood what I was saying and asked the others how they were feeling. Within minutes, the four were talking openly with one another in an exchange spiced by gentle humor about what each could do to change the situation.

Before I learned the power of Appreciation, this process would have been a much more lengthy and painful one for all of us. I probably would have interviewed each individual at length and might have requested them to fill out an elaborate team-building questionnaire. I would have reported the results of my inquiries first to the CEO and then to the entire group. I would have helped them individually and as a group to analyze what was wrong and to decide what they needed to do about it. The whole thing would have been a minimum amount of fun and maximum amount of drudgery. The results, if all went well, would probably have been about the same.

JOY—A LESSON LEARNED BY NOT
FIGHTING WITH A CHILD

An event that occurred many years ago when I was on a weekend vacation in British Columbia taught me how easily Appreciation can transform what could be irritation—even conflict—into an experience suffused with the childlike quality of joy, that innocent state we all experience when we allow ourselves to forget the murky adult concerns we insist on plastering over life, deciding instead to revel in the wonder and delight of the immediate moment.

On the first evening of the weekend, I joined a group of three other men (all of whom were already living lives powered by Appreciation) in a game of Ping-Pong. My enjoyment of a good game of doubles was marred by the fact that there was only one Ping-Pong ball in the entire resort. My ego-bound mind was on a criticism rampage: this was no way to run a resort! I was worried over the possibility that we would break that single ball, thereby bringing Ping-Pong to an end for the remainder of the weekend. While I was pursuing these less-than-joyous mental rumblings, the ball bounced off the table onto the floor.

At just that moment, a little boy about three years of age came dashing into the room. He ran to the ball, picked it up, and began to play with it.

I stood, shifting from foot to foot, waiting for one of the others to deal with what appeared to be shaping up into a disastrous situation. My alarmed mind clattered away:

"That kid has our ball!"

"What if he breaks it?"

"Why don't one of you do something before he destroys the ball—and our Ping-Pong game?"

"Just go up to the kid and ask him to give you the ball. Come on, guys, we're grown-ups, we can face down a little kid. No, wait a minute, he might get upset and cry. We don't want that. What would people think? A bunch of grown men picking on a baby."

Through all this internal racket, I managed somehow to notice that the two men across the table were talking to one another and that my partner and I were engaged in a pleasant little chat. Suddenly, I got it. *The purpose of our game was enjoyment.* It didn't matter whether we were actively batting the ball around or standing around watching a little kid and chatting. We were on vacation and enjoying ourselves. We were doing what we'd come here to do. Which was—*relax, enjoy.*

A few minutes passed and the child, as children will, grew tired of playing with the ball. One of the men from the other side of the table walked over to him and said, "Matthew, may we have the ball now?" The child said, "Yes," handed over the ball, and let us go back to the game, all wrapped in a pleasant haze of enjoyment. No muss. No fuss. And, above all, no misery and tears. Everybody was happy, delighted in fact, with this latest turn of events.

A number of far-less-pleasant scenarios might have been played out. One of the adults might have demanded that the boy return the ball immediately, arousing the child's sense of humiliation and lack of control and causing him to react by refusing our request, generating one of those all-too-familiar scenes, with the child in tears and the adults fuming and feeling like overbearing bullies.

By recognizing that our goal was en*joy*ment, we were able to act in a way that achieved that goal. We were able to do nothing, just stand around and enjoy the moment as it unfolded, leading inevitably to the next moment—and the return of our ball. The moment we enjoyed together was fresh and clean, free from any of our needs to reenact our pasts or push our fears of the future. The power of Appreciation, applied to the moment we were living, allowed us to operate more effectively, more harmoniously, in a flowing way that left us energized and feeling good about ourselves and about one another. Four adults and a toddler, all accessing with great Appreciation the meaning of joy.

CREATIVITY—THE NATURAL END PRODUCT OF APPRECIATION

A computer engineer, a client who spent years learning to bring the painstaking, "professional" tools of intellectual analysis to his work, learned from one of my workshops on Appreciation to trust that intuitive part of himself that he had tried so hard and so successfully to repress. The result, he exulted, was an almost immediate upsurge in productivity and in the quality of the solutions he brought to the problems he encountered in his work.

"Before I learned to appreciate Appreciation," he told me, "I would approach problems as *problems*, obstacles that had to be tackled in a careful, methodical, adult way. I listed all possible factors and thought my way slowly through each one, churning my mental wheels, generating all sorts of irrelevant data and approaches, eliminating them one by one until I saw through the fog what I needed to do. Granted, this approach usually got results, but it left me worn out."

This talented engineer now applies the power of Appreciation to each and every situation, beginning by redefining as "challenges" those same situations he used to define (through clenched teeth) as problems.

"I've learned to take the simple approach to my work, doing what I did naturally until I got involved in being an expert," he reports. "Applying the power of Appreciation simply means sitting back, relaxing, opening my mind to the entire situation—the problem, its context, and the vast horizon of opportunities it opens up. Instead of gearing for mental combat, I settle down, center myself, and allow the solution to appear in its own time."

That relaxed stance, he says, allows his mind "to take in the entire situation at once, instead of in the split and fractured manner the analytic approach fostered." Through Appreciation he receives detailed information in a form that gives him an opportunity to understand all the complexities and how they relate to one another and to determine "in a holistic way" what needs to be done, not to correct the problem, but *to redirect the energies that have been misused in creating the problem in the first place.*

The results, in terms of his work product, have been impressive. "I produce solutions that are at least as effective as the ones I used to produce through sheer mental shoving and pushing," he says. "But I do it faster and in a relaxed manner that leaves me feeling refreshed and energized, rather than depleted."

ENERGY—WHAT'S LEFT WHEN WE ELIMINATE STRESS

My engineer friend's experience emphasizes the fact that Appreciation is a powerful conservator of energy. An examination of energy, as conducted by Dr. Richard Heckler in *The Anatomy of Change: East/West Approaches to Body/Mind Therapy*, illustrates how important energy is in defining the quality of our lives:

> Energy is our aliveness. It is the stuff that creates the continuity of our life. We wake up with it, we go to bed with it, it is present in our waking and our sleeping dreams. It is the river that carries the meaning and significance of our daily life. We have thoughts, images, memories, sensations and emotions that are birthed and nurtured by this river. It is the ground from which our living emerges. "This current allies me to the rest of the world," says Thoreau. In various cultures and traditions, this energy has variously been called ki, chi, shabd, elan vital, prana, the life current . . . the words energy and excitement mean the same thing: the ground of our existence and that which births our experience.
>
> A primary goal in working with someone therapeutically, artistically, or educationally is to bring them into contact with their energy, that is, into the experience of their lived body. The first step is to have the person identify with what they feel, to place their attention on what is occurring in their bodily life. Attending to what we feel takes us out of our heads and into the energetic currents of our body. Living in our bodies means living in the moment. Our energy and attention weave the tapestry of who we are—bodily, emotionally, psychologically, and spiritually.
>
> We can experience our energy in a number of ways. Energy can be the rush we feel when we are surprised or suddenly jolted. The tinglings, vibrations, and streamings that arise all over the body after a series of deep inhalations and exhalations are energy. If we clap our hands and rub them vigorously

together, and then hold them about six inches apart, we feel energy as sensations in our palms. The pressure from holding our breath for as long as we can and the charge we feel after we release it are experiences of energy. The warmth and trembling of loving someone is the energy of human contact. The pulsing around our body is our energy field. In a way, energy is nothing special, but it is the glue that binds everything together and connects us to our essential self.[1]

Dr. Heckler explains that we detect this energy as various physical sensations in situations ranging from deep breathing to surprise to trembling at the touch of a loved one. This energy forms a field that pulses through and around our bodies at all times, connecting us to what he calls the "essential self."

What Dr. Heckler describes is something worth conserving. His methods for experiencing our energy are all aspects of Appreciation—being directly in touch with our experience, rather than experiencing life indirectly, as it filters through our intellectual and ego structures.

One of the minor miracles worked routinely by the power of Appreciation is that it actually seems to increase the level of energy available to an individual. That this seeming miracle is an illusion hardly matters. Appreciation does not increase energy—energy is simply there, to be used in whatever way the wondrously gifted individual human being chooses. Appreciation makes energy *seem* to be more abundant, first, by freeing the individual to focus on the feelings and manifestations of energy within his or her own being and, second, by freeing energy normally used in such learned behavior as analysis, worry, and defensive maneuvering for more productive endeavors.

As I've become more adept at practicing the art of Appreciation, I've never ceased to wonder at the vast amount of energy we are willing to sacrifice to such zappers as worry, irritability, frustration, and other negative emotions. In order to live Appreciatively, in direct and immediate contact with the present moment, we need to release those automatic, energy-depleting reactions. Our initial commitment to Appreciative living sets in process a wonderful cycle: the more negatives we release, the more energy we have available for living; the more energy we have available, the more Appreciative we become of the delight and wonder of everyday life; the more Appreciative we allow ourselves to be, the more energy we find at our disposal. On and on and on in an ever-increasing cycle, Appreciating generates an evermore expansive awareness of what it means to be alive.

TWELVE

Dancing with Resistance: Experiencing Grace in Change

■ ■ ■

It is quite possible that you have read this far in a state of "split-screen" thinking. On one screen you see a hazy, scrim-blurred mental image of yourself living a life made more vital and fascinating through the power of Appreciation, a life in which you have more time and energy to accomplish the things that matter to you because you have liberated yourself from the paralytic, joy-killing effects of ego-hooking. On the other screen, however, appears a brightly contrasted, vivid picture—a living, breathing, moving photo-drama of the life you are living now, complete with its logjams and hang-ups. The first screen has a certain appeal, but the image on the second screen is familiar, comfortable—and ever so much more detailed and believable.

You might have identified some sticky spots in your life—projects you can't seem to complete, relationships that aren't quite what you know they could be, dreams you can't bring to fruition. You suspect that a few minor adjustments to your mental scrim, just enough to let you see those spots in a new, more Appreciative way, would help you break those deadlocks. But, somehow, you can't seem to bring that "possibility" of change into focus. The reality eludes you. There's this sense that the new, improved person you envision so vaguely wouldn't be the old reliable "you," that imperfect human being you know and love.

If any of this describes what's going on with you, you are experiencing the common and necessary reaction of resistance. As you read on, you will discover that even as you endure this uncomfortable sense of inertia, you are actually taking the first step in the complex process of change.

FROM CHAOS THEORY—LEARNING TO APPRECIATE CHANGE

Since ancient times, the "hows" and "whys" of change have fascinated thoughtful people. We all have a stake in the process, since change is the constant around which we order our lives. As proponents of the emerging and much-discussed chaos theory explain, the seeds of change are present in even the most stable-appearing situation. Ilya Prigogine, Nobel Prize–winning chemist and chaos theoretician, explains that the universe consists of a series of interlocking systems that he defines as "dissipative structures"— systems that remain at equilibrium for only a short time before some minor influx or outflow of energy or information causes them either to leap upward to a new level of complexity and organization or to disintegrate into a less ordered, more chaotic level.[1]

In our thirty thousand years of civilization building, we humans have learned to live within chaos, designing our dissipative structures (which are simply structures that harness the power of chaos) so ingeniously that we no longer notice their inherent instability. We walk the narrow line of equilibrium, thinking the line is the whole of reality (as if the world were two-dimensional), and profess personal outrage when faced with change, forgetting that equilibrium is the exception and change the law.

Chaos (and the never-ending change it implies) is actually the motivating force of all life, supplying the very energy that preserves the universe, preventing it from depleting itself and disappearing down its own drain.

The Human Psyche as a Dissipative Structure

The formal definition of a dissipative structure is "an energy system that remains in equilibrium only as long as there is no influx or outflow of energy." Let that definition sit in your mind a moment, play with it, and you will soon notice that everything you value is in some way a dissipative structure. Your very body is an effort to stave off chaos, a system so highly organized that anything (even an extra cup of coffee in the morning) can throw it into a state of disequilibrium. Whether that state will result in a more orderly (healthy) or less orderly (diseased) organization depends on an almost unimaginably complex combination of factors.

Viewed in the light of chaos theory, the human psyche itself is an ingenious dissipative structure, a creation whose very function is to lend order to the chaos the infant perceives in its brand-new world. As we mature, we encounter experiences (what theorists call "perturbations") that necessitate the reordering of the structure of Self. A simple explanation of growth might be the adoption of reordering procedures that bring the psyche into a higher or more flexible order of organization. A simple explanation of psychic stagnation might be the adoption of reordering procedures that result in a lower order of flexibility within the psychic structure, diminishing one's ability to respond consciously and creatively to the environment.

At the risk of appearing to be a rude and aggressive author, I think it is time that I told you that you are stuck, hovering on the brink of change. If you find yourself having any reaction to what you have read so far in this book, you have already reached Prigogine's "point of perturbation." The energy of new ideas has entered the system of your psyche, presenting you with the opportunity for change. As always, you have a choice: you may choose to protect yourself from this input of new energy by adding yet another thread to the tight weave of your personal mental scrim, making it even more difficult for the light of expanded awareness to break through; you may simply disregard what you have read, thereby missing the opportunities inherent in a life lived through the power of Appreciation; or you may decide to relax and "go with the flow," secure in the knowledge that your dissipative psyche will reorder itself to include this new information, restructuring itself as a more complex and adaptable creation, moving forward into the bright, but still blurry, vision that is beginning to form on the screen of your mind.

A FIRST STEP FORWARD—UNDERSTANDING
   YOUR PERSONAL FEELINGS ABOUT CHANGE

All of us have mixed feelings about change. We seek change and
we avoid it—sometimes at the same time.

On the one hand, we thrive on new experiences. We change
jobs and houses, take up new hobbies, visit unfamiliar places, buy
the latest products and fashions, adopt new technologies, experiment with new diets and self-improvement courses. And most of
us would be embarrassed to be caught less than fully informed
about the latest happenings in the ever changing "news."

On the other hand, we often behave as "creatures of habit," on
automatic, doing things the same way over and over again, filling
our days with familiar routines that require little or no thought or
planning. Many of us cling to the familiar—worn-out hats, jackets, and other articles of clothing; favorite foods, restaurants,
newspapers, radio and television programs, and vacation spots.
We like outer things that confirm our inner world. We seek out information that supports our political and social attitudes. We can
be offended by music, drama, and art that's radically different
from what we're used to, have firm convictions about the kinds of
people we are and aspire to be, shy away from new experiences,
and reject people who want us to change in even the smallest
ways.

◘ **Exercise 10: Getting in Touch with Your
  Feelings about Change**

*This exercise will help you increase your awareness of your relationship
to change. Begin by listing the change experiences that have been most
important in your life.*

*These experiences could include getting married; beginning a new job,
diet, or exercise program; becoming a parent; moving to a new home or
city—anything that required you to alter a habitual pattern of behavior.*

*Remember both your positive reactions (such as excitement, anticipa-
tion, pride) and your negative reactions (fear, skepticism, boredom). On
the following page, write a brief description of the experiences and your
reactions to them:*

Change Experience

Positive Reactions

Negative Reactions

Now state your overall stance in the face of change in the following summary sentences.

1. When a change takes place in my life, the part of me that thrives on change reacts by _____

2. When a change takes place in my life, the part of me that thrives on familiar routines reacts by _____

For most of us, introducing the power of Appreciation into our lives represents a major change, one that can be expected to generate a full array of conflicting emotions, feelings that will pop up in unpredictable ways and at inconvenient times. You can make yourself more comfortable with the process if you remember that your reactions are nothing more than reactions. They don't mean that the change, in itself, is good or bad—they just mean that your Creative Self has noticed something new is happening and it does not know exactly how to react.

ORGANIZATIONAL RESPONSES TO CHANGE
Studies of organizational response to change have produced a
great deal of information about the dynamics of change that individuals can use to effect desired changes in their personal and
professional lives. Like individuals, organizations develop routine procedures and patterns of behavior—some functional, some
ceremonial, and some meaningless and even dysfunctional.

Functional Routines
Functional routines, such as procedures for sorting and distribut-
ing incoming mail, are familiar and efficient ways of getting work
done. The probability is that you have developed many personal
functional routines—systems of behavior that represent efficient
ways of accomplishing tasks.

▣ Exercise 11: My Functional Routines
*This exercise is designed to provide insight into the role of functional
routines in your life. Think about how you typically conduct an average
day. Identify (and list below) those routines you follow when you wake
up in the morning, as you are getting dressed, while eating breakfast and
other meals, when you first arrive at the office, at lunch time, and upon
your return home.*

*You might also want to review your habitual responses to such recurring
chores as opening and handling your mail, returning telephone calls,
cooking meals, and washing dishes.*

_____

_____

_____

_____

*Finish by reviewing your list, placing a star beside each routine that
makes your life easier.*

*Place a second star beside those routines that you would resist changing.
Ask yourself: Why are those routines so important? Are they really serving a valuable function or does my attachment to them reflect my own
need to resist change?*

Ceremonial Routines

Ceremonial routines are symbolic in nature. They express and reinforce values that are important to an organization or group. Ceremonial routines have great meaning to human society, often serving as a kind of cultural "glue," binding disparate forces together in a shared symbolism. Flying the flag at half-mast to recognize someone who has died, singing "The Star Spangled Banner" at ball games, saluting in the military, and staging parades to honor visiting dignitaries are just a few examples of important ceremonial routines.

I know of a manufacturing firm in which male managers come to work wearing suit coats and jackets that they promptly remove—not to put them on again until they go out to lunch or return home. This pattern of behavior symbolizes and reinforces the firm's image of itself as an informal, no-nonsense, shirt-sleeves organization.

You have most likely developed your own personal ceremonies—a glass of wine after work, washing the car on Sunday afternoons, telephoning every night when away from home.

▣ Exercise 12: My Ceremonial Routines

Take a moment to review the list you completed for exercise 11, paying special attention to those routines you marked with single or double stars. Perhaps those important functions have acquired the symbolic value of ceremony to you. If so, include them on the list below, along with other of your personal routines that you would miss because they have symbolic value for you.

Dysfunctional Routines

Now we come to the most important aspect of this discussion— dysfunctional routines, those old, outdated, even counterproductive ways of doing things that have taken on a life of their own. A surprising number of such routines can be found in even the most successful organizations and all but the most carefully examined lives. They contribute nothing to the well-being of the organizations or individuals who practice them, promoting neither the completion of necessary work nor the development and continuity of individual morale and group solidarity.

When I was director of a graduate center at Boston University, for example, we developed the custom of having a brief meeting at the beginning of each week to keep one another informed about our individual work and about the important events scheduled that week within the center. For about a year, the meetings were well attended and seemed to be accomplishing their goal of promoting communication. After that year, however, attendance began to drop off. By the end of the second year, it was clear something was wrong. We experimented, trying a variety of approaches to force the meetings to work. No success.

Convinced that Monday morning meetings were important to morale and communication, I resisted their elimination. Finally, I asked a staff committee to investigate the problem and find out why the meetings seemed to be failing. The answer—which had been apparent to almost everybody but me—was that the meetings were no longer needed. During the previous year, we had established a lounge for staff and students to use for breaks and lunch. We had also installed a bulletin board for formal announcements and had begun to circulate "hot-off-the-press" bulletins about important work being conducted by the staff. We had, in other words, developed more efficient ways of keeping ourselves informed. Reluctantly, I did away with the meetings. But I confess it took me awhile to overcome my longing for the "good old days" when the week began with a rallying of forces on Monday mornings.

In my work as an organizational consultant, I found that I was not alone in my devotion to regular staff meetings. Chief executives can cling to them long after they have become meaningless, time-wasting, dysfunctional routines, rituals that are deeply resented by those who doze their way through them.

Chances are that your work and personal lives include a number of time-wasting patterns, some of which you created and continue to maintain and others which were imposed on you and with which you comply, colluding to keep them in place because your boss or some other authority considers them useful.

In doing your personal analysis, it might be useful to remember that these useless patterns tend to carry red flags. Whenever you or someone else says something along the lines of "I guess I'm just a creature of habit," for example, you are probably revealing your commitment to an outworn routine (and sacrificing your Creative Self's right to express its natural spontaneity). How many times in the course of a week do you or an associate use that phrase and what tone of voice and attitude do you couple with it? Is the tone apologetic, Self-mocking? Does the tone convey the idea that you really don't have a good reason for what you are doing, that it even seems a little silly, but there's really nothing that can be done to change it? Or is the tone defiantly defensive, insisting that you are right and don't have to explain yourself to anyone and that you have no talent for—or intention to—change?

□ **Exercise 13: My Dysfunctional Routines**

You might begin this exercise by reviewing, once again, the list of functional routines you prepared for exercise 11. This time, place an X beside those routines that actually make your life more complicated, difficult, or dysfunctional in any way. Continue your personal analysis by listing below other dysfunctional patterns that may come to your mind.

_____

_____

_____

_____

Before moving on, take a moment to consider each item on your list— how would you feel if someone suggested you eliminate it or replace it with a more useful pattern?

RESISTANCE TO CHANGE

Freud observed that the fear of change shackled his patients to their dilemmas. Even the most desperate and emotionally tormented patients, he noticed, would sabotage his efforts to help them recover when such recovery entailed change. They found various (and often ingenious) ways to block and subvert treatment even though they wanted his help and were paying for it. He labeled this phenomenon "resistance."

Freud came to realize that it is almost inevitable for people to feel ambivalent about changing. He taught that it is necessary to deal with resistance as part of the treatment because patients need to understand and grapple with resistance (on both a theoretical and personal level) before change can occur. The analysis of resistance became a key part of psychoanalytic therapy. Since Freud, people who want to facilitate change in individuals, groups, organizations—even entire cultures—have concentrated on resistance to change and how to deal with it.

Trained as a psychoanalyst, Fritz Perls, the creator of Gestalt therapy, radically departed from psychoanalysis in his method of handling his clients' resistance to change.[2] Rather than encouraging them to work through the resistance and set it aside, he recommended using a variety of techniques to bring the resistance to the forefront (it can often remain unconscious), highlight it, and explore the part it plays in the individual's situation. As Edwin Nevis, an organizational consultant who uses the Gestalt perspective says, it is possible "to help the client-system to heighten its awareness of the forces acting for and against its moving to a new place on a problem or issue."[3]

From the perspective of Gestalt therapy, resistance represents an effort of a person, an organization, or even an entire nation to protect itself from experiences that might change the status quo and are, therefore, viewed as threatening.

For Gestalt therapists a full cycle of experience involves *sensation* (the activation of one's senses), *awareness* (interpreting what meaning the new sensations have for the individual), *mobilization* (organizing one's energies), *action* (doing what needs to be done), and *contact* (enjoying a full measure of satisfaction in what is being accomplished). Resistance to change can occur at any point in this cycle.

Resisting Sensation

Some individuals, groups, and organizations order their lives so as to resist even giving room in one's emotional house to situations that offer opportunities for positive growth and change.

Their emotional radars are notably unresponsive to even the most obvious intruders on their mental scrims. These are the rule-based people of the world for whom regulations, procedures, and carefully guarded control systems take priority over new ideas, flashes of inspiration, and unconventional forays into exploring possibilities and novel situations.

If you have stayed with this book to this point, chances are you are not a Sensation Resister: you probably do not work to protect yourself against chance by sticking to tried-and-true rules and regulations. You allow yourself the luxury of noticing new ideas and possibilities for your life.

Resisting Awareness

Once we've allowed the blip of some new idea, person, or object to appear on our emotional radar screens, we must figure out what this new thing means, especially in terms of what effect it might have on our lives. Some people resist this level of awareness by responding with full-throttle emotions to the sensations of the moment. Their emotional excitement protects them against having to face up to and perhaps fail the tough intellectual task of making sense out of what is happening.

If you are such a person, you could generate a considerable amount of excitement about what this book has to say, sharing your enthusiasm with some friends—and then promptly forgetting it as you go on to your next exciting project. You may be very good at crisis management; indeed, you may thrive on the fact that you must deal with one crisis after another in your life. But this book is not about the problems and payoffs of day-to-day crisis management, but rather about the benefits of no longer taking seriously the crises that flicker in and out of your mental scrim. The pathway of Appreciation involves a decision to go beyond your preoccupations of the moment into a new way to experience yourself, your family, and your work.

Resisting Mobilization

Resource mobilization involves gathering information, analyzing the situation, and assessing the pros and cons of various possibilities. Most important, it involves making clear decisions about what needs to be done. Resistance at this stage takes the form of diagnosing the problem. This is my favorite form of resistance. I can testify from my own personal experience that there is a kind of sardonic satisfaction in being able to figure out all the reasons why a problem exists. It's enough to diagnose and know where to pin the blame for what is happening; let someone else figure out what needs to be done.

If your form of resistance involves not mobilizing your energies for action, you may find yourself analyzing this book in terms of what others have written about the human condition. Once you've figured out how I agree and disagree with what you already know, you will have accomplished all you feel motivated to do—and enjoyed a more or less satisfying experience in the process. When you've finished the book, you can go on to the next without running any risk of figuring out how to use the power of Appreciation to change your way of being in the world.

Resisting Action

The next obvious step is to do what you have decided needs to be done. Many people, however, find that committing themselves to a course of action is fraught with negatives: losing the opportunity to pursue other possibilities, turning out to be wrong in one's assessment of the situation, risking failure, making enemies, feeling ridiculous, incurring others' scorn. The list of possible fears associated with taking action is almost endless.

If you are one of those for whom resistance is grounded in such fears, reading this book may seem a mixed blessing. Like a hound dog coming on the scent of a rabbit, you may find yourself truly excited by what you are reading. However delicious the possibilities, you hesitate to pursue your quarry. If you are like me when I first was introduced to the power of Appreciation, you may simply be afraid to take the plunge into the unknown. Or you may shy away from appearing strange in the eyes of family members, friends, and colleagues.

Resisting Contact

The difference between making and resisting contact is like the difference between steeping tea in a pot and pouring boiling water over a tea bag. In today's tea-bag society, many of us are prone to rush from one activity to another, rarely, if ever, fully engaging in situations. We thereby do not allow ourselves to be fully involved in each experience. We pass up the opportunity to reflect on what has just happened, to inquire into the deeper meaning of events, and to truly savor the relationships and activities in which we are engaged.

If you are a Contact Resister, you may notice that you've been rushing from one page to the next, eager to keep moving. Soon you will have finished reading the book. What then? Are there other books to be read? Other assignments to be completed? Other duties to be performed? To what extent will they take precedence over immersing yourself over the next few weeks in reflecting on and experimenting with the meaning of Appreciation in your life?

SELF IMAGE AND RESISTANCE

Whatever form it takes, for very good and understandable reasons, resistance to change appears remarkably early in life. By the time we've developed our image of Self, we have also learned a variety of methods to keep that image intact. The idea of Self—for children and adults—is an emotional security blanket. We feel more secure when we have that blanket to cling to—no matter how tattered and worn and thin it might become. Even when we don't like the way we are, we feel more comfortable (read that "feel safer") acting as if our personalities are cast in concrete. All of us do what we believe (again, unconsciously) is necessary to keep change at bay so we can avoid a terrifying dip in the Sea of Anxiety.

LANGUAGE AND RESISTANCE

A common—and powerful—way to avoid change is to use language that rules out the very possibility of change. Here are some recent examples from my own experience:

- Pressed by his mother to eat something he dislikes, a child whines, "I never eat rhubarb and you keep giving it to me."
- Reluctant to raise an unpleasant issue with a co-worker, a manager says, "I'm the kind of person who lets sleeping dogs lie."

- Unprepared to face the fact that his dictatorial demands create "apple polishers" who agree with everything he says, a CEO complains, "People are never willing to tell me what they really think."

By saying "never," the child projects his dislike of rhubarb indefinitely into the infinite future. He is stating quite categorically that he cannot change—and that it's not his fault; it's an impersonal, unbreachable quality foisted on him by some invisible, outside force.

By saying "I'm the kind of person who . . . ," the manager, too, is making a projection into the future. Her unstated message is that this aspect of herself is nonnegotiable—anyone who deals with her will just have to work around it, forever.

By saying "People are never willing to tell me what they really think," the CEO sends several unstated messages. First, it's not his fault that others try to placate him. Second, he's powerless to do anything about it. And, third, people will always be this way; the situation simply cannot improve so everyone but him will simply have to learn to cope.

Resistance may also be expressed in the way everyday speech conspires to make us feel vulnerable to how others treat us. Think about (and ask your friends and associates to tell you) what you say when you get angry with someone. Do you talk as if your anger belongs to you or comes from what the other person says and does? How often have you said something like, "You make me so angry!" It is very tempting to put the blame for our anger, sadness, or other negative feelings on someone else. We always feel better when we are able to make ourselves right at the expense of making someone else wrong. The problem with this is that the price we pay for the small luxury of being right is disempowerment. "You make me angry" not only pins the blame on the other person but also gives that person control over our feelings and reactions. In effect, we are saying that we have no choice; when our adversary does his or her thing, we just have to go along. We talk ourselves into being powerless victims of circumstances beyond our control. The reality is that there are few, if any, situations that will arouse anger in everyone. The event that annoys one person will "make" someone else laugh and be totally overlooked by a third. Not even the most provoking people and situations can force us to feel angry. Only we can do that to ourselves.[4]

CHANGE WITHIN A DYNAMIC EQUILIBRIUM
Psychologist Kurt Lewin, a pioneer among modern students of change, developed a simple and useful way of thinking about the whys and hows of change.[5] Central to his thinking is the idea of a dynamic equilibrium—that is, a pattern of opposing forces that balance one another out and hold one another in place. Lewin called it a dynamic equilibrium to emphasize that no living equilibrium is static. It has ups and downs, shifting and adjusting to changes in the various forces that affect it. He believes every living thing is a dynamic equilibrium. I'm a dynamic equilibrium and so are you.

The system of interlocking people, roles, procedures, and operating divisions that make up an organization as a set of forces is a dynamic equilibrium. Our society, too, can be usefully conceived of as a highly complex array of balanced forces—however much they may shift over the years, those forces are held together, unlikely to come apart, because they are a part of a dynamic equilibrium.

The opposing feelings we have about change versus stability are, likewise, part of a dynamic equilibrium, working on one another to keep the system in place.

Resistance Is a Label
Within Lewin's model, resistance is a label (usually a negative one) that we apply to those who oppose the changes we want. What we call "resistance" consists of a set of forces (namely, the individuals and groups) on one side of a dynamic equilibrium that slow down or impede some change that we favor.

If I want something to happen and you oppose it, I experience you as "resisting" what I want. Directly or indirectly, openly or covertly, deliberately or unconsciously, you are keeping me from having my way. While I am busy seeing you as the problem, you will be equally busy defining me the same way. We are both part of a dynamic equilibrium that embraces us and the situation in which we find ourselves. What we have going is a dance, possibly an endless dance, with both people locked into their steps, each convinced that the other is evil, selfish, unprincipled, or (if we are feeling generous) just terribly misguided.

We can break this deadlock (this dance of equilibrium) by recognizing that resistance (our own internal resistance and that expressed externally by the people and events that resist us) is neither good nor bad. Resistance (and the people and situations that express it) simply is. It takes on meaning only as it affects your role in the dynamic equilibrium that will be upset by change. If, for example, you are a therapist trying to help a patient move toward a broader and more fulfilling life, you will define resistance as "bad" because it is keeping your patient psychologically imprisoned. The reality is that the resistance itself is not "bad"—it is simply a force that we need to recognize whenever we initiate (or contemplate) change.

Similarly, if you are a chief executive who determines that the survival of the firm depends on the introduction of a higher profit margin into its pricing structure, you will experience the outspoken opposition of your sales manager and the foot dragging of your sales force as "bad" (very "bad") factors that, in your judgment, endanger the very existence of your business. If, however, you were a member of the French underground ("Resistance") during World War II, you (and most French citizens) considered your activities to be very, very "good." You deserved to be hailed as one of a band of heroes and heroines who helped to overcome an evil enemy.

Resisting Resistance Produces More Resistance

By recognizing that equally balanced forces in opposition to one another are necessary to keep things as they are, Lewin's notion of dynamic equilibrium suggests some basic ways to engineer change.

Anticipating the concept of boomeranging, Lewin pointed out that struggling directly against resistance is risky, increasing the amount of force being brought to bear on a situation, heightening the tension, raising the stakes, and often escalating the situation into a state of out-and-out, destructive conflict.

History is full of examples of failed efforts to counter the flow of resistance with more resistance, efforts that set up escalating conflicts that led only to widespread destruction and loss. Military history presents case after case of gallant but unsuccessful charges against entrenched (resistant) enemies. These cases (like the Charge of the Light Brigade or Custer's Last Stand) may serve as rallying points for cultural and social causes, but they achieve nothing in terms of immediate, direct change.

Even when they're nominally successful, head-on military efforts to overcome resistance usually result in an imbalance to the system that can lead to chaos. The 1991 Persian Gulf War, for example, was successful beyond all expectations in overcoming Iraqi military resistance. But the United States and other governments soon found themselves dealing with immense negative fallouts, only a few of which were predicted before the all-out assault.

In the economic arena, the annals of corporate history are replete with examples in which company officials attempted to introduce more efficient work practices—only to fail because the people required to implement the changes did so grudgingly, resisting, usually finding ways to sabotage the procedures. Union-busting executives who tried to use their authority to open their shops usually had to deal with reduced morale, lost productivity, even out-and-out hostility. Entire industries have suffered from management's failure to anticipate such side effects.

The demise of Eastern Airlines a few years ago appears to have been hastened, if not caused, by the death struggle between Frank Lorenzo (who acquired Eastern as part of his conglomerate) and the machinists and their supporters, who resisted what they considered his heavy-handed efforts to deunionize the airline.

According to Lewin, lasting and productive change is facilitated by reducing or eliminating the opposing forces that hold an equilibrium in place. This is as true on the personal level as it is in the political and economic arena. The best and most lasting results occur only when we find ways to bring the forces of opposition onto the side of the forces pushing for change. That, you may be thinking, is easy enough to say. But how does one go about doing it?

DEALING PRODUCTIVELY WITH RESISTANCE

When I studied the Japanese martial art of Aikido, I learned to treat my opponent with respect, as a necessary and valued part of my practice. In Aikido, a vigorous, wholehearted attack by an opponent is seen as a gift of "ki" (the nearest terms in English are "energy" or "life force") that one learns to receive and use for one's own purposes. One is successful if one achieves in gentling—not destroying—one's opponent.

There are several principles from Aikido that you can apply to your attempts to deal constructively with opposition in your personal or work life. These principles were designed to be applied to situations that require change in interpersonal relationships, work teams and other groups, and organizational, community, and international affairs. But, with a little refinement and practice, you can learn to use them just as successfully in those efforts that pit you against your entrenched Self.

1. Welcome the opposition and treat it as a gift. Those who oppose you care enough about the situation to spend time, energy, and, often, money on it. They are engaged in your world. Your only real challenge is to turn that engagement to your advantage.

A new CEO took over the job of running a medium-sized organization from an autocratic boss whose policy of "running a tight ship" had been very successful, creating a staff who respected him and looked to him for direction in all areas of company life. The autocrat, however, had failed to keep up-to-date with changes in his industry.

The new boss wanted to introduce more democratic, participative management methods so the firm could keep pace with changing markets and make use of the most efficient, state-of-the-art technology. He immediately set out to involve department heads and other key staff members in his new management plans. To his shock and dismay, his effort met with obvious and sometimes highly vocal resistance. The attitude of his key lieutenants was, "You're the one who's being paid to make the hard decisions. Don't expect us to make them for you. If we think you are wrong, we'll let you know."

A consultant, called in to help the new CEO cope with this un-expected resistance, produced the key to open the door to partici-pative management. "Let's see if I understand," he said to the reluctant subordinates. "You see it as a contradiction in terms for your boss to order you to be more democratic. It will only be truly participative management if everyone here, not just the boss, de-cides to give it a try." There was laughter, a chorus of agreement, and a collective sigh of relief. The consultant had hit on a crucial contradiction between the stated values of the CEO and his staff's perception of him. They had been unwilling to support the old autocracy disguised as democratic participation. By engaging in the CEO's world, they had helped him refine his own definition of democracy and hone his well-intentioned management skills.

2. Treat the opposition as a teacher working to keep you and your allies on your toes. Vigorous opposition en-courages you to sharpen your thinking, marshal your most persuasive arguments, and come up with more effective strategies and tactics.

The president of a large national membership organization acts in accordance with this principle when he makes a point of naming one or two outspoken, sincere members of the opposition to any task force he forms to study or implement change in the status quo. He believes that those who are against a change have good and sincere reasons for being so. He counts on them to force those in favor of a course of action to address their objections, thereby coming up with improved approaches that will unite, rather than divide, the organization. For him, the psychological wear and tear required to work with, rather than against, resis-tance is more than outweighed by the quality of the results.

3. Overcome the temptation to waste time and energy by venting your annoyance on opponents and wishing vainly that they would simply go away or retreat from the arena of battle. Refuse to think of them as malevo-lent spoilers, preferring instead to see them as worthy adversaries without whom you could not wage the good fight. Win or lose, they are giving you a run for your money.

4. Follow the old Native American advice to "walk a mile in the moccasins" of your adversaries. Chances are they have something to teach you about the situation in which you both find yourselves.

The application of this principle helped a small town in northern New England overcome what appeared to be irrational resistance on the part of a small group of troublemakers who lived in an isolated area near the town dump. The leaders of the town felt that the disagreeable behavior of these dissidents was contributing to the unwillingness of other residents to participate in town affairs, causing them to feel apathetic and indifferent to any activity relating to local government. The dissident group made a policy of attending all public meetings, sitting in the back of the meeting room, talking loudly among themselves, making critical comments, and cheering their leader when he monopolized the proceeding with long, rambling, irrelevant speeches.

As a consultant to a group of residents who wanted to improve their town, I suspected that the community was locked into a reciprocal boomerang. Residents living near the town dump, I surmised, were feeling like humiliated outcasts whose needs and concerns were not being heard by community leaders, including those with whom I was working. Those leaders, in turn, felt so humiliated by the dissident group's rudeness that they could no longer listen to what its members were trying to say.

At my suggestion—and most reluctantly—the town leaders agreed to invite the dissident spokesperson to join them on an improvement committee. They spent some time preparing themselves to listen carefully, to ask questions and encourage the dissident to speak his mind, to be sure they understood what he was saying, and to resist the temptation to argue with his observations or offer explanations for any possible criticism.

As expected, at the first meeting the dissident engaged in a long, rambling monologue about community mismanagement, criticizing various officials and attacking the shortcomings of the town government. Committee members, however, held to their agreement and encouraged him to speak his mind.

The dissident leader continued his monologue for the first thirty minutes of the second meeting as committee members became more and more fascinated by what he was saying. For the first time, they found themselves walking in his shoes, truly understanding the frustrations of the disenfranchised minority he represented. Suddenly, almost in midsentence, the dissident stopped and looked around the group, making eye contact with each member in turn. "You're on the right track," he said. "You don't need me." With that, he excused himself and left.

At the next town meeting, heckling from the rear was minimal and the committee's proposal was unanimously accepted. Citizen participation on town government committees increased during the following year, with some residents of the area near the dump becoming active in town affairs. By honoring the voice of resistance, the committee had interrupted a long-standing, noxious process of reciprocal humiliation and boomeranging.

To apply these guidelines to your own inner resistance to change, simply remember to treat yourself with the same respect you would show another person who was resisting some proposal or plan you support. Rather than giving way to feelings of impatience or guilt, honor your own ambivalence, confusion, and uncertainty. Learn from the inner voices that resist your effort to change yourself, just as you would listen to and learn from the outer voices that might speak against your efforts to change the outer world.

More than once in my life, I have had the experience of being convinced in my logical mind that a particular course of action was the only reasonable way to go while my Intuitive Self continued to be troubled by vague, undefined doubts. I have learned to trust those doubts—even when they don't quite make sense, often when they can't even be put into words—because I believe that those vague doubts often represent an inner voice of resistance trying to be heard. If I try to silence that voice, I may discover (perhaps after it is too late) very good reasons for taking a course different from the one I chose. At the very least, I will find myself less than totally committed to my course of action—still half-listening to those unresolved doubts.

COOPERATING WITH RESISTANCE TO
   BRING ABOUT REAL CHANGE

Those interested in bringing about organizational and community change use many different techniques to cooperate creatively with individuals and groups who oppose them. The following are a few of those techniques.

Altering

This "first-ditch" approach to change is the most common and involves nothing more than tinkering with minor details in ways that leave the basic situation unchanged. Such tinkering works best in situations, such as a marriage in which the couple need to develop a new procedure for determining what movies they will see, that have little to do with how people think or feel about themselves. In the course of fifty-three years of marriage, I figure that my wife and I made hundreds, if not thousands, of such alterations in our ways of being with one another. Here are a few that come to mind at this point: Although I enjoyed sleeping together in a queen-size bed, we switched to side-by-side single beds in order to make it easier for her to sleep through the twisting and turnings of my heavier body. Although she preferred vacations spent in rented lakeside cottages, we spent many weeks in a tent trailer in order to satisfy my yen for travel camping. Although I would have preferred to remain in the country home we had purchased in California—into which I had invested a considerable amount of sweat equity—we moved to a rented house in nearby Berkeley because of her growing discomfort over battling the winds from San Francisco Bay that frequently swept across the valley. Although she was fascinated by television and would have preferred to purchase a set early in our marriage, we delayed doing so for many years because of my fear that we would become couch potatoes as so many of our friends had done. In such relatively simple situations, altering often serves as a mechanism to allow individuals to demonstrate that they are committed to another person or idea and that they desire to cooperate in finding a mutually agreeable solution to the problem at hand. It rarely succeeds, however, when a situation requires people to change their beliefs or how they feel about themselves and one another.

Reframing

In reframing, we redefine a situation so as to uncover a previously hidden range of options. Certain kinds of reframing have been so widely used that they have become clichés. We are urged, for example, to think about "problems" as "possibilities," and "crises" are hailed as "opportunities" for developing new ways to cope. The example of the dissident and the New England town illustrates reframing at its best. The committee redefined its relationship to residents of the area near the dump by learning to respect their leader as a spokesperson rather than by treating him as a lunatic-fringe troublemaker. Exercise 5 in chapter 8 is based on the principle of reframing. It offers an opportunity to redefine rejected Not-Me characteristics of oneself in such a way as to make them neutral and even positive Also-Me qualities that in some cases can even be seen as enriching one's total personality. If you skipped that exercise, consider doing it now as a way to directly experience what reframing has to offer.

Allowing

The techniques of altering and reframing are limited by their tacit acceptance of the need to treat the Created Self seriously and to behave as if one is unable to change that Self in any fundamental way. Both approaches arise from that side of the scrim of Self on which the mental images projected on the screen are mistaken for immutable reality.

When we learn to move behind the scrim, however, we release the need to defend our Created Selves, to insist on the validity of our personal viewpoints, or to argue with what others have to say. We become fascinated with disagreement, examining it with Appreciation and wonder—valuing it as proof of the infinite capacity for Self creation that exists within the human mind. From this new perspective, disagreement and conflict become an opportunity to discover the new, unexplored possibilities that are bound to emerge as each new situation reveals itself.

Allowing is the technique of bringing the power of Appreciation to bear on all points of view, encouraging all parties to express themselves without fear of ridicule, scorn, or contempt, and illuminating the situation with wonder and fascination. Fundamental to the skills of allowing is the comprehension that we are always dealing only with interpreted reality and that we are, in effect, the creator of our own version of our experience. That comprehension is essential because it gives us freedom to approach each new situation with no fixed positions, preconceptions, or assumptions about what is—or should be—happening. I have discovered that when I tap into the awe, wonderment, and joy of Appreciative knowing, there is no fear of how others might react, no anxiety, no need to be concerned about feeling humiliated. My ego lies safely on the shelf. I have nothing to defend and, therefore, nothing to defend against. My mind is uncluttered by the images and preconceptions inscribed on my mental scrim. I am open to seeing what is and what might be; I am equally open to seeing what needs to be done.

HONOR RESISTANCE AS AN ESSENTIAL PART OF CHANGE

As we've seen, resistance is both inevitable and valuable, an integral part of the process of change. Resistance is valuable because it performs a highly desirable function in channeling and directing the process of change. It ensures that those pressing for change honor those aspects of a situation that deserve to be cherished and preserved. It can even be used to identify and eliminate humiliation and boomeranging behavior, to motivate individuals to generate more suitable solutions, and to ensure greater commitment to the end result of the change process. What can happen if resistance is not honored by those pressing for change? In one organization in which I was involved almost twenty years ago, a group of young computer professionals urged management to adopt a computer-based management information system as a way to get the jump on the competition. Feeling humiliated by what they experienced as scornful public opposition to their plan by an influential and highly vocal group of colleagues, the advocates backed off, labeled management as hopelessly old-fashioned, and passively watched over the next few years as their major competitor installed its own management information system. The result was that their own business almost went into bankruptcy. In other words, in order to avoid further humiliation, they did not deal with their colleagues' outspoken opposition. Instead they simply observed as the disastrous end that their proposal had been designed to avoid almost came to pass. In effect, by not engaging the resistance, they had, in effect, become passive, unwilling participants in a nearly disastrous process of boomeranging.

Resistance is also essential to life, fundamental to ensuring that change occurs in an orderly and constructive manner. Without resistance, change would be chaotic and life as we know it would be impossible. Without resistance, every new idea would be acted on, every impulse expressed, every possibility realized. Without resistance, all established laws, customs, rules, regulations, structured roles, and cherished values would disappear, leaving us with no dependable guides about what to expect of ourselves and others. Without the resistance of physical structure, our cells would burst open and our bodies would dissolve into streams of free floating energy particles. There would be no solid objects of any description. The universe would revert to the state it was in before the process of creation began.

Planned change (including changes we plan to alter the internal structure of the Self) works with opposing forces that serve both to create and to restrain change, forces that are designed to work toward equilibrium—that is, toward a situation in which there is no change. Resistance is so fundamental to the change process that I am willing to state that the very presence of resistance implies that the change process has already begun.

The resistance we always experience when we contemplate making changes in our personal lives is, likewise, essential, inevitable, and useful. We cannot afford to be swept away by every new possibility that comes our way. Until we are ready for change, however, we will remain firmly rooted on this side of the mental curtain on which we have painted the images of Self and others that are important in our lives.

We can move to the realm of Appreciation that is available behind the scrim only if and when we've given ourselves time to prepare to do so in a way that feels safe and orderly. Part of that preparation time involves learning to Appreciate how fully we have been involved in creating the life we are living on this, more limited, side of the scrim. If we try to change prematurely, we will find ourselves caught up in an exhausting internal struggle wherein the forces desiring change and the forces clinging to the status quo battle one another to a standstill.

The best advice I can give those who truly want to move behind the scrim of Self is to move slowly. Begin by focusing the
power of Appreciation on the life you are living now on this side
of the scrim. Give yourself permission to experience life with all
the fascination and wonder of which you are capable. Such permission has a way of enlarging life, bringing more and more of it
into focus for you to enjoy.

Begin now by Appreciating what lies just in front of you. If
you are experiencing resistance, honor it, Appreciate it, examine
it with fascination and delight, without criticism of any kind, the
way a curious child would examine a new toy. And remember—
the resistance you may be encountering is a truly fascinating
phenomenon—a device developed by your infant Self to keep
you safe until it is time to move on.

THIRTEEN

Living in the Light of Appreciation

□ □ □

How good is man's life, the mere living!
How fit to employ
All the heart and the soul and the senses
Forever in joy.

—Robert Browning

In the next few pages, I will give you a powerful, motivating vision of what your life might be like when you release the resistance that freezes your current equilibrium of Self in place.

Before we begin, take a few moments to acknowledge that resistance. Pay attention to any voices of inner resistance that arose as you have been reading. Have you often disagreed with me? Have you heard yourself muttering (quietly, I hope) phrases along the lines of "rubbish," "airy-fairy psychobabble," or "interesting theory, but not quite right for me"?

Don't judge or fight those voices and the resistance they express. Just notice them and move on, adopting the most receptive attitude possible under your particular circumstances. Try to stay open to both experiences—the experience of reading and the experience of resisting and judging what you read. From that dual stance, I am going to ask you to relax and consider the following domestic scene:

A husband and wife are eating breakfast together, preparing to begin their respective workdays. The husband says, "Oh, I forgot to tell you. We're supposed to meet the Joneses for dinner this evening. Can you get a sitter?"

"You forgot? Again?" the wife responds. "You know how hard it is to find a sitter at the last minute. Or maybe you don't—since you're never the one who has to do it."

"Oh, great—the Miraculous Martyred Mother," the husband sighs. "Look, do you or do you not want to join me for dinner this evening?"

The wife snaps to attention over her grapefruit. You can almost see the wheels in her head turning as she prepares to launch her most caustic rebuttal. Before the first three words have left her mouth, it's obvious that both husband and wife are caught, trapped in the first movements of what will develop into an(other) intense and bitter argument.

We are witnessing that all-too-familiar phenomenon—the marital "number," the argument that unfolds according to a pattern so predictable that the couple might as well be reading their lines from a script. Over their years together, most couples perfect quite a variety of these numbers. Like barnacles on a ship, these prerecorded dramas become encrusted in the relationship, consuming increasing amounts of energy, slowing both partners down, and depriving them of the freedom to move and grow within the marriage.

Unless you are very unusual (and incredibly fortunate), you have developed a series of numbers that you play out with your close friends, your spouse, your parents, possibly even the people with whom you work. Once a number has been created (and numbers are created with the cooperation and collusion of both players), it takes almost nothing to set them in motion. A remark, a sigh, a frown—whatever the unconsciously accepted stimulus—and presto! Everything else ensues right on cue. From the first stimulus, the patterned argument unfolds as if the participants had rehearsed it dozens of times—which, in point of fact, they have.

Let's get back to the couple at the breakfast table, who by this time have managed to work themselves up into a state of undeclared ego-hooked war.

"Sure, oh, sure, oh, sure, sure, sure, I'll find a baby-sitter, just like I always do," the wife announces. "You just relax and give orders and let Mama take care of everything. But, right now, Mama has got to get herself off to work."

With that, she rises and makes a point of clearing every item off the table, including her husband's half-finished grapefruit—and the spoon he has poised above it. She slams the items into the sink, grabs her purse off the counter, and sweeps out the door, banging it dramatically behind her.

As soon as she's gone, her husband drops his nonchalant air, slumps gloomily into his chair, and drops his head into his hands, muttering, "Oh, damn! Not again."

Suddenly, however, the mood of the husband (who happens to have been me some forty years ago) begins to brighten.

"Oh boy, we've just given an outstanding performance," he thinks. "We were exceptional. Her exit was brilliant; her timing impeccable. And, me, I'm a master. Sitting here with my head in my hands, I must look like a study in human misery. It's time to ring down the curtain or black out the stage. Applause, applause!!"

I went about the rest of the day in high spirits—stopping at 10:00 A.M. to call my wife to tell her I had found a student to watch the boys and to share my excitement over our "performance." I learned, to my amazement, that she had been thinking all morning along the same lines. We had a fine time that evening, basking in the comfortable glow of understanding, love—and Appreciation. A minor miracle had occurred—we had overcome a major obstacle in our relationship; we had found a way through (not around) the rigors of ego-hooking, opening the door to the development over the years of a mellow, resilient marital relationship, one based on our constantly expanding abilities to Appreciate the human miracles we are. As the power of Appreciation became more and more influential in our lives, the incidents of ego-hooking and boomeranging all but disappeared (I say "all but" because we always gave ourselves the freedom to run through our favorite numbers once in a while). Allowing became our preferred way to deal with the changes and challenges of our shared life.

The miracle my late wife and I experienced that day cannot be explained in terms of logic or theory. But it can be illustrated by using the metaphor of the scrim. Before that morning, we played out our lives in *front* of our personal mental scrims. The curtains of mental scenery we had created about ourselves and our relationship were locked in place, unmovable, limiting the ways in which we could express the drama of our lives. Woven into the very warp and woof of these scrims were all the old hurts and buried resentments that accumulate in any real, growing relationship. The scenes on the scrim were not mere scenery to us—they were solid and real.

What happened that morning was a change in our psychic lighting. With that change, we discovered that our scrims were no longer opaque. Just as the audience can see, when the house lights go up, that the scenery onstage in a theater (which looks so real when the stage is lit low for the drama) is nothing but a fabrication, so were we able to see the nonreality of the scenery that had formed the background for so many of our marital dramas.

Please understand: what occurred for my wife and me that day was not a matter of subscribing to a new theory or set of ideas but rather one of allowing a whole new world of perception and understanding to open for us. What we saw in one another—the possibilities, the talents, the creative genius—had always been there. But they were hidden behind the opaque images on our mental scrims. The light of Appreciation threw all those hidden treasures into bold relief, made them available to us on a day-to-day basis. But how did we get there?

DEVELOPING THE ART OF APPRECIATION

As we saw earlier, the first essential step to gaining access to the state of being I call Appreciation is to accept the fact that we each create the Self we call Me. It's not enough to gain an intellectual understanding of this idea. When I say "accept," I mean you need to know in your very bones that the Me you've been so quick to defend is nothing more (and need be taken no more seriously) than a character in a play or novel. When you are able to accept this fact with no reservations, you have arrived at a point at which you may no longer want to think about your Self as anything more than your own wonderful creation. At this point, you may decide to take the second step: that is, to set aside your ego.

Many people never make this decision. If you turn out to be among them, you will be in good, traditional company. By resisting the simple, yet far-reaching change, your mind (like the minds of those whose company you share) is acting in your behalf, doing its best to defend and maintain the Self you have so painstakingly created over the years.

You may, on the other hand, be one of those lucky few for whom this decision comes automatically, without effort or anxiety. If so, you are fortunate indeed.

Most of us exist somewhere in between the two extremes. Faced with this important (and life-changing) decision, we react with powerful resistance. It's understandable—we've spent a longer or shorter lifetime defining our Selves as something we must defend to the death. The thought of setting our egos aside sounds more than a little dangerous! No matter how much torture we've endured from our egos—and most of us have experienced an enormous amount—the idea of letting go of that very basic Self-created structure has the ring of death to us.

My personal experience was probably fairly common. When it first became apparent to me that clinging to the Self-created ego (and the ghost patterns it cast on my mental scrim) did nothing to empower my life, I was elated. Merely by changing my relationship to my artificial Created Self, I could transform my life! What a thought! As long as it remained a thought, I remained elated. It wasn't until the thought became a call to action that I began to experience discomfort.

My Ego Mind, sensing that things were about to get out of hand, leapt into action, questioning the validity of my proposed endeavor. "Well, Don, you've come up with an intriguing idea here, this business of learning to live on the other side of the ego—behind the scrim, as you so picturesquely put it," my mind said to me. "But what makes you think this is really possible—or practical? And, more to the point, what will happen to me if you persist in this foolhardy project?" I couldn't answer my Self—part of the adventure of setting your ego aside is that you don't know what will happen; you are opening your Self to possibilities you've never allowed it to see before. I was asking my Self to do something that felt almost (but not quite) as safe as jumping from a high diving board through a mist into a hidden (possibly nonexistent) pool.

My Mind invented whole armies of ghosts and goblins, all huffing and puffing their dramas against my opaque mental scrim. I remember talking with a colleague, a psychologist who had already taken the step I contemplated. "The ego holds all the disparate parts of the human psyche together," I explained in my most authoritative academic voice. "There is the possibility that an effort to set the ego aside could result in psychic disintegration. How do I know I won't dissolve into microscopic particles?"

My friend refused to fuel this resistant argument with debate. He just laughed—giving full expression for his newfound freedom to Appreciate me and my fear-driven mental acrobatics. "If you disappear, I'll send out search parties," he assured me. I found his nonchalant response reassuring—this guy had embraced the powers of resistance and lived to laugh about it.

The well of resistance seemed unfathomably deep. I developed some highly creative tactics for delaying change. I worried that I would lose the finer qualities I had worked so hard to incorporate into my personality. What about the integrity I modeled from my father? And that quality of childlike sweetness I had managed to preserve through the years? I didn't tell my friends how proud I was of that particular quality, but I did argue that I felt parts of my Self were worth taking seriously, parts that deserved to be defended against any and all assaults.

"Nope," my friends (and my own better sense) informed me. "Everything must go. You must remove your investment in any quality that you consider essential to the Me you call Don Klein. You must recognize all aspects of your personality as nothing more than Self-created constructs—fabrications of your own invention, developed to meet the needs you perceived in your environment."

I spent several painful days at this endeavor, trying to find a way to release my Self from my ego-limited cage. I wavered, I argued, I worried and fretted over concerns I can see now (from a safe distance of more than thirty years) were nothing more than disguised attempts to hang on to my sense of importance. It was not an easy decision. I expected my world to quake.

It didn't. There was no shaking or quaking, only the revelation of a whole new set of exciting, lovely, and loving realities—possibilities that automatically come into focus when one gets in touch with that inborn capacity that I call Appreciation, but for which others have used such labels as "ecstasy," "bliss," "wonder," and "fascination." The label isn't important; only the reality matters. And the reality is that the obscuring screen of Self importance hides many positive, happy, and loving experiences and feelings, experiences you may not have enjoyed fully since you were a child.

When you move behind your mental scrim, lovely, gentle changes like those precipitated by the scene in our kitchen will become common in your life. You will come to expect the subtle changes that herald yet another widening of your perspective, yet another deepening of your capacity for joy. But you need expect no radical changes in your lifestyle, no soul-rattling transformations, no trips to the mountaintop. There will be just a continuing expansion of one fundamental realization—the realization that all those things about your Self that you consider so important aren't so important after all, no more important than the roles children assume and discard in their ongoing games of "pretend." That realization will alter forever how you feel about and handle the routine (and not-so-routine) matters of your life.

To repeat, the essential step in arriving at this realization is to recognize that you are not your beliefs. I am told that in the Talmud it is written: "We do not see things as *they* are. We see them as *we* are." But this and all other such wisdom remain theory until we know in our bones that we are truly looking at life through the lenses of our attitudes, beliefs, and ideas about who we are and what the world is all about. As storyteller Rachel Naomi Remen writes in her book *Kitchen Table Wisdom: Stories That Heal*:

> With our sun glasses on, life looks green to us. Knowing what is real requires that we remember that we are wearing glasses, and take them off. *One of the great moments in life is the moment we recognize we have them on in the first place.* Freedom is very close to us then. It is a moment of great power.[1]

As you contemplate taking these steps to rediscover and activate your capacity for Appreciation, it may help to remember that it is not a matter of developing a new set of skills. As I pointed out in chapter 11, entering the realm of Appreciative

knowing is an art, not a science. I have tried to describe faithfully
the path I followed and the struggles I experienced when I became aware of what might lie beyond my mental scrim. It remains for you to discover what happens if and when you decide
to set aside your ego, to no longer take your Self seriously, and to
take the leap of faith in moving beyond the intricate mental images that are inscribed on your mental scrim. Perhaps—as some
others have done—you will slide easily and happily into that
realm. Perhaps you will find your resistance, like mine, putting
up a valiant struggle to keep you from taking that leap. If so,
your struggles will surely be uniquely yours and your path, although it may resemble mine in certain respects, will also be
unique. In any case, I invite you to find your way to rediscover
your inner realm of Appreciative knowing, knowing that if and
when you find your Self in that realm, you will have transformed
your life.

APPRECIATION IS NOT DENIAL OR SUPPRESSION

Counselors and therapists often ask how Appreciation differs
from such unproductive defense mechanisms as denying the existence of a problem or putting a lid on the intense, unacceptably
strong feelings that occur when we encounter a difficulty.

The difference may best be described in terms of the quality of
the psychic energy involved. Defense mechanisms are designed
to do exactly what their name implies—defend the Humiliated
Self. In order for them to be activated, the Humiliated Self must
experience an event as threatening—an experience that is, in itself, very energy draining. The attempt to defend the Humiliated
Self through denial or suppression consumes even more energy:
when we deny the seriousness of a situation, we first use energy
to judge it as "serious" and then expend additional stores of energy to contradict that judgment and act as if nothing were
wrong. Suppressed anger or other "unacceptable" emotions consume both the energy of the emotion itself plus the energy needed
to keep it hidden underground within the psyche.

In contrast, Appreciation frees energy. There is no longer, as we
have seen, a need to expend energy on defending one's Humiliated

Self against ridicule or scorn. While defense mechanisms work as psychological blinders, restricting one's understanding and hampering one's ability to see the range of available options, Appreciation removes the blinders and enhances our ability to perceive all available options, including options that can be negotiated with minimal expenditure of psychic energy.

THE FALLACIOUS THEORY OF EXTERNALLY DERIVED APPRECIATION

Because the capacity for Appreciation is inborn, we have all experienced it and retain an intuitive understanding of what it is and how it manifests itself. It is a pure state of being that we only need to remember and learn to access at will. We all cherish memories of moments when we felt vitally alive, at one with the world around us. Unfortunately, what we tend to remember are the special circumstances that might have surrounded those moments— the sunset, the inspiring music, the terrific sex. And remembering those circumstances, it is easy to assume that the wonderful feelings derived, somehow, from those external events.

This theory of externally derived Appreciation, however, fails to pass the most basic tests of logic and rationality. Where did that wonderful feeling come from? And where did it go when the sun set, the music stopped, or the lovemaking came to an end? The answer is that the feeling arose from within you—and disappeared back into that same internal place, where it stayed dormant, awaiting another opportunity to surface. The logical conclusion from this observation is that the feeling of Appreciation is, like all other aspects of human reality, Self generated. It was not the external events but your responses to them that produced those momentary highs.

This is the good news. It means that, quite literally, it is possible to live every moment of your life—regardless of the circumstances that characterize that moment—in a state of Appreciation. All you need do is rediscover your inborn talent for accessing that state and practice the talent until it becomes natural again. I can assure you that it is possible to feel fully alive even when the external circumstances of your life are as stimulating as a cocktail party hosted by a crashing bore.

THE FALLACIOUS THEORY THAT
PRACTICE MAKES PERFECT

Appreciation is not a skill, like tennis or bridge, that we can learn, practice, and perfect. This is one case where practice does not make perfect. Take, for example, watching a beautiful sunset as the occasion for tapping into one's inner feelings of peaceful contentment, wonderment, and awe. Many people do so. When weather conditions are suitable, hundreds gather at Mallary Dock in Key West to witness the sunset and to join one another in applauding as the sun seems to disappear into the ocean. Suppose you decided to watch the sunset night after night on the theory that sooner or later you'd perfect your ability to tap into those wonderful feelings on any and all occasions. The chances are that just the opposite would happen. After only a few repetitions of that wonderful experience, you'd find that sunsets had become commonplace—they would be no longer able to arouse your capacity for Appreciation from its slumber within you. There is no way that practice in sunset watching would sharpen or increase your ability to experience wonder and joy. Quite the opposite.

So long as we confuse our capacity for Appreciation with that which we Appreciate, repetition of experience leads to dulling of our enthusiasm and ultimately to boredom.

Years ago, my wife and I tried an experiment while driving down the coastal highway in California. On an impulse, we turned east off the highway onto a narrow, twisting road into the coastal hills. Here's what we discovered about our Selves and new experience. For seven miles until the road deteriorated into an impassable rutted path, we noticed and enjoyed all manner of flora and fauna, including a lone peacock that spread its luxuriant tail feathers for our exclusive delight!

When we retraced our path, however, we no longer experienced the excitement of newness and discovery. Instead, we were attracted to familiar items. We noticed objects that had attracted our attention the first time through the territory. By the time we had returned to the starting point, we knew that the bloom was definitely off the rose. We had been unable to maintain the excitement of discovery while traveling through more-or-less familiar territory.

▣ Exercise 14: The Effects of Repetition

To conduct this experiment for yourself, drive out into the countryside and pick a deserted side road to explore.

Step 1:

Drive very slowly down that side road. Remember, you are an explorer, discovering territory that is new to you. Every tree, every flower, every rock, every fence, every field, every bird, and every animal is something you have not seen before. Notice the shapes, the colors, and the shadows. Listen for sounds. Be aware of odors, temperature, the feeling of the breeze on your face and arms.

What is it like to be an explorer, to discover new things, to experience this road for the first time?

Step 2:

After no more than five miles of this journey of discovery, turn the car around and, still driving slowly, retrace the drive until you return to the starting point.

Notice what it's like to venture through territory you have already explored once. How is the experience of retracing your steps different from seeing the territory for the first time? Which experience is more exciting? Satisfying? Boring?

THE (CLOSELY RELATED) FALLACIOUS THEORY OF NOVELTY

Another lesson was clear from our drive into the California hills. By assuming that external events and situations "caused" us to react in certain ways, we had surrendered our Selves to needing novelty and variety in order to experience the excitement and wonder of being alive. In their search for happiness, many people engage in an endless quest for novel experiences that quicken their senses, fill them with the thrill of discovery, and satisfy their desire to savor the joy of life.

Another, similar group of people hope to find fulfillment in the endless search for material wealth. Although temporarily satisfying, both novelty and material goods provide only temporary, quick fixes in the search for Nirvana. Like heroin, cocaine, and other addictive substances, they sometimes become goals in and of themselves. Here are the thoughts of Mihaly Csikszentmihalyi, a psychologist who has specialized in the subject of happiness:

> Material advantages do not readily translate into social and emotional benefits. In fact, to the extent that most of one's psychic energy becomes invested in material goals, it is typical for sensitivity to other rewards to atrophy. Friendship, art, literature, natural beauty, religion, and philosophy become less and less interesting. . . . Eventually a person who only responds to material rewards becomes blind to any other kind and loses the ability to derive happiness from other sources. As is true of addiction in general, material rewards at first enrich the quality of life. Because of this, we tend to conclude that more must be better. But life is rarely linear; in most cases, what is good in small quantities becomes commonplace and then harmful in larger doses.[2]

THE THEORY OF POSITIVE THINKING

When I was growing up, the power of positive thinking was all the rage. My mother was one of the legion of moms who warned their kids not to scowl. "Watch out, one of these days that expression will freeze on your face!" My mother was also raised on the familiar dictum "If you don't have something good to say, don't say anything at all." The expression "Smile and the world smiles with you" was one of many ways in which we were urged to present a happy face to those around us. The culture was filled with well-meaning advice about the power of positive thinking. For example, the radio often featured George Gershwin's 1927 popular tune:

> Accentuate the positive,
> Eliminate the negative,
> Don't mess with Mr. In Between.

In the early 1900s a French physician and hypnotist named Emile Coué became internationally renowned when he preached the idea—revolutionary at the time—that suggestion was the engine that made individual change possible.[3] Documenting many instances in which Self suggestion was far more powerful than reason or intention in creating states of well-being or illness, he made liberal use of positive suggestion when he dispensed medications to his patients. Coué ended up believing that all he needed to do was deliver positive suggestions in order to bring about change in his patients. He gained many devoted followers, who followed his instruction to repeat over and over again just before going to sleep the sentence "Every day, in every way, I am getting better and better."

The power of a genuinely positive attitude toward life is beautifully expressed by a tale that has been ascribed to the Sufi tradition:

> A Sufi master was sitting in the shade beside the road from Alexandria to Damascus. A weary traveler on his way to Damascus sat down next to him. "Where are you from?" asked the Sufi master.
>
> "Alexandria," the traveler replied. "I'm moving to Damascus. Do you know Damascus?"
>
> "Yes," the Sufi replied.
>
> "What are the people like in Damascus?" the traveler asked.
>
> "Tell me," the Sufi countered, "what were the people like in Alexandria?"
>
> "Terrible," the traveler said. "That place is filled with crooks and people who have no respect for life or property."
>
> Well," the Sufi said, "I'm afraid you will find that Damascus is no better."
>
> A few hours later another traveler to Damascus joined the Sufi master. The conversation went very much the same way. "What are the people like in Damascus?" the traveler asked.
>
> "What are the people like in Alexandria?" the Sufi countered.
>
> "Marvelous!" replied the traveler. "They are friendly and caring people. I hated to leave, but I'm forced to move because of my business."
>
> "That's too bad," the Sufi said. "But I have good news for you. You'll find that Damascus, too, is filled with marvelous people."

I have no doubt that we are much more likely to achieve the results we want, even in the face of adversity, by maintaining a positive attitude than by wasting energy on useless complaints and recriminations. An Appreciative orientation to life, however, is not the same thing as putting on a positive attitude about events in one's life, which requires us to do the near-impossible—adopt a cheery attitude just at those times when our minds are most filled with bitter thoughts and fears. About the best that most of us can do at such times is to remember that "this, too, shall pass" or to cling to the old saying "Every cloud has a silver lining." In other words, simply adopting a positive attitude is rarely possible when we are caught up in negative emotions. When we try to appear to be happy under such conditions, we run the risk of earning—and deserving—the nickname of Pollyanna, the legendary girl who insisted on putting a positive spin on whatever awful tragedies she faced.

A modern version of the Theory of Positive Thinking called "Appreciative Inquiry"[4] is sweeping like wild fire among organizational consultants and social researchers. Developed by experts in organizational behavior at Case Western Reserve University, Appreciative Inquiry rests on the basic assumption that those who seek to understand and do something about organizational change create the world they discover by virtue of the methods they use. Its many enthusiastic advocates point out that the traditional problem-solving approach focuses on deficiencies, failures, and factors that cause organizations and community groups to fall short of their goals. By contrast, Appreciative Inquiry focuses on successes, accomplishments, and factors that are operating at those times when organizations and community groups achieve their objectives and live up to their ideals. It is, in other words, a glass-half-full rather than a glass-half-empty approach. Appreciative Inquiry represents a profound change in orientation from one of rational, analytic skepticism about the world to one of almost mythical reverence for the life-giving potential that the universe has to offer. In the words of its creators:

> *Serious consideration and reflection on the ultimate mystery of being engenders a reverence for life that draws the researcher to inquire beyond superficial appearances to deeper levels of the life-generating essentials and potentials of social existence.*[5]

In the comparatively few years since Appreciate Inquiry came upon the scene, its practitioners have come up with ingenious methods for helping people transform how they think about themselves and their organizations from a problem-solving approach to ways that evoke images of what is possible, generate hope, mobilize affirming energies, and enable them to create the positive approaches they can imagine. For those who have experienced the transforming possibilities of Appreciate Inquiry in action, it does not require a major leap for them to move behind their mental scrims and enter the realm of Appreciative Knowing.[6]

SOME COMMON SMOKE SCREENS
Most of us have a huge investment in the smoke screen of ideas created by the mind to maintain and protect our sense of Self importance. That smoke screen keeps us from recognizing and using our power of Appreciation.

If you are convinced that what I am describing when I talk about Appreciation is the often-recommended practice of "reframing" a situation to provide new perspectives, you have adopted a very common smoke screen. Reframing involves choosing a new word to describe an established situation, calling someone "svelte" instead of "skinny," for example, or referring to the body type we used to call "fat" as "substantial."

Another smoke screen might take the form of insisting that I am simply repackaging the old cliché about every cloud having a silver lining, suggesting that we all should struggle to find reasons to Appreciate situations that no one in their right minds would want to Appreciate.

Both those screens imply that Appreciation is an overlay, something that can be added like a coat of paint, by sheer force of will, to the objective reality that exists outside ourselves.

That is not what I am saying. *When I talk about Appreciation, I am describing a whole new way of seeing the mini-dramas of everyday life.* Appreciation is, in effect, an illuminating feeling state. It does not have to be justified. It just is. The following anecdote may clarify this subtle, but essential, distinction:

Some years ago I was teaching an evening course at Johns Hopkins University. Late on a mid-March afternoon, in a year that had been distinguished by an exceptionally long, snowy, and cold winter, I walked across campus to the Eisenhower Library, thrilled to notice that the snow had at last melted and the trees were beginning to bloom. I felt light and liberated as I trudged down three flights of library stairs to my basement classroom.

I emerged three hours later to encounter a transformed world. It was snowing hard, with no sign of letting up. I stood hunched at the top of the stairs in front of the library, zipped my jacket, and pulled the hood over my head, full of resistance against the unexpected winter weather. Cursing the elements, I mushed through the snow to my car, dreading the long, slippery drive home. I was not a happy man.

I was unlocking my car door and stamping the moisture from my unbooted feet when an uninvited thought occurred to me. "What if this were Christmas Eve? How would I be feeling then?"

With that thought, I snapped to. "If this were Christmas Eve," I reminded myself, "I'd react quite differently. I'd welcome the snow as part of the larger package of holiday delights—sparkling lights highlighted on fresh new snow, mulled cider in front of the fire, and sledding down the neighborhood hill."

I decided to take another look at the uninvited snow, bringing the power of Appreciation to bear on this unexpected event. What I saw then was a lovely winter scene worthy of Currier and Ives. The campus lay soft and quiet under a clean blanket of pure white snow, unshoveled, untrampled, unblemished. The air was still, with that serenity that feels almost supernatural. The snow fell straight and soft, reflecting the twinkling lights of the campus buildings. My life had changed and I had changed with it—I was no longer a beleaguered professor pushing his way home after a twelve-hour winter day. My shoulders relaxed and straightened; my mind stopped resisting the drive ahead and refocused on the beauty of the scene. I stood there a few minutes, watching the reactions of other people as they emerged from the library. One after another, they bundled up, hunched their shoulders, and trudged off into the night, no doubt complaining bitterly to themselves about the nasty weather, cheating themselves of the opportunity to enjoy a winter wonderland.

Our egos are adept at glomming on to almost any reason to feel upset, imposed on, or bent out of shape by the events and situations that compose our lives. But we don't need a reason to appreciate those same events. All we need is the willingness to experiment with another way of viewing things. No, Christmas Eve does not fall in mid-March. But the feelings of Christmas Eve are available anytime, waiting inside each of us to illuminate life with the radiant glow of Appreciation.

My experience that night on the urban campus of Johns Hopkins brought home for me the enormous transformation that occurs whenever we allow the scrim of illusion to disappear. I was not expecting to find beauty in the desolate cold around me—but it was there, almost waiting to ambush me, as it always does when we illuminate a person or situation with the pure light of Appreciation. Appreciation, unlike the forced optimism of the silver-lining philosophy, has the power to reveal whole new vistas of possibility. When we are lighting our lives with the lamp of Appreciation, we see more clearly and understand more precisely what we want to achieve and how to go about achieving it.

APPRECIATION WORKS EVERYWHERE

The power of Appreciation can be harnessed at work, at home, in the community—anywhere you use your energies to understand problems and solve them, to define goals and achieve them, to bring people together and unravel the tangled webs we usually let pass for communication.

One of the simplest ways to put the power of Appreciation to work—and for me one of the most interesting—is to pay special attention to the mental scenery of your life. By mental scenery I mean the images of your Self and the world around you that you've so lovingly and painstakingly painted on your mental scrim. Don't try to do anything about those images. Neither apologize for nor boast about nor defend them. Simply note what those images are. Talk about them if you have a spouse, companion, or good friend who's willing to hear you out. Remember, it's not a matter of explaining or analyzing your Self. It's about Appreciating the subtlety and imagination that you've used over the years in developing these ideas about who you are, the people who are important to you, and the world in which you live. The idea is to get to the point of truly acknowledging and owning the mental scenery that has meant so much to you.

I am suggesting that you view your mental images of your Self and your world from the perspective of a fascinated spectator who can see that both problems and payoffs are involved in your everyday mental scenery and who can also Appreciate the irony and humor in the fact that all those images, without exception, are products of your own fabulously creative imagination.

One of the most important by-products that I receive from taking playful views of the images of Self and others painted on my mental scrim is that I am much freer of the need to defend, justify, or explain away this Don Klein character that I've maintained and refined over all the years of my life. All the energy that used to be tied up in protecting my ego is now available for more creative and pleasurable purposes. Take the matter of humiliation, for example. Once I was able to view my fear of humiliation from an outside cosmic perspective, I saw that—as Buddha and many others have pointed out—any effort to avoid ridicule, scorn, and various other kinds of put-downs from others would be like locking the proverbial barn door after the horse was already stolen. I'd already been humiliated many times and no doubt would feel its sting many more times before I died. Instead of wasting energy in a vain effort to avoid it, better to get on with and enjoy life. And if that meant feeling and even being ridiculous, on with the show!

UNEXPECTED GIFTS

Several wonderful dividends have come from using the power of Appreciation in the way I have described.

First, I've enjoyed simply getting to know the scenery on my mental scrim. It's been like revisiting a museum to examine favorite works of art over and over again, noting different aspects of the work each time, gaining new insights into what the creator of the work was trying to do, and finding new meaning in both subject matter and technique.

Second, except for brief intervals when my ego has been hooked temporarily, I've been able to give up any need to waste energy on defending my ideas and my actions in the face of criticism.

Third, the most marvelous gift of all, I find myself admiring and enjoying other people's mental scenery, which means their ways of being in the world, their ideas, and their actions. For me, they, too, have become artistic creations, creative products of their own imaginations, incomplete works of art always in progress, always holding the possibility of change.

A friend uses different words to describe the impact on his life of viewing the images on his mental scrim from the combined emotional and intellectual state of knowing that I call the power of Appreciation, calling the Appreciative state "the place of consciousness where we are all connected." Born and raised in a working-class family, this brilliant, dedicated, and enormously creative man carved out a successful and highly remunerative business career. Looking back from this "place of consciousness" on his transition from a working-class to an upper-middle-class position in society, he describes the process "as a kind of catharsis, something similar to beating the dirt out of an Oriental rug."

"The process," he writes in an autobiography, "can be filthy, but the end result is a dazzle of color unseen in years." He concludes: "The journey has been psychologically enlightening, sometimes oppressive, and sometimes liberating."

In my work as a consultant, I have learned to view the problems my clients bring to me through the lens of Appreciation, a technique that produces insights that are often far more helpful (and less threatening) than the critical analysis that was once my primary tool. Critical analysis, a purely intellectual technique, made me a whiz at diagnosing what was wrong with an organization—information that my clients were often less than thrilled to receive. As I have learned to experience similar situations through the experiential lens of Appreciation, I have gained the ability to understand that everyone involved in a corporate or an organizational dilemma is behaving perfectly if the goal is to ensure that the problem continues to exist. With that understanding comes power—my clients are quick to see that if they are able so easily to keep the problem in place, they are equally empowered to remold the situation to fit a more productive configuration.

Appreciation was my most effective information-gathering tool in the situation I described in chapter 11 involving the CEO who was experiencing bewildering difficulties with his three most trusted lieutenants, capable young people who had virtually stopped speaking with one another. If you will remember, it took me only one meeting with the individuals involved to discover the core of the problem—that they all felt their boss acted unfairly because of his susceptibility to pressure and that they were afraid to confront him with their complaint because they did not want to hurt his pride. Because I was able to Appreciate what I was hearing and understand how much all of them wanted to resolve the problem, I was able to present my findings in a way that met with minimal resistance. The entire effort, which might once have consumed weeks, was completed in less than two days—and we had a remarkably good time. By the end of the second day, we were all poking gentle fun at our own foibles, enjoying the ingenuity with which we manage to mess up our lives.

During the past year, at a deeply personal level, I have been faced with the most awful tragedy by far in my life, the death of my beloved wife, Lola. At age eighteen we met and fell in love as freshmen in college and married five years later. We had been married fifty-three years. Nothing in my life had prepared me for the pain I experienced. Not the ten years I had spent working with Dr. Erich Lindemann, a pioneer in the study of grief. Not the deaths of my father, mother, brother, other close relatives, and dear friends. My intense grief has been with me at all times. Experiencing my bereavement through the lens of Appreciation, I have opened myself to it. I have been able to allow my tears and to claim all the manifestations of my great loss. I have wept, wailed, sobbed, cried on a daily basis. I have discovered facets and depths of sorrow, loneliness, loss, and despair that I barely knew existed. I have been able to reach out to friends and family, to allow their sorrow to blend with mine, to welcome their offers of support and comfort, and to participate with them in honoring and celebrating Lola's life. Most important, I have been able to embrace my loss and my great love for Lola fully and directly without denial, repression, or disguise of any kind. At the same time I have continued with my work, entered into living alone for the first time in my life, and begun what I expect will be a long process of discovering the shape, direction, and purpose of what lies ahead for me. Appreciation has enabled me to embrace this awful turning point in my life and to discover in it the great beauty that is inherent in all of life experience, including deep sorrow.

APPRECIATIVE HUMOR, THE DEATH OF NEGATIVITY, AND MORE

One sign that the power of Appreciation is operating is the emergence in any situation of a gentle, spontaneous, and caring humor. Here's how one observer of the human condition puts it:

> Among the riches that deserve savoring are life's absurdities . . . humor . . . helps us stay the course, preventing us from taking ourselves too seriously, helping us put life's bruises in perspective, enlarging our vision. Humor gives us ways to come to terms with pain, loss, and failure, yet also look beyond it.[7]

I think of humor as Appreciation's solvent, used to dissolve the rigid Self importance the ego finds so necessary to protect the Humiliated Self. Humor brings a new fascination with the incredible complexity of the human mind and a delight in the endlessly absurd situations we so effortlessly generate.

From my own experience and that of others, there are a number of wonderful by-products of approaching life from an Appreciative perspective. First of all, without conscious decision or effort on my part, I have discovered that I spend far less energy on unproductive mental gymnastics, such as regrets, pinning blame, and worrying. I'm very good at blaming others, perhaps not a world-class champion blamer but at least a first-class amateur. Once in a while I still find myself playing the blame game, but my heart is no longer in it. I never was a very committed worrier or regretter, even before I tuned into my capacity for Appreciation. But I have friends who are quite talented at these pursuits and I'm also far better than I once was at keeping myself from being drawn into their episodes of worry and regret. Occasionally, I even find ways that help them Appreciate those episodes, take charge of them, and draw them to a close.

In addition, I have discovered that both compassion for others' struggles and forgiveness for hurtful behavior are inevitable by-products of the Appreciative state. I know that many religious leaders have preached that compassion and forgiveness are virtues to be required of truly devout followers of their faith. For me, no moral position is involved. My experience is that both compassion and forgiveness are inevitable when one enters the realm of Appreciation and sees beyond the scenery inscribed on one's mental scrim. Virtues they may be. Tests of faith they are not. Rather, they are indicators that a certain level of what some call spiritual consciousness has been reached. Within that realm of consciousness, it makes sense neither to require that others ask for forgiveness nor to withhold forgiveness whether or not it is requested. There is no need to waste one's energy on holding a grudge, seeking revenge, or otherwise making one's compassion conditional on whether or not the other person is ashamed, feels guilty, or has been properly humiliated. Those who experience life from the perspective of Appreciation find that the demands of emotional reparation are unnecessary, energy draining, Self justifying, and ultimately destructive.

Of all the reasons I can give to encourage you to make the leap away from an ego-driven and toward an Appreciation-powered life, perhaps the most important is this: such a leap (and it is really more of a leaplet) will enable you to experience once again those moments of transcendent happiness that are a part of everyone's childhood. You will, in fact, remember your entire childhood differently—gaining a new access to memories that have been overcast by the need of your Humiliated Self to be in charge of remembering what happened to you while you were growing up, allowing that new memory to fuel the powers of childhood to work in the life you are living now, making you a happier, more productive, and more deeply satisfied adult.

FOURTEEN

Fanning the Flames of Appreciation: Simple Approaches to Transparency

◩ ◩ ◩

If you've read this far, chances are you have moved past your personal iron curtain of resistance. You've made the decision to change; you're ready, even eager, to reclaim your birthright. Now comes the really tricky part—beginning to master this new way of life.

The way to begin is simply to begin, confident that you cannot fail. You may experience moments, even days, when your hooked ego plays tricks on you. You may even continue to endure more than your share of boomeranged mess-ups. Those predicaments may even increase initially as your ego begins to sense that you are "deserting" it. Just be assured, when those moments sneak up on you, that there is no such thing as failure when it comes to playing your part in this drama we call life. You can continue to speak your lines on cue, living many moments unconsciously in front of your scrim as you have done all your life. Accepting those moments with grace and humor, as growth-enhancing opportunities, is just part of the process.

SIGNS TO WATCH FOR

As you practice using your inborn talent for Appreciation, you will begin to notice more quickly the signals that your Humiliated Self has regained center stage, that you have entrenched yourself in front of your scrim and are responding, not to the grand possibilities of your life adventure, but to the painted images that compose your mental scenery. Included among those signals are negative emotions, Self justification, conditional emotions, Self denigration, and filing new experiences in preexisting categories.

Negative Emotions

The first, and probably the most obvious, indicator that you have begun to replay an outdated drama is the onset of such negative emotions as fear, frustration, anger, contempt, deprivation, and hurt feelings. These symptoms are almost infallible in signaling that your ego has been hooked and that you are about to engage in futile efforts to restore, maintain, or enhance your wounded Self esteem.

Self Justification

Once your ego has been hooked, you are very likely to begin the circular process of conjuring up explanations (some of them highly imaginative) for your behavior in a given situation. You may begin to notice how lame some of your reasons sound, how you try to shore up your logic with emotion. You might even begin to feel some compassion for the friends or acquaintances who are politely (or not so politely) hearing you out.

Conditional Emotions

It may take you longer to sense the importance of this signal because it is very subtle, consisting primarily of associating even your pleasant emotions—such as joy, love, admiration, or Appreciation—with an external person or event, rather than realizing that those positive experiences arise from within yourself.

You are experiencing your emotions conditionally whenever you feel the need to explain or rationalize them. If someone, for example, remarks that you appear to be feeling very good today and you respond by saying, "I have a reason to be happy; I just got a five-thousand-dollar raise," you are responding conditionally, as if you have to have a reason for joy. You may, of course, choose to share your good fortune with those around you, but recognize that fortune, in and of itself, has no power over your emotions. Any conditional emotion arises in front of the scrim, existing only as a response to the images that we emblazon on the curtain of our minds. Behind the scrim, all emotions are unconditional, dependent on nothing but our recognition for their existence.

Self Denigration

Self denigration is the defining component of those moments during which we allow ourselves to feel inadequate or small in comparison to others, those times when we take it on ourselves to heap coals of shame and guilt on our own heads. There's a poisonous paradox at work in Self diminishment—although it disguises itself as an expression of our sense of "smallness," it is actually an expression of our attachment to our own sense of Self importance. When we truly release our attachment to ego, we release with it our need to punish ourselves for not living up to those arbitrary standards we have set to evaluate our performance in front of the scrim.

Filing New Experiences in Preexisting Categories

Whenever you agree or disagree with something you hear or read, you are working to keep preexisting images and ideas in place on your mental curtain. In like manner, you reinforce what you already think or feel when you associate new ideas with something you've already learned. What you are doing is filing new ideas and information in mental categories that are already well entrenched on this side of the scrim, rather than allowing them to assume a new and unique place in your thinking. By refusing to hear an unfamiliar idea in all its newness, you more or less ensure that it will have only minimal impact on your thinking and behavior.

Consider, for example, the progression of your response to the ideas I've been presenting in this book. As we discussed in chapter 12, you probably found yourself engaged in many forms of resistance at various phases of your reading, including an unconscious effort to evaluate what I was saying by comparing it to other concepts with which you may already be familiar. There is nothing really wrong with this intellectual endeavor. It is, in fact, essential to any discriminating learning experience. The problem is that discrimination, while necessary, works against the very sense of wonder that lies at the basis of Appreciation. It is only as we allow ourselves to become comfortable with the new, to release our compulsive need to compare and discriminate, that we free ourselves to experience the wonder that underlies all human thinking. It was only as you began to move past your normal resistance that you were able to share in the fascination I feel for the amazing capacity humans have for existence on both sides of our mental scrims. To the extent that you have allowed yourself to become fascinated, you are experiencing directly—that is, without thought or judgment—the transparency of your psychic scenery. To that same extent, you will know directly (without having to justify our intuitive knowing with theory or argument) that Self importance, feelings of humiliation, ego-hooking, and boomeranging behavior are all creations of your own ingenious mind, creations that can be set aside anytime you choose.

SELF-IMPORTANT EGO FLACK

The dynamics of ego flack became clear to me as I shared drafts of this book with friends and colleagues. Almost universally, those individuals (all of whom I like and respect) were aroused by my use of phrases such as "no longer taking one's Self so seriously." Most of them demanded to know what was wrong with taking our Selves seriously. Life is a serious matter; anger in a just cause has value; a modest level of pride in one's accomplishments is a good and healthy thing.

As if with one voice, these valued people spoke up to remind me that the Self is a valued part of one's being, that a strong ego is essential if a person is to survive and thrive in this rough-and-tumble world.

It was months before I realized what I was experiencing—the Self is so important to most of us that we will rise up in defense when even the idea of Self appears to be under attack. What I was hearing from my friends with all their well-thought-out half-truths was nothing more than "ego flack"—unconscious efforts to protect the ego from even the threat of attack. My friends had taken it upon themselves to furnish me with a series of living, breathing examples of the ego's need to uphold the validity of its own sense of importance.

That uncomfortable (almost uncontrollable) urge to uphold and defend one's definition of Self is the most dramatic expression possible of how tenuous are our holds on our own creations. Our Created Selves cannot do the job we ask them to do—keep us safe and insulated from the changing world. We are made to experience life directly, free from the limiting, artificial constraints of Self. Only by recognizing the impermanence of the Created Self, its essential permeability, can we derive from it the strength it was created to impart, freeing ourselves to do the important work that the world so desperately needs to get done.

THE IMPORTANCE OF TRANSPARENCY

What my friends were all telling me, each in his or her own way, was that they still felt the (very understandable) need to hide from the world, to protect themselves behind the barricades of Self. They were not convinced, yet, that it is safe to live without the security of their scrims. That kind of life, with its vast potential for clarity, joy, energy, and creativity, demands a willingness to recognize that the images we see on our scrims are not opaque, but transparent, liable to evaporate at the slightest adjustment of our mental lamps.

What my friends (and possibly my readers) needed to hear was that the Self never really disappears. It remains with you, ready for your conscious use whenever you decide you need it to play out the roles and fill the relationships that exist for you in front of the scrim. Unlike the old days, however, when you felt honor bound to take your Self "seriously" (possibly even when you knew you were being ridiculous), you will no longer be the slave of your ego, but its skillful master. You will be able to act out whatever part you choose with great gusto and devotion, energized by the security that comes when you know you are safe from the stress of such "serious" preoccupations as success or failure, approval or ridicule. With transparency, in other words, you will purchase the right to let your true Self shine through.

Throughout human history, many have felt the call to innocence that is the lamp of transparency and a few have actually achieved it, either through dint of personal effort or by a happy accident. Transparency may be obtained, humans wiser than I have discovered, through sudden illumination, as a response to a crisis, and through meditation. But the approach I find most productive is one I call "seeing through fresh eyes."

Sudden Illumination

A relative minority of people have achieved transparency when they were least looking for it—in a blinding flash of unexpected enlightenment that came on them without advance preparation or effort. The lives of the religious saints are often characterized by unexpected, transforming instants that removed them once and for all from the common lot of joy and sorrow, triumph and travail, fulfillment and frustration that are the inevitable lot of those who play out their lives unconsciously in front of the scrim.

The lives of those who are granted this shortcut to Appreciation serve as models of what can be achieved through the clarity, joy, energy, and creativity that is available just beyond the scrim. The problem, of course, is that these model lives provide little information to those of us who are not illuminated, who must work to find our ways around the scrim. If all we had to do to achieve transparency was to sit around and wait for inspiration to strike, I doubt I would have felt motivated to write this book.

Response to a Crisis

Some individuals come through a life crisis to a moment of sudden illumination and transformation.

During a television interview recorded when he was ninety, pianist Artur Rubinstein described how such a moment transformed his life when he was a very young man. Overwhelmed by loneliness and despair, and alone in a hotel room in Paris, Rubinstein attempted to take his own life. He awoke some hours later, realizing that his suicide attempt had failed and that he still had a long life ahead of him. Delighted to find himself alive, young, and very talented, he rushed out into the Parisian street, only to be overwhelmed yet again—this time by a newfound ecstasy in the simplest things of life: the sights, sounds, and odors of the French night.

What the great pianist discovered that night was the power of Appreciation, the thrill of experiencing life directly, without limitations or expectations. When the interviewer asked him which was his favorite piano composition, he considered a moment, then smiled and said, "Whatever piece I'm playing at the moment."

Meditation

Many time-honored meditative techniques have been recommended as pathways to Appreciation. There is no doubt that meditation is a path that leads one toward the realm of fascination and wonder that lies behind the scrim. I have even less doubt, however, that a path always remains a path—nothing more. As long as one is on a path, any path, one has not yet arrived where one is going.

People have been known to devote entire lifetimes to a spiritual discipline designed to produce a state of enlightenment they are never able to transfer to their daily lives. Most of those people experience some truly awesome moments during their meditations, enough to encourage them to continue their pursuit. Once in a while, a meditator is fortunate enough to discover that meditation is not the path—it is, indeed, the destination.

I recommend the use of meditation as an exercise that provides an occasional glimpse of the realm that lies beyond everyday consciousness. Remember, however, that while a daily ritual of meditation may be good preparation for moving beyond the scrim, it is only preparation, nothing more.

▣ Exercise 15: Appreciative Compassion

Recently, a person who had just returned from India described on the World Wide Web several days of meetings with the Dalai Lama. Toward the end of their time together, the Tibetan spiritual leader shared the following practice with the group and asked everyone present to share the practice with as many people as possible.

In my view, the Dalai Lama brings the power of Appreciation to bear on the complex political, religious, and social challenges with which he must deal. I am delighted to share his four-step practice with you.

Step 1: *Spend five minutes at the beginning of each day remembering that we all want the same thing—to be happy and loved—and that we are all connected.*

Step 2: *Spend five minutes cherishing yourself and others. As you do so, let go of all judgments—of yourself, of others, and of events in the world. As you breathe in, cherish yourself; as you breathe out, cherish others. If faces appear in your mind's eye of people with whom you are having difficulty, cherish them as well.*

Step 3: *During the day extend that attitude of cherishing to everyone you meet. Remind yourself each time, "We are all the same; I cherish myself and I cherish you." Do so with everyone, including the clerk in the supermarket, a client, a co-worker, family members—everyone with whom you make contact.*

Step 4: *Remind yourself to stay in the practice no matter what happens.*

Seeing with Fresh Eyes

I once read about a man who, born with normal vision, lost his sight as a young child (as many of us lose our insight, the power that allows us to see life from the core of our beings). In his mid-forties, he underwent an operation that completely restored his vision. He described his new life as a continuing series of small delights as he experienced for the first time the ordinary sights—like watching a leaf fall to the ground—that most of us take for granted.

I think of this wonderful story as a lovely metaphor for what happens when someone reclaims his or her birthright of seeing the world through the lens of Appreciation. As I have pointed out earlier, we are born with the gift of this vision. Most of us lose the use of that gift in everyday life because we have reserved it for sunsets and other special occasions. Most of the time we accept the scenery of images and ideas inscribed on our mental scrims as the only reality. When we reclaim the gift, however, every moment of every day becomes special and worthy of note. Washing dishes, mowing the lawn, chopping weeds, working at the computer, chatting with a friend . . . there is an infinity of such moments. Like the falling leaf for the man who recovered his sight, even the most simple, mundane routine takes on a wondrous glow.

I am not alone in making this happy discovery. I remember watching the man whom a friend hired to clean his apartment. My friend was away. I watched as the cleaning man—who called himself "Mark the Maid"—went about his work. There was something about the way he moved that attracted my attention—he seemed so concentrated and yet so relaxed. He moved efficiently from one task to another and yet did not appear to be rushing. He was very deliberate; his every move seemed conscious and purposeful. As I watched him dust a vase on my friend's coffee table, I realized that Mark the Maid was doing his work with complete and total awareness. For him, cleaning my friend's apartment was nothing less than a moving meditation.

I observed with total fascination as he knelt on the rug in front of the coffee table, reached for the vase with his left hand, pulled a feather duster from his back pocket with his right hand, and, with complete concentration, dusted the vase inside and out. Returning the duster to his pocket, he held the vase in both hands, looked at it for what seemed to me an endless moment, returned the vase to its place on the table, then got up and moved to the next task. I was reminded of what I'd read and heard about the almost mystical aura that surrounds the Japanese tea ceremony. For me, watching Mark the Maid dust the vase was a moment of blinding beauty.

A few years ago I heard of a similar incident involving a cleaning lady who had just been hired by a woman who was a very successful and busy lawyer. After showing the new maid around her apartment and discussing what needed to be done, the employer settled down with some work in her office. An hour or so later, the maid interrupted the woman's work and, seeming pleasantly excited, urged her employer to "Come see!" Somewhat reluctantly, she followed the maid to the doorway to the kitchen. "Look," said the maid. "Isn't it lovely!"

Having just finished waxing the kitchen linoleum, the maid was obviously thrilled by the beauty she had created and wanted to share the moment with her employer. The maid's excitement was contagious. The busy lawyer dropped her impatience, joined her maid in moving beyond her mental scrim, and found herself transfixed by the beauty she allowed herself to take in. A mundane act, which many people would have hurried through with their attention elsewhere, had become a wondrous moment for both women. So it can be with all moments in life when they are attended to within an Appreciative frame of mind and heart.

The following exercise is intended to help you experience what the man felt when his vision was restored, the way in which Mark the Maid approached his work in my friend's apartment, and how the cleaning lady and her employer felt when they allowed themselves to take in the beauty of a waxed kitchen floor.

◉ Exercise 16: Experiencing for the First Time

This exercise, which is sometimes used as an orientation to the practice of meditation, encourages us to experience fully and directly the true textures, forms, shadings, and colors of objects, instead of living with our tired, abstract ideas of what those objects are like. I'd like to suggest that you tape-record the instructions so you can follow them with your eyes closed.

Select a simple, small, everyday object such as a matchstick, and find a comfortable place to sit. Take a deep, long breath and as you exhale imagine that all the tension in your body is being released into the air. Relax as completely as you can. Repeat the process with two or three more breaths, each time releasing more tension and relaxing more deeply.

PAUSE

When you feel completely relaxed, hold the object gently in your fingers or cupped in the palm of your hand. Close your eyes and experience how the object feels to your touch. Try different ways of touching and stroking the object. Slide it from one hand to the other. Give yourself plenty of time to get acquainted with how it feels to lift, touch, and stroke your object.

PAUSE

Continue examining the object with your eyes closed. How heavy is it? What is its texture? Is it rougher in some places, smoother in others? How hard is it? Does it feel cool or warm? What does your touch tell you about its shape?

PAUSE

Eyes still closed, imagine that this object is a precious gift from someone you love, someone who loves you. Let the object be filled with loving energy. Allow the energy to flow into your fingers and from there to the rest of your body until you are filled with the wonder of loving feelings. Let these feelings of wonder radiate from you back into the object you are holding. Let them fill the space that surrounds you.

PAUSE

Allow those feelings of wonder to intensify as you very slowly and gently open your eyes and let yourself gaze on the object. See the appearance of the object rather than relying on your preexisting idea of what the object looks like. If the name of the object comes to your mind, simply let the name drift away until it is out of sight of your mind's eye. Bring your good feelings of wonder with you to the experience of seeing the object. Give yourself plenty of time to continue gazing on the object. See its colors, its shadings of light and dark, its lines and shapes.

PAUSE

Continue to gaze steadily at the object. Notice the feelings you experience. Perhaps you feel excitement and delight, perhaps mild discomfort or boredom. Whatever you feel is okay. Just register the feeling and continue to let yourself look on the object. Notice how different qualities of the object come to your attention. Notice, too, if your mind sends you negative messages telling you, perhaps, why you should stop this activity. Let these messages, too, drift away until they disappear.

PAUSE

Finally, remind yourself that this object was given to you by someone you love and who loves you. It's filled with loving energy. Let that energy come in through your eyes and spread to your entire being. Gaze on this object as if you have never seen anything like it before. Allow yourself to experience as fully as you can those feelings of wonder and fascination that reside in you and that you are capable of bringing to new experiences.

Be like the man who recovered his sight, gazing ecstatically at a falling leaf. Give yourself the gift of experiencing this object as if for the first time, fully and completely and through your feelings of Appreciation.

PAUSE

Slowly put the object aside while you allow your feelings of Appreciation to remain. Remember: these are your feelings. They don't belong to the object. They belong to you. It was you who brought them to awareness.

Take these good feelings with you as you relax, return to your everyday activities, or resume reading this chapter.

You have just given yourself an experience of what it is like to live in the world of Appreciation that lies behind your mental scrim. You now have a standard for recognizing the experience that can be yours every day as it becomes more and more natural for you to power your life with Appreciation.

◙ Exercise 17: A Group Experiment in Appreciative Problem Solving, or the Cosmic Chuckle

Here's a four-step experiment you can try with a small group of friends. Its purpose is to show how the power of Appreciation can help resolve stubborn interpersonal problems. I've used this experiment many times in workshops. Almost everyone enjoys it and most people end up discovering hopeful new ways to approach situations that until then had seemed hopeless. For this experiment you'll need a timer that will signal when five or ten minutes have gone by. You'll also need writing materials.

In workshop situations the experiment works best with no fewer than three and no more than five members of a group. Depending on the number of people involved, it takes from one and one-half to two and one-half hours. Make sure you have enough time to complete the experience and do everything possible to avoid telephone or other interruptions.

Preparation

Take a few moments to allow each participant to think of a conflict situation that involves at least one other person. The conflict can be with any person in your life—a close family member, a distant relative, a friend, or a co-worker. Don't choose a situation involving a stranger or someone you'll never see again or a situation involving someone with whom you don't have a personal relationship such as a public figure.

Make notes about the situation. During this exercise you will be telling the other group members about this conflict four different times.

Round 1: PROBLEMS

Each person tells the other members of the group about the conflict situation and all the problems it causes. When each person's story of woe is complete, the others act as "coaches of doom." Their job is to suggest possible problems in the situation that the person with the conflict hasn't already mentioned. As coaches of doom, group members should do their best to make sure that no snag, snarl, or snafu has been overlooked. Because people vary according to how willing they are to talk about uncomfortable situations in their lives, use the timer to make sure that everyone takes no more than ten minutes for telling his or her story and having the others respond to it.

Important: *It's not okay to try to help the person solve the problem by making comments (such as "I wonder what would happen if you told your son that he can't use the family car until he's gotten his school grades back up to A's and B's") or by asking questions (such as "When was the last time you told your son that you love him very much?"). Remember, this person has been doing his or her best to deal with the problem for days, weeks, months, possibly even years. It may even be in-*

sulting to think that after less than ten minutes group members are wise enough to offer a solution that will clear everything up!

Round 2: PAYOFFS

Each person has no more than five minutes to tell his or her story once more. Instead of emphasizing problems, however, this time the person talks about all the "payoffs" he or she gets from being involved in the conflict situation.

A payoff is some form of benefit—psychological or material—that we get when we are party to a painful clash or dispute. You may wonder, What benefits could I possibly get from such a painful, disagreeable situation? The answer is that, whether we realize it or not, there are always payoffs when we are caught up in conflict, however unpleasant. For example, we have the built-in benefit of knowing we are right. That's a given; otherwise, why would we not simply acknowledge that we are wrong and remove ourselves from the situation? In conflicts, as in other dances of life, "it takes two to tango!" Another common payoff is the opportunity to gain others' sympathy for having been made the victim of someone else's mistaken, misguided, or even downright evil behavior.

This time, group members act as "coaches of payola." Their job is to think of other payoffs that the person hasn't mentioned.

Again, avoid the temptation to help resolve the conflict.

Round 3: PERSPECTIVE

Once again, each person has five minutes to tell the story of the conflict. This time, however, the challenge is to disengage from the situation, putting psychological distance between the person and the dilemma. The storyteller should try to see the humor in the situation. (It helps to imagine yourself as an elf or a fairy perched above and some distance away from the conflict situation. As you describe the situation, give yourself a cosmic chuckle. Remind yourself: "what fools these mortals be.")

This time group members are "coaches of playful paradox." Their job is to help the storyteller view the situation as if it were theater of the absurd. They should offer comments about elements in the situation that might be seen as amusing, entertaining, even hilarious. Done with enough zest, this round may even be able to transform depressing tragedy into enlightening farce!

Round 4: POSSIBILITIES

In this final round, each person has up to five minutes to tell the story, emphasizing possible new ways in which he or she can approach the situation. The question is: Now that I've explored how the conflict creates problems in my life, provides personal payoffs for me, and can be viewed from a cosmic perspective, what different approaches come to mind that I might explore from now on?

Almost invariably, group members complete this exercise laughing, energized, and feeling far less stressed by a situation about which they have been feeling considerable psychic pain. The conflict that seemed indelibly engraved on their mental scrims has either disappeared or been transformed into a far more hopeful situation. They have tapped into their capacity for Appreciative knowing.

▣ Exercise 18: An Individual Experiment in Appreciative Problem Solving

Appreciation has far more practical potentials than the mere production of a happier, less burdened life for its practitioners. It can also open up more effective, less energy-draining ways to deal with life's challenges. I would like to ask you, even if you have chosen not to participate in earlier experiments, to take part in one final experiment, which may help demonstrate this practical power.

For this experiment, select a problem that, despite your best efforts, you have been unable to resolve. If possible, choose a current situation, one that is presently consuming your thoughts, time, and energy. If you are one of those fortunate people who have no current problems, choose a problem from your past. Don't forget to tape-record the instructions.

Find a comfortable place in which you can relax, undisturbed. When you are ready, close your eyes and take a few long, slow, deep breaths. Each time you exhale, imagine that all the burdens and tensions of the day are flowing out of your mind and body. Invite all the muscles in your body to relax. Let go of all tightness and tension. Allow yourself to be as relaxed as possible.

Let an image of the problem you have selected to develop in your mind's eye. Notice exactly what's going on in this situation. Who is involved? Where are you in the situation and what's it like for you to be there?

What are you doing? How are you feeling? What other problems is this situation creating in your life? What unsuccessful efforts have you made to deal with the situation? For the next thirty seconds, allow yourself to experience as fully as you can all the frustration, anger, despair, and other negative feelings this situation summons up in you.

PAUSE

Let the image of the problem situation fade, taking all the negative feelings and frustrations with it. Watch the situation and all its accompanying problems and feelings slip away until your mental screen is completely blank.

Now, recall an event, situation, or activity in your life when you were filled with a pure sense of fascination, wonder, and delight about being alive and in the world. Let an image of the time come into focus in your mind's eye. See as vividly as possible exactly what is happening. Just watch for a while.

PAUSE

Now, let yourself become part of the scene, reexperiencing as directly as possible what it is like to be filled with Appreciation. What do you see as you look around? Listen for the sounds. Feel the sensations in your body and notice any odors. What are your emotions? For the next thirty seconds, let yourself be as fully present to the situation as you can.

PAUSE

Gradually let this image fade from your mental screen, but continue to allow yourself to experience the feelings of fascination, wonder, delight, and Appreciation with which you originally responded to the scene. Notice, again, that since these feelings arise from within you, you are able to experience them even when the situation that stimulated them is no longer present. Allow yourself to carry these feelings with you to the next part of this experiment.

Return to your problem, bringing your Appreciative feelings with you. As the image of the problem situation becomes clearer in your mind's eye, let the feeling of Appreciation become part of the situation. Allow yourself to experience what's going on through the lens of Appreciation. For the next thirty seconds, let the situation unfold in any way it seems to want to unfold. Don't force anything. Simply notice what happens.

PAUSE

*Gradually let the scene fade. Bring your Appreciative feelings with you
as you return from the image to real time and space. Take your time.
When you are ready, open your eyes and look to see how this space you're
in looks now. Notice how you are feeling. Notice, especially, whether you
are still in touch with your powers of Appreciation. If so, are those feelings revealing anything to you about yourself, the situations in your life,
or the world in which you live?*

*My hope is not that you arrived at some amazing insights into your prob-
lem, but that you allowed yourself to Appreciate yourself fully throughout
this experience, without worrying about whether you were "succeeding"
or not. Many people have reported their problems seemed much less hopeless after they completed this exercise. They even found themselves generating new solutions and had an eagerness to try them as soon as possible.
If you were able, through the power of Appreciation, to enjoy such an experience, I share your delight. If you did not arrive at a new, creative solution, but only at an expanded definition of your problem, you have still
gained a great and useful, if not totally formed, insight.*

*There are individuals, however, who are unable to experience the Apprecia-
tive situation or to transfer their feelings of fascination and wonder to the
problem situation. If you found yourself in that group, I hope you will
give yourself permission to Appreciate whatever you experienced and
whatever scenario unfolded for you. Perhaps you are feeling frustrated or
apologetic because your results were not those you imagine were intended. You may find your mind doing a great job of finding flaws with
the experience itself, perhaps arguing that it proves that Appreciation
isn't really relevant to you or the problems in your life. If that is your experience, remember: when we are living life in front of the scrim, we are
always right in our own minds. I hope you will Appreciate your mind's
dedication to doing the job of keeping you right.*

TAKING THE LEAP
To make that final move behind the scrim demands not only desire but also an active decision. Savoring the delights of a vacation
on a Caribbean or South Pacific paradise island is one thing; moving one's entire life and livelihood to such a location is quite an-

other. We may be in awe of people who make such life-changing relocations. We admire their courage; we may envy their lives. But few of us follow their examples. We prefer our perfect dreams of life in paradise to the reality of living there. Reality, even in paradise, entails the details of everyday life—earning a living, maintaining nurturing relationships, coping with injury and illness, and dealing with whatever opportunities and challenges arise in the course of our routines.

It might be just as well that most of us relinquish our dreams of moving to a magical geographical place that transforms us and our lives. For the reality (and the magic) is that the place of transformation lies within, not outside in some faraway place. When we make the decision to live our lives on both sides of the scrim by allowing ourselves to tune in to the inherent power of Appreciation, we transform the places, the people, and the relationships in our lives. When we move behind the scrim, we don't have to renounce the lives we know now, lives that most of us have spent years building. Our lives remain the same. Only the feeling that pervades the events of our lives is transformed.

When we live behind the scrim, we discover, like Artur Rubinstein, that each new day, each new event, each new composition is our favorite day, event, or masterpiece of all.

One thing is certain. You will know when you're living within the transforming realm of Appreciation. The signs are easy to read. They are wonderfully described in the following tongue-in-cheek e-mail message that flashed its way around the Internet during the closing days of the old millennium:

> Be on the lookout for symptoms of inner peace. The hearts of a great many have already been exposed and it is possible that people everywhere could come down with it in epidemic proportions. This could pose a serious threat to what has, up to now, been a fairly stable condition of conflict in the world.
>
> Some signs to look for:
>
> - A tendency to think and act spontaneously rather than on fears based on past experiences.
> - An unmistakable ability to enjoy each moment.
> - A loss of interest in judging other people.

- A loss of interest in interpreting the actions of others.
- A loss of interest in conflict.
- A loss of the ability to worry (this is a very serious symptom).
- Frequent, overwhelming episodes of Appreciation.
- Contented feelings of connectedness with others and with nature.
- Frequent attacks of smiling.
- An increasing tendency to let things happen rather than to make them happen.
- An increased susceptibility to the love offered by others as well as the uncontrollable urge to extend it.

Notes

■ ■ ■

CHAPTER 1: OUR SHARED REALITIES

1. Maxine Hong Kingston, *The Woman Warrior: Memoirs of a Girlhood Among Ghosts* (New York: Vintage Books/Random House, 1977), 184.

2. Harry Stack Sullivan, *The Interpersonal Theory of Psychiatry* (New York: W. W. Norton, 1953).

3. Willis Harman, "Two Liberating Concepts for Research on Consciousness," *Noetic Sciences Review* (spring 1993): 15.

4. Jiddu Krichnamurti, *You Are the World* (New York: Harper and Row/Perennial Library, 1972), 6.

5. David Bohm and Mark Edwards, *Changing Consciousness* (San Francisco: Harper, 1991), 8.

6. Ibid., 4.

7. Ibid., 151.

8. Roger Mills with Elsie Spittle, *The Health Realization Primer: Empowering Individuals and Communities* (Long Beach, Calif.: R. C. Mills and Associates, 1998), 8. See also Sidney Banks, *The Missing Link* (Vancouver, BC: Lone Pine Publishing, 1998); Roger Mills, *Realizing Mental Health* (New York: Sulzberger and Graham, 1995); and George Pransky, *The Renaissance of Psychology* (New York: Sulzberger and Graham, 1998).

9. Mills, *Health Realization Primer*, 10.

10. Bohm and Edwards, *Changing Consciousness*, 212.

11. Ibid.

12. Ibid.

13. Gurudev Chitrabhanu, *Ten Days Journey into the Self* (New York: Jain Meditation International Center, 1974), 49–50.

14. Krishnamurti, *You Are the World*, 40.

CHAPTER 2: HOW FREE ARE WE, *REALLY?*

1. Eric Berne, *What Do You Say After You Say Hello?* (New York: Bantam Books, 1972), 31.

2. Paul Loeb, *Soul of a Citizen: Living with Conviction in Cynical Times* (New York: St. Martin's Griffin, 1999), 139.

3. John D. W. Andrews, *The Active Self in Psychotherapy: An Integration of Therapeutic Styles* (Needham Heights, Mass.: Allyn and Bacon, 1991), 24.

4. Berne, *What Do You Say*, 131.

5. Ibid., 102.

6. Ibid., 102.

7. Ibid., 97.

8. Ibid.

CHAPTER 3: THE MIRACLE OF SELF CREATION

1. John D. W. Andrews, *The Active Self in Psychotherapy: An Integration of Therapeutic Styles* (Needham Heights, Mass.: Allyn and Bacon, 1991), 6.

2. See especially: Charles Horton Cooley, *Human Nature and the Social Order* (New York: Scribner, 1902). Also: George Herbert Mead, *Mind, Self and Society* (Chicago: University of Chicago Press, 1934).

3. For a more extensive discussion of collective dis-identity, see Donald Klein, "Collective Dis-Identity," in *The Promise of Diversity*, ed. Elsie Cross et al. (Burr Ridge, Ill.: Irwin Professional Publishing, 1993).

4. Erik Erikson, in personal communication, 1952.

CHAPTER 4: THE SCRIM OF SELF (OR HOW WE SEE THROUGH A FILTER DARKLY)

1. Susanne Langer, *Philosophy in a New Key: A Study in the Symbolism of Reason, Rite and Art* (Cambridge, Mass.: Harvard University Press, 1957).

2. I came across this story years ago and have used it many times since to illustrate how we function to create our own realities. My most recent encounter with the story was in the book *Inventing Reality: Physics as Language* (New York: Wiley, 1990), in which astrophysicist

Bruce Gregory makes the point that even the scientific concepts of physics are creations of the human mind.

3. Richard Schweder, *Thinking through Cultures: Expeditions in Cultural Psychology* (Cambridge, Mass.: Harvard University Press, 1991).

4. Ibid., 155.

5. Daniel Goleman, *The Meditative Mind: the Varieties of Meditative Experience* (New York: G. P. Putnam Sons, 1988).

CHAPTER 5: THE PRISON OF THE PROTECTED
SELF: THE HUMILIATION DYNAMIC

1. Alice Miller, *The Drama of the Gifted Child* (originally published as *Prisoners of Childhood*) (New York: Basic Books, 1981), 88.

2. Carl Goldberg, "The Daimonic Development of the Malevolent Personality," *Journal of Humanistic Psychology* 35, no. 3 (1995): 12.

3. Graham Greene, *Doctor Fischer of Geneva* (New York: Simon and Schuster, 1980), 71.

4. Alex Ayres, ed., *The Wit and Wisdom of Mark Twain* (New York: Harper and Row, 1987).

5. Matthew Brelis, "Humiliation," *The Boston Sunday Globe*, 9 May 1999, p. E2.

6. William Ian Miller, *Humiliation and Other Essays on Honor, Social Discomfort, and Violence* (Ithaca, N.Y.: Cornell University Press, 1993).

7. Harvey Hornstein, *Brutal Bosses and Their Prey* (New York: Riverhead Books, 1996).

CHAPTER 6: THE ELEMENTS OF HUMILIATION:
THE DANCE OF DISGRACE

1. Tom Wolfe, *The Bonfire of the Vanities* (New York: Bantam Books, 1987), 512.

2. Donald Klein, "The Humiliation Dynamic: An Overview," *The Journal of Primary Prevention* 12, no. 2 (1991): 98–99.

3. Thomas Cahill, *The Gifts of the Jews* (New York: Doubleday, 1998).

4. Haig Bosmajiian, *The Language of Oppression* (Washington, D. C.: Public Affairs Press, 1974), 6.

5. Matthew Brelis, "Humiliation," *The Boston Sunday Globe*, 9 May 1999, p. E2.

6. See Aaron Lazare, "Shame and Humiliation in the Medical Encounter," *Archives of Internal Medicine* 147 (1987): 1653–58.

7. J. Steven Smith, "Humiliation, Degradation, and the Criminal Justice System," *The Journal of Primary Prevention* 12, no. 3 (1992): 209–22.

8. Scott Adams, *The Dilbert Principle* (New York: Harper Collins, 1996), 20.

9. Natasha Josefowitz and Herman Gadon, *Fitting In: How to Get a Good Start in Your New Job* (Reading, Mass.: Addison-Wesley, 1988), 30.

10. Cited in Marcia Westkott, *The Feminist Legacy of Karen Horney* (New Haven, Conn.: Yale University Press, 1966), 75.

11. Helen Luke, *Old Age* (New York: Parabola Books, 1987), 105.

CHAPTER 7: HOW HUMILIATION KILLS THE CREATIVE SELF

1. James Gilligan, *Violence: Our Deadly Epidemic and Its Causes* (New York: Grossett/Putnam, 1996), 48–49.

2. Ibid., 54–55.

3. Ibid., 54.

4. Ibid., 110.

5. Matthew Brelis, "Humiliation," *The Boston Sunday Globe,* 9 May 1999, p. E2.

6. Ibid.

7. Willard Gaylin, *Feelings: Our Vital Signs* (New York: Harper and Row, 1979).

8. Marcia Westkott, *The Feminist Legacy of Karen Horney* (New Haven, Conn.: Yale University Press, 1966).

9. Donald Klein, "The Humiliation Dynamic: An Overview," *The Journal of Primary Prevention* 12, no. 2 (1991): 111.

10. Erik Erikson, *A Way of Looking at Things: Selected Papers from 1930 to 1980,* ed. Stephen P. Schlein (New York: W. W. Norton, 1987), 342–43.

11. Daniel Jacobs, "Learning Problems, Self-Esteem, and Delinquency," in *The Development and Sustaining of Self-Esteem in Childhood,* ed. J. Masck and S. Ablon (New York: International Universities Press, 1983).

12. Helen Lewis, *Psychic War in Men and Women* (New York: New York University Press, 1976), 241. The passage illustrates how Lewis and others have used shame and humiliation interchangeably or have treated the two as members of the same family of shame-related emotions. According to Lewis, shame-related emotions include what we ordinarily refer to as shame, embarrassment, chagrin, mortification,

humiliation, and feeling dishonored. Although both shame and humiliation involve reactions to others' disparagement, the two have quite different dynamics from one another. I believe that it is useful to make a clear distinction between the two. We feel ashamed when we feel we have failed to live up to our ideals in our own eyes as well as the eyes of others. We feel humiliated when we are scorned, ridiculed, held in contempt, or otherwise disparaged in ways that we feel we do not deserve. *People believe they deserve their shame, they do not believe they deserve their humiliation.* In specific situations it's easy to blur the distinction in one's own mind. I keep the two separate in my own thinking by making the following distinction: if my wife commits adultery and I find out about it, I feel humiliated; if I commit adultery and my wife finds out about it, I feel ashamed.

13. For Erich Fromm's views on sadomasochism, see his important book on cruelty entitled *The Anatomy of Human Destructiveness* (New York: Holt, Rinehart and Winston, 1973); Horney's views on the subject are well summarized in Marcia Westkott, *The Feminist Legacy of Karen Horney* (New Haven, Conn.: Yale University Press, 1966).

14. Karen Horney, *Neurosis and Human Growth* (New York: W. W. Norton, 1950).

15. Jill Montgomery, "Countertransference Identification," in *Masochism: The Treatment of Self-Inflicted Suffering*, ed. Jill Montgomery and A. Greif (Madison, Conn.: International Universities Press, 1989), 75.

16. Klein, "The Humiliation Dynamic," 109.

17. Larry Gernsbacher, *The Suicide Syndrome. Origins, Manifestations, and Alleviation of Human Self-Destructiveness* (New York: Human Sciences Press, 1985).

CHAPTER 8: THE PRISON OF THE DISOWNED SELF: BOOMERANGING (OR HOW WE GET HIT BY WHAT WE THOUGHT WE THREW AWAY)

1. Florence Scovel Shinn, *The Game of Life and How to Play It* (Brooklyn, N.Y.: Gerald J. Richard, 1941).

2. Dean Rusk, *As I Saw It: As Told to Richard Rusk* (New York: W. W. Norton, 1990).

3. Ibid., 270.

4. Ibid., 360.

5. Peter Senge, *The Fifth Discipline: The Art and Practice of the Learning Organization* (New York: Doubleday, 1990).

6. Ibid., 250.

7. William Hinton, *Shenfan: The Continuing Revolution in a Chinese Village* (New York: Random House, 1983), 47.

8. George J. Church, "The Coup Plotters," *Time*, 6 January 1992, 40.

9. William Raspberry, "The Evil Evolution," *Washington Post*, 1 September 1995.

10. Frank Norris, *McTeague* (New York: W. W. Norton, 1977), 10–11.

11. Peg Bracken, *A Window Over the Sink* (New York: Harcourt Brace Jovanovich, 1981).

12. For a more detailed explanation of the Me, Not-Me, Also Me exercise, see *Power: The Infinite Game* written by Michael Broom and Donald Klein, published in 1999 by Sea Otter Press (e-mail address: SeaOtter@Klein.Net).

CHAPTER 9: EGO-HOOKING: BOOMERANGING GONE WILD

1. Aldous Huxley, *The Perennial Philosophy* (New York: Harper-Collins, 1990), 101.

2. The basic idea of ego-hooking, as presented in this chapter, was introduced to me at least fifteen years ago by my friend and colleague Dr. Michael Broom.

3. Eric Berne, *Transactional Analysis: A Systematic Individual and Social Psychiatry* (New York: Ballantine Publishing, 1973).

CHAPTER 11: THE PSYCHOLOGY OF APPRECIATION

1. Richard Strozzi Heckler, *The Anatomy of Change: East/West Approaches to Body/Mind Therapy* (Boulder, Colo.: Shambhala Publications, 1984), 58–59.

CHAPTER 12: DANCING WITH RESISTANCE: EXPERIENCING GRACE IN CHANGE

1. Chris Welch, *Works in Progress*, a workbook prepared for his Mastery of Learning Workshop (Houston, Tex.: 1993).

2. For more information about Gestalt therapy and resistance, the following sources are recommended: Frederick Perls, *Gestalt Therapy Verbatim* (Lafayette, Calif.: Real People Press, 1969); Erving Polster and Miriam Polster, *Gestalt Therapy Integrated* (New York: Random House, 1974); Edwin Nevis, *Organizational Consulting: A*

Gestalt Approach (New York: Gardner Press, 1987); Taylor Stoehr, *Paul Goodman and the Origins of Gestalt Therapy* (San Francisco: Jossey-Bass, 1994).

3. Nevis, *Organizational Consulting*, 60.

4. Some linguists teach new ways of speaking to help us stay in touch with how we (1) create our own internal images of people and events and (2) react emotionally to those images as if they were real and separate from our own reactions. If we were to use the percept language created by John and Joyce Weir, for example, we would no longer say, "You made me angry." Instead, we would use this awkward, grammatically questionable, but far more accurate construction: "I angered myself with what the you in me did."

5. Kurt Lewin, "Quasi-Stationary Social Equilibria and the Problem of Permanent Change," in *The Planning of Change*, ed. Warren Bennis, Kenneth Benne, and Robert Chin (New York: Holt, Rinehart, Winston, 1969), 235–38.

CHAPTER 13: LIVING IN THE LIGHT OF
APPRECIATION

1. Rachel Naomi Remen, *Kitchen Table Wisdom: Stories That Heal* (New York: Riverhead Books, 1996), 77.

2. Mihaly Csikszentmihalyi, "If We Are So Rich, Why Aren't We Happy?" *American Psychologist* 54, no. 10 (1999): 823.

3. Emile Coué, *Self-Mastery Through Conscious Autosuggestion* (1922; reprint, Kila, Mont.: Kessinger Publishing, 1997).

4. David Cooperrider and Suresh Srivastva, "Appreciative Inquiry in Organizational Life," in *Research in Organizational Change and Development*, ed. Richard Woodman and William Pasmore (Stamford, Conn.: JAI Press, 1987).

5. Ibid., 131.

6. To learn more about Appreciative Inquiry, see the following: *OD Practitioner: Journal of the Organization Development Network* 37, no. 1 (2000)—devoted to articles on Appreciative Inquiry; David Cooperrider, et al., eds., *Appreciative Inquiry* (Champaign, Ill.: Stipes Publishing, 1999).

7. Paul Loeb, *Soul of a Citizen: Living with Conviction in a Cynical Time* (New York: St. Martin's Griffin, 1999), 317.

Index

ABOUT THE AUTHOR

Donald C. Klein, Ph.D., is a clinical/community psychologist and applied behavioral scientist with a distinguished career as a clinician, a consultant to organizational and community leaders, and a faculty member at Harvard University, Boston University, Johns Hopkins University, and The Union Institute. He is the author of numerous professional books and articles and has conducted extensive research in the area of use and abuse of power, focusing on the use of humiliation as a dysfunctional control and socialization tool in families and organizations.

HAZELDEN TRANSITIONS is an initiative between Hazelden Foundation's Information and Educational Services division and Transitions Bookplace, Inc.

Hazelden Information and Educational Services helps individuals, families, and communities prevent and/or recover from alcoholism, drug addiction, and other related diseases and conditions. We do this by partnering with authors and other experts to deliver information and educational products and services that customers use to aid their personal growth and change, leading along a wholistic pathway of hope, health, and abundant living. We are fortunate to be recognized by both professionals and consumers as the leading international center of resources in these areas.

Transitions Bookplace, Inc., founded in Chicago, Illinois, in 1989, has become the nation's leading independent bookseller dedicated to customers seeking personal growth and development. Customers can choose from more than thirty thousand books, videos, pamphlets, and musical selections. Authors appear frequently for special events or workshops in the Transitions Learning Center. Also available in the store is a legendary collection of exquisite international gifts celebrating body, mind, and spirit.

This Hazelden Transitions Bookplace initiative is dedicated to all brave souls who seek to change courses in their lives, their families, and their communities in order to achieve hope, health, and abundant living.

Transitions Bookplace
1000 West North Avenue
Chicago, IL 60622
312-951-READ
800-979-READ
www.transitionsbookplace.com

Hazelden Information and Educational Services
15251 Pleasant Valley Road
Center City, MN 55012-0176
800-328-9000
www.hazelden.org